DEATH ON DEMAND

DEATH ON DEMAND

Jack Kevorkian and
the Right-to-Die Movement

Michael DeCesare

ROWMAN & LITTLEFIELD
Lanham • Boulder • New York • London

Published by Rowman & Littlefield
A wholly owned subsidiary of
The Rowman & Littlefield Publishing Group, Inc.
4501 Forbes Boulevard, Suite 200, Lanham, Maryland 20706
www.rowman.com

Unit A, Whitacre Mews, 26-34 Stannary Street, London SE11 4AB,
United Kingdom

British Library Cataloguing in Publication Information Available

Library of Congress Cataloging-in-Publication Data

DeCesare, Michael, 1975–
Death on demand : Jack Kevorkian and the right-to-die movement / Michael DeCesare.
pages cm
Includes bibliographical references and index.
ISBN 978-1-4422-4213-5 (cloth : alk. paper) — ISBN 978-1-4422-4214-2 (electronic) 1. Right to
die. 2. Euthanasia. 3. Suicide. 4. Kevorkian, Jack. I. Title.
R726.D446 2015
179.7—dc23
2015009212

∞ ™ The paper used in this publication meets the minimum requirements of
American National Standard for Information Sciences Permanence of Paper
for Printed Library Materials, ANSI/NISO Z39.48-1992.

Printed in the United States of America

To Afshan, Aleena, and Lilah,
for always holding my hand

Then is it sin, / To rush into the secret house of death, / Ere death dare come to us?

—Shakespeare, *Antony and Cleopatra*, Act IV, Scene XV

CONTENTS

ACKNOWLEDGMENTS

I thank my colleagues in the Sociology Department at Merrimack College for their support and encouragement. Ray Dorney, in particular, has been incredibly generous with his advice and guidance on countless occasions; he also read and provided helpful feedback on drafts of several chapters of this book.

Christina Condon, the outstanding head of access services at Merrimack's McQuade Library, tracked down and delivered a number of obscure publications with a speed that never ceased to amaze me.

I am grateful for Merrimack's Faculty Development Grant program. Two separate grants, in 2008 and 2014, helped me enormously during the research and writing stages. A sabbatical leave during the fall 2014 semester enabled me to finish writing the manuscript.

The encouragement, thoughtfulness, and enthusiasm of Sarah Stanton, my editor at Rowman & Littlefield, made this project that much more enjoyable to work on.

My largest debt of gratitude is to my family. Afshan Jafar has given me years of love, support, and strength. In her roles as partner, editor, and sociologist, she read the entire manuscript, posing sharp questions and offering constructive criticism that helped me clarify the story. At the same time, our wonderful young daughters, Aleena and Lilah, helped me simplify the story through their innocent questions about Jack Kevorkian. They also patiently abided their pappa's time in front of the computer at night and on weekends. For these reasons and so many others, this book is dedicated to them and their amazing mamma.

INTRODUCTION

From Janet Adkins to Brittany Maynard

In April 2014, Brittany Maynard was told that she had six months to live. The Berkeley graduate had begun suffering from debilitating headaches since getting married a year and a half earlier. She was ultimately diagnosed with stage IV *glioblastoma multiforme*, the most aggressive form of terminal brain cancer. She was twenty-nine years old.

Upon receiving the prognosis, Brittany decided to move from her home in San Francisco to Portland, Oregon, along with her husband, her mother, and her stepfather, so that she could access the state's seventeen-year-old Death With Dignity Act. She wanted the option to end her life with a doctor's help. On October 6, she posted a video to YouTube in which she explained her condition and said that she had received a prescription for medication that would kill her, if she chose to ingest it. Within a week the video had been viewed more than six million times. Shortly afterward, in an exclusive interview with *People* magazine, Brittany announced that she would, indeed, take the medication and end her life on November 1, 2014.[1]

I write these lines on November 4, 2014. Brittany Maynard committed suicide three days ago, in her own bedroom, surrounded by her husband and family members. The act, and the preceding publicity campaign sponsored by right-to-die group Compassion & Choices, has once again put the "right to die"—also called "aid in dying" or "death with dignity"—literally on the front pages. The cover of *People*'s October 27 issue featured Brittany alongside the headline "My Decision To Die." Her YouTube video has now been viewed eleven million times. An online initiative by Compassion & Choices called "The Brittany Maynard Fund" has been collecting donations to support legislative action in states that currently prohibit assisted suicide, like Brittany's home state of California.[2] Her death was perhaps the first in human history to go "viral."

Multiple national and international news stories and opinion pieces in the wake of Brittany's suicide have credited her with reigniting the right-to-die movement while referring to her as its new "face."[3] That is with good reason. Assisted suicide has not garnered this much sustained attention, from either the public or the media, since before the turn of the century. Twenty-five years ago, on June 4, 1990, another individual suddenly became the face of the right-to-die movement when he helped an Alzheimer's patient kill herself in the back of his Volkswagen camper. And with that act, he single-handedly ushered in the most tumultuous and visible decade in the movement's history.

❈ ❈ ❈

There was nothing physically outstanding about Michigan Prisoner #284797. He was frail with a drawn, wrinkled face and large features. He had a small frame, standing five foot eight and weighing about 115 pounds, and his right eye sometimes seemed to wander to the right even as his left eye stared straight ahead. The thin hair he had left on his head was completely white. According to his lawyer, he suffered from hepatitis C, diabetes, and other ailments.

Michigan's Lakeland Correctional Facility, which housed Prisoner #284797, opened in the southern city of Coldwater in 1985. It provides mainly dormitory-style housing to its all-male population. As a Level II prison, it does not hold the state's worst criminal offenders; they can be found in the Level IV facilities scattered around the state. Still, Lakeland features double fences topped by razor-ribbon wire and an electronic detection system, and a patrol vehicle constantly circles its perimeter. It also boasts both a law library and a general library, and like many prisons, offers education and development programs.

Lakeland was the last stop for Prisoner #284797, who had been transferred among different state correctional facilities since his incarceration in 1999. On April 13 of that year, an Oakland County, Michigan, judge sentenced him to ten to twenty-five years for murder in the second degree and delivery of a controlled substance. He had injected a man with a lethal dose of drugs, and shown the videotape of it on national television. Given the nature of his crime, he and many others believed that he would remain in prison until his "maximum discharge date" of August 10, 2019. But in December 2006, just a few months after being transferred to Lakeland, it was announced that he would be granted parole on June 1, 2007. When he was released that day, at the age of seventy-nine, he had served close to 3,000 days for his offenses.[4]

Despite his unspectacular appearance, his nearly eight-year absence from public life, and his physical deterioration while in prison, many Americans immediately recognized Prisoner #284797 when they watched the news footage of his release. Some recalled his face and nickname—"Doctor Death"—from a May 1993 *Time* magazine cover; others recognized him from popular talk shows and news programs of the time like *The Phil Donahue Show* and *60 Minutes*. Most, perhaps, remembered him as the man who, over eight years, very publicly assisted in more than 100 suicides. His celebrity alone made him anything but the typical prisoner at Lakeland Correctional. His name was Jack Kevorkian.

During the 1990s, there were few more publicly recognizable activists—or more controversial ones—than Dr. Kevorkian. Like Brittany Maynard today, he was, quite literally, the face of the right-to-die movement during most of the 1990s. As such, he also left an indelible mark on the broader culture. Terms like *Kevorkianesque* and *Kevorkian pact* entered the lexicon. The doctor and his famous "suicide machine" were referenced on countless Top 10 lists on the *Late Show with David Letterman*. Kurt Vonnegut published *God Bless You, Dr. Kevorkian* in 1999. A restaurant in Toronto began serving up the Big Kevorkian, a burger that boasts a day's worth of fat and salt. In 2010, just a year before Kevorkian's death, a movie was made about his life starring Al Pacino.

Between 1999 and 2007, however, Dr. Jack Kevorkian was simply Prisoner #284797. While his opponents had spent the better part of a decade hoping for such an end for Kevorkian, very few observers, whether they supported or opposed the doctor, anticipated the fire-storm he would create during the 1990s when he took a pleading phone call from Ron Adkins in the fall of 1989. Ron's fifty-four-year-old wife, Janet, who was in the early stages of Alzheimer's disease, became the first person to kill herself with Kevorkian's assistance. Literally over-night, the retired pathologist from Michigan was thrust to the forefront of the American right-to-die movement and under the media spotlight. He would remain there for the rest of the decade.

$$* * *$$

Toward the end of the twentieth century, two authoritative observers correctly asserted that the right to die had replaced abortion as "America's most contentious social issue."[5] They had witnessed perhaps the liveliest decade in the right-to-die movement's history. They had also witnessed the most controversial activist in the movement's history. Yet the few subsequent books on the movement's activities and accomplish-ments during the 1990s all but ignored the crucial part that Jack Kevorkian played. Even as they described Kevorkian as a "national celebrity,"[6] a "cultural icon,"[7] or the person "who did the most for the right-to-die movement in twentieth-century America,"[8] to take just a few examples, these and other books did not adequately examine his role.[9]

Death on Demand attempts to do just that. Although we are now nearly twenty years removed from Kevorkian's final assisted suicide, the reverberations from his actions during the 1990s are as strong as ever. Between 2008 and 2014, four states decided, either by referendum or by legislative action, to join Oregon in allowing terminal patients to seek help in dying.[10] At the time of this writing, death with dignity bills are in front of the legislatures of seven other states.[11] Public opinion polls consistently show majority support for assisted suicide for terminally ill patients. On a broader scale, people around the world have recently taken to leaving their homes to travel to countries that have vague or no laws against assisted suicide for help in ending their lives. The most popular destination for what has come to be called "suicide tourism" is Switzerland, which saw the assisted suicides of 611 people from thirty-one countries between 2008 and 2012. "Going to Switzerland," at least in the United Kingdom, has become a euphemism for assisted sui-cide.[12] In that context, Brittany Maynard's decision to move from California to Oregon can be seen as a local manifestation of a trend that is local and global; that is, a trend toward controlling the circumstances of one's death.

As we will see throughout this book, Jack Kevorkian pushed harder than anyone in the history of the right-to-die movement to force that trend into existence. This book tells the story of how he did so. It recounts Kevorkian's criminal trials, the publicity stunts, his public feuds with opponents and advocates of assisted suicide—and the more than 100 assisted deaths along the way. The book also attempts to position Kevorkian against the backdrop of the right-to-die movement and its cultural, legal, and political twists and turns. The 1990s saw more of them than any other decade: the end of the now-famous Nancy Cruzan case, the approval of a referendum in Oregon making it the first state to legalize physician-assisted suicide, repeated attempts by the Michigan legislature and judiciary to clarify state law in response to Kevorkian's actions, and two U.S. Supreme Court rulings on assisted suicide.

In short, I show that before he became Prisoner #284797, Dr. Jack Kevorkian was a lightning rod throughout most of the stormiest decade in the history of the right-to-die movement.

I

"A SELF-IMPOSED MISSION"

Four Decades of Lone Activism

About thirty dollars. That was the cost of the prototype Mercitron, Dr. Jack Kevorkian's homemade suicide machine. Kevorkian's description of it as a "Rube Goldberg apparatus" was a bit inaccurate, for there was nothing complicated about the way it worked. The device—three vials suspended from a rack over an oblong box—consisted of little more than an electric clock motor, a switch, a solenoid, a pulley axle, and some scrap aluminum. The doctor purposely designed it so he would not have to operate it himself. All he had to do was insert an intravenous line into the patient, which would deliver a saline solution. After that, it would be up to the patient to press a button that would stop the saline solution and inject sodium thiopental. The drug would induce a coma, and potassium chloride would be injected automatically to stop the patient's heart. Kevorkian estimated that any individual who used the Mercitron would be dead in three or four minutes.[1]

The sixty-one-year-old retired pathologist built the machine in his two-room apartment in Royal Oak, Michigan, over a few weeks at the end of August and beginning of September 1989. He was inspired to do so after having met David Rivlin, a quadriplegic who had died in July of that year after the state of Michigan granted him the right to turn off his ventilator. "Anyone who saw [Rivlin] would say, 'My God, that's not a life,'" Kevorkian later said. "But a couple of religious nuts were keeping him alive against his will. That's when I knew I needed a device."[2] A few months later, he completed the Mercitron. Kevorkian's plan was to use it to assist in the suicides of people like David Rivlin.

The doctor was seemingly tireless in promoting the machine and his unusual services. He extended his first request to advertise the Mercitron to the Oakland County Medical Society. Its seven-member board quickly turned him down. Eventually, he managed to attract the interest of a writer at the *Oakland Press*, his local newspaper. The paper ran a feature story in October 1989, complete with a picture of Kevorkian and his device. The *Detroit News* soon requested a similar interview and picture, and the subsequent article resulted in a deluge of invitations to radio and television talk shows. It all must have seemed overwhelming for the son of Armenian immigrants who bought most of his clothing from the Salvation Army and who had not held a job in seven years.[3]

Amid the flood of interest in Kevorkian and his machine was a phone call from Ron Adkins, an Oregon man who had seen a November 1989 *Newsweek* article about Kevorkian. Ron was calling on behalf of his wife, Janet, who had been diagnosed with Alzheimer's disease four months earlier. After Ron explained that Janet was eligible for an experimental drug trial at the University of Washington in Seattle, he and Kevorkian agreed that she should enroll in the program. Kevorkian later explained that "any candidate for the Mercitron must have exhausted every potentially beneficial medical intervention, no matter how remotely promising."[4]

Janet was a fifty-four-year-old grandmother and former English teacher who enjoyed playing the piano and flute, hiking, and playing tennis. She was also, even before the onset of her disease, a member of the Hemlock Society. Based in Eugene, Oregon, it was the country's largest right-to-die organization. Janet had been terrified when she began to forget some of the notes to her piano and flute music, and how to spell certain words. By the time of Ron's first phone call to Kevorkian, she could no longer read words or music notes as easily but she could recognize her husband and carry on a conversation.[5]

Ron Adkins called Kevorkian again at the end of April 1990, after he and Janet saw the doctor on *The Phil Donahue Show*. Janet had entered the University of Washington's experimental drug program in January, Ron explained, but the new drug had proven ineffective. In fact, her condition had gotten worse. She was more desperate than ever to end her life. Kevorkian was sympathetic, and studied her medical records for himself. He then talked to Dr. Murray Raskind, Janet's physician in Seattle, who urged Kevorkian not to go through with the assisted suicide. "I felt his plan was totally inappropriate," Raskind wrote in his medical notes, "and that, in my opinion, Mrs. Adkins could expect several more years during which she would be able to maintain self care and enjoy the types of experiences (spending time with her grandchildren, outdoor activities, etc.), she was currently enjoying." On top of that, Raskind observed that "Mrs. Adkins was in good spirits and did not appear to be suffering." Kevorkian, though, was convinced after talking to Ron that "her doctor's opinion was wrong and that time was of the essence." His decision to assist in her suicide was, from his perspective, a simple one: clearly, to him, "she was aching to get this done." Partly for that reason, he told the Adkinses that he would assist Janet's suicide free of charge. In fact, he would never accept payment from any of his patients over the next eight years.[6]

Kevorkian's next step was to find a suitable site for the procedure. He quickly ruled out his own apartment and his sister's apartment "because of lease constraints." No matter where he ended up carrying out the assisted suicide, he felt obligated to inform whomever was in charge of the location because, he predicted, "if they didn't know beforehand, they would sue me for emotional distress later." Kevorkian faced a series of rejections. The owners or managers of motels, funeral homes, places of religious worship, rental office buildings, and various other potential sites all turned him down. One of these men was Reverend Douglas Gallagher, a minister at a local Unitarian Church, who, despite not allowing Kevorkian to use his church, was nonetheless impressed by the doctor's zeal. "He is singularly committed to the concept" of assisted suicide, Gallagher remarked. "This is something to which he seems passionately dedicated." Kevorkian's dedication eventually paid off: After several weeks of being turned away, a friend in Detroit agreed to let him and the Adkinses use his house for Janet's suicide.[7]

With the place set, Kevorkian suggested carrying out the procedure at the end of May. The Adkinses postponed the date to June 4, preferring to avoid the hassle of airline travel over the Memorial Day weekend. During the negotiation of the date, Kevorkian's friend, acting on the advice of a doctor, withdrew his offer of letting them use his home. By this point, though, Janet, Ron, and one of Janet's close friends,

Carroll Rehmke, had already purchased their airline tickets. Frustrated, Kevorkian had to quickly find another site. "I had made a Herculean effort," he later wrote, "to provide a desirable, clinical setting. Literally and sadly, there was 'no room at the inn.' Now, having been refused everywhere I applied, the *only alternative* remaining was my 1968 camper and a suitable campground."[8]

The Adkinses were also undeterred. They and Janet's friend flew from Seattle to Michigan on June 2. Kevorkian and his two sisters, Margo and Flora, met with the threesome in their hotel room that afternoon so they could all get acquainted. During the meeting, Flora videotaped a forty-five-minute interview by her brother with Janet and Ron. Janet made it clear that she did not want to live to see the progression of her disease. "I want to get out," she told Kevorkian during the interview. "I just . . . want to get out."[9]

The entire group enjoyed a seven-hour dinner at a local seafood restaurant that night, during which they had a wide-ranging conversation. They even told jokes; indeed, it was Janet who "kept us all happy prior to her death," according to Kevorkian. Ron felt the same way. "She was the one who kept everyone up—even to the last hour," he said afterward. Kevorkian explained the procedure over dinner, and believed Janet understood everything. He also asked her to sign several detailed documents. "They're not legally binding," he would later say, "but it shows that I meant well." The party left the restaurant at 12:30 in the morning on June 3. Janet and Ron spent the day of June 3 by themselves. It would be their last together.[10]

At 8:30 on the chilly, overcast morning of June 4, Kevorkian drove his 1968 Volkswagen camper van into a rented space in Lot 73 at Groveland Oaks County Park in north Oakland County. He chose the park, in part, because it had electrical hookups for campers; he would need one for the electrocardiograph (ECG) machine that he was going to use to monitor Janet's heart. He quickly, and somewhat nervously, began to prepare for the procedure. Indeed, he would admit a few days later that Janet was the "calmest person" on the scene that day. While setting up and testing the Mercitron, the doctor accidentally knocked over the container of thiopental—the solution that would induce unconsciousness—and lost about half of it.[11]

Meanwhile, Margo and Flora had gone to pick up Janet at her hotel. They arrived at the campsite at about 9:30, leaving Ron and Carroll at the hotel, as Janet had wanted it. The three women agreed to ride with Kevorkian back to his Royal Oak apartment—a two-and-one-half-hour round trip—to retrieve more thiopental. They got back to the park around noon, and while Kevorkian and his sisters prepared and tested the Mercitron, Janet waited alone in the car. Two hours later, at about 2:00 p.m., Janet climbed into Kevorkian's van through its sliding side door. It was the last place on earth she would see.

Much would later be made by critics and journalists of the doctor's "rusty" camper; most news stories made a point of describing the van with that particular adjective. Naturally, the twenty-two-year-old Volkswagen had some spots of rust. But the facts are also that Kevorkian had installed a cot in the back of the van, upon which he had put new sheets and a clean pillow covered by a new case; that he had cleaned and vacuumed the van's interior in preparation for the procedure; and that he had sewn the new green curtains himself. In what would become a characteristic maneuver, he later defended himself against the attacks on his "rusty van" by using carefully chosen symbolism and emotional appeals: "Where was Christ born? The world's worst conditions—in a haystack with manure and animals all around." [12]

Kevorkian proceeded, with Janet's permission, to cut holes in her nylons at the ankles. There, and at her wrists, he attached the ECG electrodes. He then covered her fully clothed body with a light blanket. Other than Flora's reading of a brief note from Carroll to Janet, and a reading of the Lord's Prayer, little was said by anyone. [13] Finally, the doctor repeated his earlier instructions to Janet about how to activate the Mercitron. After four attempts to insert the syringe, Kevorkian finally got an adequate puncture on Janet's right arm. Janet nodded to him, and Kevorkian turned on the ECG. "Now," he said. Janet hit the Mercitron's switch with the outer edge of her hand. Thiopental, and then potassium chloride—which would stop her heart—began flowing through her body. Her eyelids quickly began to droop. She looked at Kevorkian and whispered, "Thank you, thank you." Her eyes closed, and the doctor replied, "Have a nice trip." She was clinically dead, of a massive heart attack, six minutes after she hit the switch. It was 2:30 in the afternoon.

Even if Kevorkian's comparison of Janet Adkins's death to Jesus Christ's birth was hyperbolic, the fifty-four-year-old woman's suicide was a pivotal event in the American right-to-die movement. With this single, desperate act, Jack Kevorkian became a household name, his dream of *obitiatry*—the practice of assisted death—became a reality, and the movement was reborn.

❁ ❁ ❁

Few people realize just how long of a road Jack Kevorkian had traveled to arrive at the side of Janet Adkins's cot. The doctor's "self-imposed mission," his "righteous crusade," as he referred to it in his 1991 book *Prescription: Medicide—The Goodness of Planned Death*, began shortly after he graduated from the University of Michigan's Medical School in 1952. Kevorkian, the only son of immigrants who fled the Armenian Holocaust during World War I, was an idealistic resident in Michigan's Pathology Department. He was fascinated by the controversial idea of medical experimentation on condemned criminals. It was his reading of one article in particular—published in German in 1932—that represented "a turning point in my career," as he later put it. "In time," he continued, "I became convinced that its impact shackled me with the responsibility to promulgate a profound idea which, whether I liked it or not, would somehow and sometime be a major, if not the predominant, goal of my professional life." The article described the mandated execution, by means of medical experimentation, of condemned criminals in ancient Alexandria. Although direct evidence of the executions does not exist, two Roman historians' criticisms of them, roughly 400 years after they were supposedly carried out, were all that Kevorkian needed to read. For the thirty-year-old doctor, "the spark had been lit."[14]

He insisted, however, that unlike in ancient times, condemned criminals of the 1950s must be given the choice "between conventional methods of execution and irreversible surgical depth anesthesia for the purpose of medical experimentation."[15] Here is an early example of Kevorkian's insistence on individual choice and autonomy. Emphasizing the importance of individual decision making—and defending it from government interference—would become one of the major ways in which he would frame his actions over the rest of his career as an activist. It would prove to be a sound strategy, as we will see in later chapters.

Kevorkian's time in medical school coincided with a period of retrenchment, or to use sociologist Verta Taylor's term, "abeyance," for the right-to-die movement in the United States.[16] According to historian Ian Dowbiggin, who has written the most detailed and comprehensive history of the movement, two "revolutions" had set the stage for the movement's birth two decades earlier, during the 1930s: the expansion of scientific knowledge in the late 1800s and the advent of Progressivism in the early 1900s. "Each trend in its own way," Dowbiggin argued, "helped to undermine orthodox religious faith, question the authority of tradition, and engender a taste for daring social experimentation in the name of justice, efficiency, public health, and human emancipation."[17] In addition to these broad social and cultural shifts, the media began printing stories on mercy killing for the first time, and prominent figures like Jack London and Helen Keller publicly expressed their support for euthanasia. From Dowbiggin's perspective, the founding of the Euthanasia Society of America (ESA) in 1938 was an outgrowth of forty or so years of widespread changes associated with science and Progressivism: massive urbanization, immigration, and industrialization; a rapidly growing belief in Darwinism and positivism; a weakening of religious ties; and consequent shifts in Americans' attitudes toward birth, sex, life, and death. The time was ripe during the 1930s for a public debate over end-of-life issues.

But the movement lost much of its momentum during the 1940s and 1950s, in large part because of the Nazi atrocities during World War II. Many Americans became sensitive to the possibility that euthanasia could be used on this country's weakest and least protected citizens. The Catholic Church also positioned itself as a major opponent of euthanasia, at a time when the Church "enjoyed a unity, rigor, power, and influence that propelled it to the very center of American life."[18] Coupled with successful efforts by euthanasia opponents to equate support for euthanasia with allegiance to Communism, the opposition proved difficult to overcome. These were decades of "setbacks and grave disappointments" for the right-to-die movement.[19] It simply could not compete against the joint forces of fervent anti-Nazism, strong Catholicism, and rapidly growing anti-Communism.

Jack Kevorkian, meanwhile, went on to earn his medical degree and began publishing the results of various research projects. His earliest publications in medical journals emphasized simple medical procedures and the practical, positive uses of medical research, whether he was discussing the use of various staining methods to detect carcinoid tumor cells[20] or entering the debate over so-called "nuclear pellets" in pineal cells and glands.[21] Consistent and highly specialized studies such as these early efforts by Kevorkian—he was not even board certified yet— would likely have served him well in making a traditional career as either a medical researcher or a practicing physician.[22] His research was practical and rigorous, and it had real potential to deepen physicians' knowledge of the human body and to advance the practice of medicine. But he simply could not hide his true interest at the time: using the bodies of condemned criminals for medical experimentation.

Kevorkian's first step in making this idea a reality was to find out what convicted criminals themselves thought of it. On a day off in October 1958, he drove three hours to the nearest prison, the Ohio Penitentiary in Columbus, to inquire about interviewing death row inmates. This was, he believed, "the key event in the evolution of my mission, the cornerstone of its early development."[23] Much to the nervous visitor's surprise, Warden Ralph Alvis allowed him to talk to two condemned prisoners in their twenties. Both men had been convicted of murder. And, although only one of them put it in writing for Kevorkian, both opted for his proposed alternative of anesthesia and experimentation. Kevorkian was ecstatic. He drove home to Ann Arbor in his 1956 Ford, daydreaming about the possibilities.

Two months later, he delivered a paper on the topic, entitled "Capital Punishment or Capital Gain," to the Criminology Section during the annual meeting of the American Association for the Advancement of Science. Both the presentation and its subsequent publication in June 1959 further encouraged Kevorkian in what he referred to as his "controversial death penalty campaign."[24] His colleagues back in the Pathology Department at Michigan were not as enthusiastic, however, and Kevorkian was promptly informed that he had to either abandon his crusade or leave the residency program. "The decision was easy," he later claimed.[25] Kevorkian resigned, and soon became a third-year resident in pathology at Pontiac General Hospital, about forty miles northwest of Ann Arbor. His new position left him free to pursue his unusual interest in what he described as the "extraction of human benefit from death."[26]

And pursue it he did. Among his other activities in the Department of Laboratories at Pontiac General were experiments in transfusing blood from corpses into living human beings. He summarized this work in three scholarly papers. The first appeared in 1961. Kevorkian and his coauthor, Glenn Bylsma, had stumbled upon the "startling idea" that for thirty years, Russian doctors had been successfully transfusing cadaver blood. They decided to replicate their Russian colleagues' work by transfusing two pints into each of four living patients. The authors recognized that Americans would have "a natural tendency merely to shrug the matter off as something which could never be performed or regarded as worthwhile," but took the position that "baseless rejection [of the idea] is unjustified." The pair also admitted "an ostensible undercurrent of repugnance" to the idea "which makes it difficult to view objectively," but nonetheless believed it had "obvious advantages."[27]

Before explaining what the benefits were, Kevorkian and Bylsma went to some lengths to counter possible objections to their work. They allayed readers' fears about seeking permission from the donor's next of kin, notifying the patient's physician of the source of the blood, obtaining consent from the patient, and exposing the patient to possible toxins in the donor's blood. In these paragraphs, Kevorkian can be seen developing his ability to anticipate and preempt his critics' arguments—and to belittle them as irrational. "Most of these objections are more imaginary than real—a sort of emotional reaction to a new and slightly distasteful idea," he and his coauthor wrote.[28] As we will see, this would not be the last time that Kevorkian accused his detractors of "emotionalism" while trumpeting his own indisputable rationality. Ironically, he would continue during the 1990s to use emotional appeals to make his own arguments, at the same time that he demonstrated complete intolerance for his opponents' reliance on emotional arguments.

The advantages of using cadaver blood were several, according to Kevorkian and Bylsma. First, the procedure always raised the recipient's hemoglobin level and hematocrit value to a degree comparable to that of a blood bank. In addition, individuals who would normally require multiple transfusions, such as victims of emergencies, could get it all from one donor. This would serve at least two important purposes: reducing the number of possible antigens introduced into the patient and saving the technician's time. Third, cadaver blood was free. A fourth advantage was that "the technic of obtaining it is simple, and it is stored and dispensed exactly as is conventional donor blood."[29] Finally, because donors would have undergone both gross and microscopic autopsies that verified their overall health and that of each of their organs, their blood would offer "the *least possible* chance for transmission of infectious hepatitis."[30] These advantages far outweighed the potential costs and dangers, and convinced the researchers of the procedure's "merit and practicality." They concluded thus: "From our limited experience, we know it can do no harm and that it offers tremendous potential good which warrants widespread and thorough investigation."[31]

Evidently, Kevorkian himself was one of the very few researchers who were willing to carry out further investigation, despite the potentially positive, practical advantages of using corpse blood in transfusions. Three years after his and Bylsma's 1961 article appeared, Kevorkian and two assistants, Neal Nicol and Edwin Rea, published an article describing the team's experiments in transfusing cadaver blood into living human beings. The recipients were volunteers who were chosen solely on the basis of having a blood type that was compatible with the donors. All of the donors were "fairly young, previously healthy persons who died suddenly and unexpectedly, preferably due to trauma."[32]

The first was a thirty-four-year-old white male who had been dead for five-and-a-half hours. His body was placed head down on a tilt-table in the autopsy room. The first recipient was one of Kevorkian's coauthors, twenty-three-year-old Neal Nicol, who would go on to participate in many of Kevorkian's assisted suicides thirty years later. After donating a pint of his own blood, Nicol lay down on the floor of the autopsy room, about two feet from the donor's head. The experiment proceeded with Kevorkian inserting a sixteen-gauge needle into Nicol's jugular vein and pumping in 400 cc (a little under one pint) of the cadaver's blood. Post-transfusion studies indicated that Nicol "felt well and vigorous during and after the procedure." The authors excitedly pointed out the possibilities: "In this instance over 3 pints could easily have been transfused in less than 10 minutes if the clinical situation so demanded." Two more transfusions went just as smoothly, and were possibly of more consequence because the researchers had to puncture each of the two donor's hearts in order to extract enough blood. Every previous donor in Kevorkian's research had had blood removed from the jugular vein. The authors stated with more than a little satisfaction: "All three recipients are working and well."[33]

Kevorkian claimed he had two motivations for carrying out the research. The less important of the two "was plain inquisitiveness—to try something new and see what happens."[34] More important to Kevorkian was "the tremendous potential military value of direct cadaver blood transfusions."[35] The key word here was "direct." Kevorkian was partly trying to argue against the opponents of using cadaver blood to treat combat wounds in the field: "It is the *direct* aspect which unequivocally destroys the two most prevalent arguments against military use of cadaver blood."[36] First, he argued, "the needed equipment is now minimal and easily capable of being carried in a corpsman's kit." He had, over the course of his experiments, purposely honed his equipment from "fragile and bulky" vacuum bottles to a short list of relatively simple materials. Having served for fifteen months in the Korean War during 1954 and 1955, Kevorkian understood very well the need to minimize medical bulk on the battlefield.[37] Second, Kevorkian believed that the "procedure is simple enough to be carried out anywhere—in a battalion or regimental aid station, field hospital, base hospital, or even in a foxhole on the battlefield itself. This," he argued, "effectively removes the second objection of the need to take the time to gather corpses."[38] The direct body-body method that he and his associates had successfully demonstrated could be used wherever there were dead or dying soldiers. As a matter of fact, the doctor continued, "once the civilian population makes universal [the] use of personal blood-type identification of some kind, the procedure might possibly be employed in the treatment of victims of any natural or man made disaster of catastrophic proportions."[39] Practical benefit and simplicity were, again, Kevorkian's primary concerns.

The end of the article has hints of the defiant, self-righteous rhetoric of insistence, urgency, and idealism that Kevorkian would later employ during his assisted suicide campaign:

> We know that the United States Department of Defense has been reluctant officially to endorse the use of cadaver blood because of its controversial nature and practical drawbacks. But we feel that this study has effectively "lowered the threshold" of acceptability and that there is no justifiable reason for ignoring the matter. We can only suggest that official military recognition be given. But we emphati-

cally insist that military medical service personnel, including nurses, be made aware of successful use of the procedure—whether it is taught or not. If in the future the life of even a single member of our armed force is saved under these circumstances, then our present effort will have been more than vindicated.[40]

Several aspects of this paragraph are worth pointing out since they foreshadow many of Kevorkian's later framing techniques. First, he sets up a supposedly obstinate and timid institution—specifically, the Department of Defense—as an obstacle to beneficial change. As we will see in later chapters, public tirades against the "establishment," which would eventually come to include a host of institutions and groups, would be an important part of Kevorkian's arsenal during the 1990s. A second noteworthy aspect of the selection is the doctor's matter-of-fact insistence that he is right, even if his position has little support. To flatly claim that "there is no justifiable reason for ignoring the matter" is essentially to argue that opposing perspectives are unworthy of being heard. In short, his is the most reasonable position. In later years, Kevorkian would make use of much more colorful dismissive language when talking about his ideological opponents. There is a final point to be made about this passage. By invoking the possibility of saving the lives of American soldiers, Kevorkian gives his readers a grand and hopeful vision that goes far beyond the bloody details of any particular medical experiment. He is appealing to rationality here, as he would do countless times in the decades ahead. At the same time, interestingly, he is trying to tap into his readers' sense of patriotism and loyalty to their soldiers; in other words, into their emotions and feelings. It is a clever way of mustering support for any idea, but especially for a controversial one.

In a third article describing his ongoing experiments in transfusing blood between cadavers and living humans, Kevorkian and John Marra, the Chief of Laboratories at Pontiac General Hospital, set out four purposes. The first three were "to document our experience with three human recipients; to corroborate statements published long ago by Russian pioneers; [and] to help justify and support further clinical probes of non-Russian investigators interested in the topic." The fourth objective was ideological; namely, "to help dispel some of the aura of 'untouchability' connected with corpse blood in this country because of emotionalism, politics, or fear."[41] Kevorkian's denigration of "emotionalism" should be familiar by now. He would continue the habits, especially during the 1990s, of chiding his critics for being fearful of the consequences of his ideas being put into practice, and of impugning political motives to his detractors. As in his two previous studies, the transfusions went smoothly. The researchers concluded that the clinical use of cadaver blood was "at best valuable therapy, [and] at worst an interesting study."[42]

One year later, Kevorkian and a coauthor examined the survival of red blood cells that had been transfused from cadavers into living humans. They found very little difference between cadaver blood and live-donor blood, in terms of the survival rates of red cells, and believed that theirs was "the first such demonstration recorded in the United States." The researchers concluded with unwavering self-assurance: "There is no doubt in our mind [sic] that cadaver blood is safer to use than routine live-donor blood, because it is never given until all gross and microscopic examination of the donor has been completed."[43] Indeed, the live-donor blood had produced hepatitis in all three recipients in the study.

Kevorkian's research on cadaver blood transfusions during the early and mid-1960s convinced him "that the Russians are right."[44] Nevertheless, his enthusiasm for the notion of transfusing corpse blood into living human beings was not contagious. He himself moved on to other research areas after 1965. Assisted suicide and euthanasia were not yet among them, despite Kevorkian's continued interest in studying the potential benefits of human death. "Back then," he later remarked, "I wasn't concerned with euthanasia."[45] Given Americans' widespread rejection of euthanasia during the 1950s, the reasons for which were described earlier in this chapter, it seems unsurprising that Kevorkian would have occupied himself with other pursuits at the time.

What is surprising, however, is how long it took him, given his ongoing interest in death, to come around to euthanasia as a personal and professional interest. At the same time that Kevorkian was studying blood transfusions from cadavers, the right-to-die movement resurfaced and quickly grew. It would maintain its newfound strength through the end of the 1970s. Faced with the threat of nuclear war, the horrors of the Vietnam War, an aging population, and the increasing use of medical technology to prolong life, Americans became obsessed with death during the 1960s.[46] The movement became an outlet for people to express their fledgling beliefs, new ideas, and lingering insecurities. In the social upheaval and rights culture of the 1960s, euthanasia—which during this time began to be replaced by the phrase "the right to die"— was transformed from a social and biological issue into a personal matter. The right of each individual to choose how and when to die was increasingly viewed as a civil liberty, as a tangible freedom from the state's interference in its citizens' personal lives. In hindsight, one would have expected Kevorkian, with his interest in the "extraction of human benefit from death," to have at least a passing interest in the rejuvenated social movement to critically reexamine the ways in which people die.[47] He had a personal reason to do so as well, as his mother had been suffering from a long and painful illness that she would ultimately succumb to in 1968. Her only son, however, simply tried to make her as comfortable as possible toward the end. Assisted suicide did not cross his mind even then.

Between 1970 and 1976, Kevorkian served as the Director of Laboratories and Chief of Pathology at Sarasota General Hospital in Detroit.[48] The right-to-die movement was continuing to pick up steam during this time, even as it underwent organizational changes. Despite, or perhaps because of, the reinvigoration of the movement in the previous decade, its purpose became less clear and internal divisions began to become apparent. To that point, the Euthanasia Society of America (ESA) had been the dominant movement organization. In 1967, the society's president, Pauline Taylor, formed the Euthanasia Educational Fund (commonly known as The Council) in an attempt to solve the ESA's ongoing financial problems. It was hoped that The Council, as a tax-exempt charitable organization, would raise revenue for the movement through donations. The parent organization, the ESA, changed its name to the Society for the Right to Die (SRD) in 1974, and The Council became Concern for Dying (CFD) in 1978.

The importance of these name changes was twofold: Dropping the term "euthanasia" further distanced the movement from images of Nazis, and adding terms like "right to die" and "concern" recast the practices in a compassionate way and as a human right. In addition, according to Ian Dowbiggin, "the founding of the SRD marked a renewed dedication to pursuing the legalization of active euthanasia, a reenergized campaign to seek euthanasia laws through the political process."[49] The SRD, in other words, would not only continue to support the removal and withholding of medical treatment from terminally ill and severely incapacitated patients (passive euthanasia), but would begin to pursue legalizing the killing of consenting, competent patients, typically by administering medication (active euthanasia). The only, but crucial, difference between passive and active euthanasia was the nature of the doctor's role—passively allowing a patient to die by disconnecting a feeding tube versus actively bringing about a patient's death by way of a lethal injection, for example. The SRD would advocate for both acts while CFD would abandon the right to die altogether and focus instead on "hospice and palliative care and better communications among patients, their families, and health care providers."[50]

The disagreement over the direction of the movement soon grew bitter. In 1979, the two organizations—which were the two arms of the same original body, the ESA—officially separated. With the founding of the Hemlock Society in the following year by Derek Humphry and his then-wife, Ann Wickett, there were now three different, and competing, right-to-die organizations in the United States. By 1980, a "social movement sector," as it has been called, had developed for the first time around the right to die.[51] It was characterized by organizations with competing interests, agendas, leaders, and definitions of what the "right to die" actually meant.

Jack Kevorkian spent the late 1970s and early 1980s working at several hospitals in southern California. His general interest in human death remained as strong as ever, regardless of where he practiced medicine. In fact, at the Beverly Hills Medical Center, he continued a habit he had developed during his residency at the University of Michigan during the 1950s: "I used to take what I called death rounds. I would go around to all of the people who were about to die and watch. I wanted to see at what point they could no longer be resuscitated. All the other doctors laughed at me."[52] His "death rounds" involved "photographing the retinas of dying patients in an effort to establish the point at which death becomes irreversible."[53] It was not something Kevorkian took personal pleasure in; it was professional curiosity that pushed him to do it: "I don't like to watch someone die," he later admitted. "It is a traumatic, wrenching experience."[54]

Indeed, it was his medical curiosity, but also his interest in the practical benefits of studying dead and dying people's eyes, that had spurred him to publish a series of papers between the mid-1950s and early

1960s on using changes in the human eye to document the onset of death. The first, which appeared while Kevorkian was still a resident at the University of Michigan, argued that observing changes in a dying patient's retinas was a most effective technique for determining the exact time of death. The author's pragmatism is clear throughout the article, but nowhere more so than at the end, where he outlines two types of situations in which his technique "may find useful application." The first was in general clinical practice "to determine a state of death; to differentiate between real and apparent death and to determine re-suscitability of victims of fainting, pathologic sleep, electrocution, deep coma, profound shock; narcosis (barbiturates, chloroform), asphyxia-tion, or drowning; to differentiate real shock from cardiac arrest or fibrillation during surgery; and to determine death in patients in respi-rators." The second was in forensic medicine "to estimate time of death in minutes . . . or hours . . . ; and to determine the position of the head at death." This was no mere medical or intellectual exercise; observing ophthalmoscopic changes, as far as Kevorkian was concerned, had tan-gible benefits, especially for the living. From his perspective, changes in the retina and the retinal vessels "provide a readily available means of determining the fact of death, of differentiating apparent and actual death, of estimating (within a certain range) the elapsed time after death, and, *of great importance*, of indicating the possibility of success from efforts at resuscitation."[55]

In a related article published in the *Journal of the American Medical Association* one year later, Kevorkian again argued that "there is an urgent need for a rapid, easy, and accurate method for determining the absence of cardiac output"—in other words, determining when death occurs.[56] Demonstrating his knowledge of and interest in history, he cited a French doctor who, in 1863, had used the newly invented oph-thalmoscope to describe "the most nearly infallible sign of death"; namely, the segmentation of blood vessels in the retinas. Kevorkian performed eye examinations at the operating tables of eight patients, and described in detailed text, as well as with one photograph and three drawings, the changes he observed in each one's retinas. Simply and directly, he concluded that "the ophthalmoscope can serve as an accu-rate aid in the rapid determination of circulatory arrest and as a de-pendable guide in the institution of therapy."[57]

The young doctor published two more papers in 1961 on his observations of cadavers' eyes. One, simply titled "The Eye in Death," was more of an instructional essay than a research article.[58] By this point, Kevorkian had become supremely confident in the efficacy and superiority of his method: "After a careful study of the literature and personal experience in the examination of the fundus of 25 patients and numerous animals during their agonal period . . . , it is our belief that 30 seconds with an ophthalmoscope will provide more accurate information to pinpoint the time of complete biologic death than can be obtained with all other methods combined."[59] This level of precision had practical benefits; namely, it could "provide more accurate information on the circulatory status and the exact time of irreversible biologic death, and the time since death," and could help medical teams essentially determine whether a patient was worth saving.[60]

In the second article, Kevorkian describes his experiments in using color changes in corpses' retinas as a "post-mortem clock" to estimate their approximate time of death.[61] After all, at the time, according to Kevorkian, "current methods are by no means satisfactory." His method was simple: "The only tool used was an ordinary ophthalmoscope. Each morning I checked the morgue for new admissions but carefully avoided learning the recorded time of death or of admission to the morgue. Each case was an unknown whose time of death could be in the range of the previous 1 to 15 hours. It was up to me to 'guess' when using the ophthalmoscope and my own judgment."[62] Kevorkian carried out his original observations at University Hospital in Ann Arbor, and then, one year later, made additional observations at both Pontiac General Hospital and Pontiac State Hospital.

His estimates were fairly accurate: The average "error per case" was 1.2 hours, which compared well to the practices then in use.[63] But the young doctor's most important result was that experience meant everything: "The signs are difficult to teach. Only a description of the essential changes can be imparted by instruction, but without experience one is lost. The most fruitful road to proficiency is through actual observation and guessing, by trial and error. Each must achieve mastery by doing for himself."[64] Indeed, Kevorkian described what an "authority" on the subject should look like: "As a tentative rule, I propose that anyone who has examined the retinae of 50 unknown cases and has shown consistent or increasing accuracy might consider himself to be in a position to use the signs with authority."[65]

Even if Kevorkian's colleagues at the Beverly Hills Medical Center two decades later could overlook some of his odd behavior—such as sleeping overnight in the hospital parking lot in the same 1968 Volkswagen van in which Janet Adkins would end her life in 1990—his ongoing practice of intently observing dying patients' eyes must have made some of them uneasy. Nevertheless, the most vivid memory that Trudy Staler, a lab technician at Beverly Hills Medical, had of the middle-aged doctor was not of his "death rounds," but of one of his inventions: "What I remember most is that, in his spare time, he invented a contraption that would cut up prostate tissue in the lab, so you wouldn't have to use a knife." Kevorkian still had not demonstrated any interest in the subject for which he would eventually become internationally famous. In fact, Dr. Fred Hodell, the chief pathologist at Pacific Hospital in Long Beach, California, who hired Kevorkian as his assistant in 1981, didn't "remember him talking about suicide."[66]

The year 1982 would be the last in which Kevorkian held a job, even though he continued to apply for various positions throughout most of the 1980s. The last straw was being rejected for a job as a paramedic in 1988, despite the description of him offered by his former boss: "He's a very brilliant man. He was very friendly with people at the hospital," said Dr. Hodell. "I don't apply anymore," Kevorkian said in an interview two years after his failed attempt at becoming a paramedic. He knew that he was "unemployable because of the controversy surrounding my work." He had grown frustrated, telling one reporter, "I've written off the medical profession. I'm an outsider. I'm the lowest in the profession. I'm tired of beating my head against a wall."[67] In these comments, we can see Kevorkian setting himself up for the role he would play so well for most of the 1990s: the maverick doctor, the "outsider" railing against the medical establishment.

Kevorkian's careful management of his public image would help propel him to his position as the face of the right-to-die movement. It was a movement that continued to grow during the 1980s. The World Federation of Right-to-Die Societies was formed in Oxford, England in 1980. The body was composed of twenty-seven groups from eighteen countries. From the outset, European members of the World Federation tended to be more sympathetic than Americans—which included the SRD and CFD—to active euthanasia. The more radical tendencies of the international movement quickly drove a wedge into the American movement.[68] For the first time, right-to-die organizations in the United States were forced to take a clear and definite position on the various forms of euthanasia. The wedge was driven even further by the newly founded Hemlock Society, which had ballooned to 50,000 members by the time Kevorkian appeared on the scene in 1990. Its rapid growth was due in large part to its official support for active euthanasia and assisted suicide and to its dual mission of legislative reform and grassroots education. Unable to handle the national and international competition, the SRD and CFD reunited in 1991 to form Choice in Dying (CID). Nevertheless, Hemlock would continue throughout most of the 1990s to be the most widely recognized right-to-die organization in the country.

Without a job, Kevorkian devoted himself almost entirely to pursuing his research interests. His published work during the 1980s was noticeably more dogmatic than his earlier research efforts and papers. Nearly all of it focused on "the ethics and practices of euthanasia, assisted suicide and judicial executions," as he later described it.[69] One of the first articles to come out of this period represented a return to one of his earliest interests. It was called "A Brief History of Experimentation on Condemned and Executed Humans."[70] Kevorkian later explained that once he finished drafting the essay, he realized that it was "not 'academic' enough to please the fastidious editors of journals devoted exclusively to historical research." At the same time, he continued, "because I had no academic credentials and because the subject of my paper is anathema to medical authorities, I knew that it would never be accepted by editors of so-called prestigious journals" such as the *Journal of the American Medical Association*. As a result, he turned to the *Journal of the National Medical Association*, which published the paper in 1985.[71]

Because the article represented both a return to an early interest of Kevorkian's and a preview of an argument he would make during his assisted suicide campaign of the 1990s, it is worth examining in detail. The purpose of the essay was simple: to raise the "now denigrated, but honorable, concept" alluded to in its title "to the dignity of an open, fair, and thorough assessment."[72] Kevorkian begins from the dual premises that "the altruistic desires of many now languishing on death row are being ignored,"[73] and that the topic is "of little interest or importance in today's scientific community, perhaps because it is accorded the emotionally charged repugnance of the death penalty."[74] Again, Kevorkian resorted to juxtaposing science, or reason, and emotion. He hoped to kill two birds with one stone: "ameliorating such judgments" by chronicling the "pertinent historical facts and ideas,"[75] while offering death row inmates, whose "insignificant voices are lost in the din of society's ethical chaos,"[76] more autonomy over how their bodies are used after they are executed. In short, Kevorkian saw an opportunity to simultaneously take advantage of the 1976 U.S. Supreme Court decision to reinstate the death penalty and to meet medical researchers' constant need for "risky" human experimentation.[77]

Kevorkian's essay goes on to offer detailed accounts of experiments in ancient Greece and Alexandria, among the Mayans, during the Renaissance and the Enlightenment, and during the nineteenth and twentieth centuries.[78] His discussion was, in his own later judgment, "the most comprehensive history of the topic ever published in medical journals in the United States, if not the world."[79] To Kevorkian, the conclusion was straightforward and indisputable, if for no other reason than that it would thin out the crowds on death rows across the country: "In the United States where death rows are once again becoming overpopulated, all condemned persons should be allowed to choose to submit to experimentation, or to organ donation, under strictly controlled anesthesia before ultimate death by lethal thiopental injection." And even if there was some disagreement, Kevorkian continued, again privileging individual autonomy and choice over institutional interference, "the decisive argument should be that of the condemned themselves."[80]

In the same year, 1985, Kevorkian published two articles in the Israel-based international journal *Medicine and Law*. Three more would follow, in the same journal, in 1986, 1988, and 1989. Kevorkian chose this particular outlet time after time because "no American medical journal would accept" the articles. The reason was simple: The editor of *Medicine and Law*, from Kevorkian's perspective, was "less intimidated by potential controversy" than his American counterparts.[81] The ideas he set forth in this series of five articles were nothing if not controversial.

The first three also represented a return to his medical school obsession with experimentation on condemned criminals.[82] Although he claimed to be neutral on the question of whether capital punishment should be legal, he reiterated his old argument that death row inmates should have the freedom to choose to have their organs donated and their bodies experimented upon after their execution. He also expanded his original argument from thirty years earlier to indict physicians and the medical establishment:

> No matter what his personal feelings or convictions, it is a physician's moral duty to insist that *if* and *when* men and women are to be destroyed by law in any of our states, that law should also grant them the opportunity to donate organs. No matter what its stand on capital punishment per se, the medical profession has a moral duty to help society prove that vengeance alone is not the ultimate aim of it all.[83]

Individual doctors' feelings and personal morality did not make any difference to Kevorkian. What mattered most was the profession's moral obligation to patients. He was so sure of his position, in fact, that he felt justified in chalking up any opposition to his ideas as simply "a result of subjective emotionalism comfortably insulated from direct experience with the reality of the matter at hand."[84]

Kevorkian published two more articles the following year. The first outlined a detailed and comprehensive "bioethical code" for carrying out medical experiments on condemned criminals.[85] The theme of the second article was even more radical. Kevorkian called for the establishment of a new medical specialty, which he termed "bioethiatrics" or "bioethiatry." Like practitioners in any of the other many fields of medicine, bioethiatricians would have a specialized role: Embodying "a unique combination of ethical action and moral judgment," they would be called upon to decide matters of life and death, such as euthanasia.[86] To Kevorkian, the new field would be no different from any other medical specialty, some of which—rheumatology and gerontology, to use examples he cited—had been considered equally outlandish several decades earlier.

In what type of case would a bioethiatrician be called upon? Kevorkian's hypothetical scenario was a poignant one that was still fresh in Americans' minds. If a board-certified bioethiatrician had existed when Karen Ann Quinlan lay in a persistent vegetative state during the late 1970s and early 1980s, he suggested, the situation would have turned out very differently: "Instead of precipitating the unfortunate contro-

versy that actually ensued, the family's request could have been referred by attending physicians to the hypothetical bioethiatrician." He
continued:

> After in-depth interviews with the next of kin, analysis of the entire
> family situation, review of the patient's clinical course as recorded in
> the chart, thorough examination of the patient, and consultation with
> colleagues in other pertinent specialties, the bioethiatrician would
> use his or her abilities to make the necessary diagnosis of inescapable
> and imminent biologic death due to an irretrievably vegetative state
> and to write the necessary orders to accomplish the called-for "treat-
> ment."[87]

Once the bioethiatrician had made the decision, it would stand: "nothing and nobody could justifiably override or gainsay the preemptory
role of the board-certified bioethiatrician."[88]

 Kevorkian failed to drum up any professional or public support for
his latest ideas, but he forged ahead. In a 1987 letter to the editor of the
Canadian Medical Association Journal, Kevorkian argued that physicians should be allowed to remove the organs of a condemned criminal.
Once the extraction was done, "a lay executioner" would cause "death
with a lethal injection."[89] The doctor was optimistic, but realistic, about
the impact of his letter:

> This letter may not influence the debate in Canada on capital pun-
> ishment, but it could kindle a bit of concern in the United States,
> where humans are being destroyed by law, and many patients are
> dying with them, and where access to a proper medical forum is
> blocked by a blasé and, on this issue at least, a *socially criminal
> profession*.[90]

The last three words were characteristically dramatic and hyperbolic. In
his view, he was undoubtedly right, and his former colleagues in the
medical profession were all wrong. This manner of sharp criticism of
the medical profession would eventually become Kevorkian's stock-in-
trade, as I demonstrate in later chapters.

 The final two articles Kevorkian published in *Medicine and Law*
explored his related interests in bioethics, "planned death," and organ
harvesting.[91] "The Last Fearsome Taboo: Medical Aspects of Planned
Death" was the piece that would be most often referred to by journal-

ists after Kevorkian became famous in 1990—and not surprisingly, for it outlined his most controversial and radical notion yet. The doctor's idea was to establish "obitoria," or medical clinics, to which people could go to carry out a "planned death," which Kevorkian defined as "the purposeful ending of human life by direct human action." It included capital punishment, suicide, "justifiable" infanticide and pedicide, and "both intra- and extrauterine" feticide.[92] Medical doctors—"obitiatrists"—would staff the clinics and carry out the procedures.

Planned death was, in Kevorkian's estimation, an idea whose time had come—or was inevitably to come very soon. Typically, he blamed both the legal and medical establishments for the delay: "It is now anachronistic laws that dictate what is moral or ethical. And the medical profession continues its futile hair-splitting of platitudes in the face of inexorably changing taboos."[93] In typical fashion, Kevorkian saw his position as the most logical, and his critics as unreasonable: "Criticism of this proposal cannot withstand rational analysis," he wrote.[94] The article ends in passionate, moralizing language:

> Perhaps the greatest advantage [of implementing planned death] would be the further unshackling of the primal human right of what shud [sic] be absolute personal autonomy within the bounds of reasonable law. The operative word is "reasonable," for human history is a sad narrative of misery wrought through strictly sectarian dogma (religious or secular) which zealous proselytizers strive to have universalized as dispassionately punitive law. Such indecent coercion makes certain extraordinary and well-reasoned actions of otherwise law-abiding "infidels" or "heretics" into "criminal acts," though the consequences are relevant and meaningful to their immanence alone.[95]

In three somewhat rambling sentences, Kevorkian managed to dismiss religious officials, ethicists, and legal professionals—in short, anyone who was "unreasonable" enough to disagree with his idea. At the same time, he called upon readers to apply their reason and to elevate personal autonomy above all other considerations. These, as we have seen, had become common pleas from Kevorkian over the previous thirty-five years.

Kevorkian's final *Medicine and Law* article recalled his earlier arguments about the benefits of harvesting organs. In this piece, however, he took his idea one step further by asserting that a commercial market for human organs and tissues should be established. This was Kevorkian at work, again, on what he saw as an important and practical problem: the shortage of available organs for those in need of transplants. The shortage, Kevorkian believed, was due to the "delusion of hypocrisy" called altruism.[96] He reasoned that potential donors would respond much more favorably to monetary incentives—the "profit motive," as he termed it.[97] So, he concluded, a commercial market for organ donation was the logical answer. He painted a by-now familiar picture of medical professionals who balked at the idea of commercially marketing tissues and organs. "It is sheer folly," he wrote, "to expect a lone and flimsy beacon of purely altruistic organ donation to withstand . . . an invincible deluge of commercialism. The transplant council's guidelines perpetuate a deeply ingrained tradition of hypocrisy which, now more flagrant and pervasive than ever, continues to undermine ethical sobriety by affronting rational judgment."[98] The medical establishment, in Kevorkian's view, was profit-hungry, irrational, moralistic, and indifferent toward patients.

Kevorkian's preoccupation with new death-related interests did not stop him entirely from promoting old ones. In 1988, he read an article in the *Western Journal of Medicine* by two California doctors who proposed applying a nuclear medicine study—essentially, the use of state-of-the-art imaging procedures—to determine the onset of brain death. Doing so required an intravenous injection and a portable gamma camera.[99] Kevorkian was not convinced of the need for such complexity, and immediately wrote a letter to the journal's editor. "There is a neglected, far quicker, cheaper, and easier way," Kevorkian, ever the pragmatist, began, "to conclude whether or not cerebral blood circulation exists than the complex nuclear imaging procedure advocated by Drs. Braunstein and Wang." His proposed method required only an ophthalmoscope, tap water, and a patient without cataracts, and referenced his own research on "the eye in death" during the 1950s and early 1960s. After describing how his technique would work, he concluded dismissively: "Here is one area where a 'high-tech' approach would seem to be ostentatious and wasteful frippery."[100]

By early 1989, Kevorkian was more publicly promoting his idea of harvesting the organs of the roughly 2,000 people then on death rows across the country. "Each condemned prisoner could save five, six, seven lives," he said. "They're young, they're in good shape. What a waste." Hearts, lungs, kidneys, livers, pancreases, small intestines—all were on the doctor's wish list for transplants: "We need organs," he argued, "and these men owe society a debt." Kevorkian even had new business cards printed, on which he referred to himself as an obitiatrist—"the world's first," he declared proudly. What little response there was to Kevorkian's notion was, perhaps predictably, not positive. Infamous serial killer John Wayne Gacy was among the very few people who publicly supported it. By contrast, the director of the Illinois Coalition Against the Death Penalty called Kevorkian "Dr. Frankenstein." The comparison to Mary Shelley's fictional doctor was, to Kevorkian's mind, "a compliment." After all, he pointed out, "Frankenstein was a benevolent man. It's society that made the monster bad."[101] Despite his embrace of the epithet, Kevorkian moved another controversial idea to the back burner. It would remain there for a few years, thanks to the sudden notoriety that he would soon achieve by making one of his other ideas a reality in the summer of 1990.

2

"THEY'LL BE AFTER ME FOR THIS"

Lighting a Movement's Fuse

It was not until the summer of 1990—more than twenty-five years after he carried out his experiments that transfused blood directly from corpses into living humans—that sixty-two-year-old Jack Kevorkian finally got another chance to put one of his many unusual ideas into practice. In so doing, the retired pathologist almost immediately set off a decade-long national debate over the right to die, complete with courtroom theatrics, hunger strikes, and a media feeding frenzy. "My ultimate aim is to make euthanasia a positive experience," he declared. "I'm trying to knock the medical profession into accepting its responsibilities, and those responsibilities include assisting their patients with death."[1] When Kevorkian helped Janet Adkins die in June 1990, he instead ushered in the most tumultuous period of the American right-to-die movement's history.

❖ ❖ ❖

Jack Kevorkian had cycled through a number of unconventional, obscure, and provocative research interests between the 1950s and 1989: medical experiments on death row inmates, observations of dying patients' retinas, blood transfusions from the dead into the living, organ harvesting, the commercialization of human tissues and organs, and the establishment of death clinics and a new medical specialty. Despite

Kevorkian's efforts, none of his ideas resonated with anyone outside of the medical community—or with many people within it, for that matter—before 1990. He spent these four decades as a lone activist, outside of both mainstream medicine and the public's view.

Regardless of which idea he was studying and advocating, his emphasis was typically on its practical advantages, as we saw in chapter 1. His arguments also relied on setting up a dichotomy: reason versus emotion, scientific evidence versus personal opinion, and individual autonomy versus institutional meddling. Throughout the 1990s, Kevorkian would continue his habit of splitting issues into two clear sides. Most often, he positioned himself on the rational, scientific, individualistic, "right" side, with anyone and everyone who disagreed with him on the other. His technique was remarkably successful for much of the decade, as we will see.

☼ ☼ ☼

The first things Dr. Kevorkian did after Janet Adkins's electrocardiograph showed a flat line were to disconnect the intravenous line and call the authorities to tell them what he had done.[2] Calling the police himself was a critical part of Kevorkian's approach. He wanted as many people as possible to know exactly what had happened, and that he had been directly involved in Janet's death. Over the next couple of years, Kevorkian would rely on the tactic of contacting the authorities as he tried to persuade the public that he had nothing to hide. He was not secretly killing people without their consent, he was not hiding his actions, and he continually made it clear that he was not going to run away from any consequences he might have to face. These quickly came to be the implicit messages of Kevorkian's campaign. And they would endear him to a large proportion of Americans, who quickly came to see him as a crusading hero who was willing to sacrifice himself for his desperate patients' wishes.

Detective Sergeant David Haire and his partner, both of the Michigan State Police, were the first to arrive at the scene of Janet's death. Kevorkian began by informing them that he had been contacted by the Adkinses, who had heard of him and his suicide machine through the press. He went on to tell the story of how they ended up carrying out Janet's suicide at the campground in his van, rather than in a more agreeable place. After he described the details of the procedure and showed the officers Janet's body, he allowed them to photograph and search the van.[3] It is unlikely that the officers had ever encountered such a scene.

There was so much blood smeared on Kevorkian's hands and clothes that one eyewitness thought he "looked more like a fisherman than a doctor."[4] Kevorkian explained to Michael Podeszwik, an investigator with the Oakland County Medical Examiner's office, that he had experienced "some difficulty inserting the needle" into Janet's arm. Podeszwik also collected two pieces of paper from the doctor. Both were notes from Janet. The first said that she wanted to end her life before her disease progressed, and the second requested that her eyes be donated for transplantation.[5]

It was not until four hours after her death that Janet's body was finally removed from Kevorkian's van. Kevorkian would later complain that they were four wasted hours of investigators "walking around and scratching their heads." Such a long delay irritated the doctor, if only because it offended his pragmatic sensibility: "You could have sliced her liver in half and saved two babies and her bone marrow could have been taken, her heart, two kidneys, two lungs, a pancreas. Think of the people that could have been saved." Kevorkian's complaint harkened back to his earlier published arguments in favor of organ harvesting. This time, a doctor publicly disagreed with Kevorkian's claim, calling it "nonsense." The medical director of the New England Organ Bank, Dr. Robert Kirkman, continued: "The way she died precluded the diagnosis of brain death and that would have made impossible the removal of any organs for transplantation." In fact, even if she had died another way, according to Dr. Kirkman, Janet's age made it likely that only her kidneys could have been donated.[6]

While the police investigated the suicide scene, Kevorkian and his two sisters drove to the state police barracks in Pontiac, where he wrote a voluntary statement describing the circumstances of Janet's death. Kevorkian, again, wanted to be as open as he could be about his role in her suicide. The next night, June 5, Ron Adkins and two of his and Janet's three sons, Neil and Norman, held a press conference back home in Portland, Oregon. Ron said that his wife had decided to die almost a year earlier, when she was first diagnosed with Alzheimer's. Though he supported his wife's decision, none of his three sons did. He also read a brief suicide note, which Janet had written just a few hours before her death: "I have decided for the following reasons to take my own life. This is a decision taken in a normal state of mind and is fully considered. I have Alzheimer's disease and do not want to let it progress any further. I don't choose to put my family or myself through the agony of this terrible disease." The note was signed "Janet E. Adkins" and cosigned by two witnesses: Carroll Rehmke and Ron Adkins.[7]

Despite his obvious and admitted assistance in Adkins's suicide, Kevorkian was not immediately arrested. Several aspects of the case tied the prosecutor's hands. For one, Michigan had no specific law against suicide, let alone against assisting in it. Oakland County Prosecutor Richard Thompson, who would eventually charge Kevorkian with murder, knew that no law existed. He had to buy himself some time. Thompson claimed that the police investigation and the medical examiner's report would take two months; it was only after they were both completed that he would decide whether to bring charges against Kevorkian. A second problem, from prosecutors' point of view, was that the onus of Janet Adkins's death was on Janet herself: She was the one who had activated the Mercitron. Kevorkian's careful design of the device, which required that the patient activate it, was what made this particular case different from other, similar ones in which the assisting doctor had been charged with homicide.[8]

Before Jack Kevorkian had ever even met Janet Adkins, Michigan prosecutors had disagreed over the legality of assisted suicide. Responding to Kevorkian's promotion of the device during the fall of 1989, one assistant prosecutor in Oakland County had claimed that anyone who provided such a device could be charged with murder. But the chief of the Wayne County prosecutor's appellate division, Jim Baughman, had disagreed: "If you actually take part in the act, that's criminal. If you provide the means to do it, that's not."[9] It was a distinction that Jack Kevorkian understood very clearly, and was able to exploit to further his cause. He had taken great pains to build a device that could be operated by the patient. All he had to do was insert the intravenous line—and then sit back and watch. He believed he could not be successfully prosecuted for that. As it turned out, he was correct.

Kevorkian's understanding of Michigan's current statutes—or lack thereof—regarding suicide and assisted suicide allowed him to take advantage of what sociologist Doug McAdam has referred to as the "political opportunity structure."[10] McAdam believed that shared grievances and sufficient resources were not enough to generate collective behavior such as a social movement, as earlier theorists had asserted. Political opportunities also had to exist, and people needed to successfully take advantage of them, as leaders of the civil rights movement had done during the 1960s. Political opportunities, of course, come in many shapes and sizes, including receptive government officials, support from powerful preexisting groups, and, in Kevorkian's case, legal loopholes. Three times during the 1990s, as we will see in later chapters, Kevorkian would be acquitted by a jury because of the vagueness and limitations of extant Michigan law. He knew exactly how far he could legally go each time he assisted in a suicide.

Another possible reason that Kevorkian was not immediately arrested for his part in Janet Adkins's death was that he did not have a criminal record. He was so clean, in fact, that since becoming licensed to practice medicine in Michigan on July 24, 1953, there had not been a single complaint registered about him or any disciplinary action taken against him. His medical record was impeccable. Despite not being arrested on the spot, Kevorkian made a prediction that would, by the end of the year, prove correct: "They'll be after me for this."[11]

But first, Dr. Jack Kevorkian became a celebrity. On June 7, just three days after Janet's death, he appeared on *Geraldo* and the *Today Show*.[12] In subsequent chapters, we will see that with the help of his flamboyant attorney, Geoffrey Fieger, Kevorkian would go on to manipulate the media more successfully and for a longer time than any other right-to-die movement leader had before—or has since. He was articulate, well educated, and a licensed medical doctor, which gave him instant credibility in the eyes of the public. He appeared as an amiable older man, if also a bit eccentric, in televised interviews. In addition, he nearly always found common ground with viewers and interviewers, whether he was touting the importance of individual freedom or criticizing organized medicine. He framed the discussion of the right to die in ways that would resonate with people, and he used the media to do it. Audiences seemed naturally drawn to him.

Thanks to burgeoning technologies, the news of Janet's suicide—and Kevorkian's assistance in it—quickly spread around the world, from Canada to the United Kingdom to Australia.[13] Kevorkian appeared on the ABC's *Couchman* television program in Australia at the beginning of July.[14] Part of the interview focused on Kevorkian's current interest in establishing special death chambers—or obitoriums—to be set up in Melbourne and Sydney. They would be run by doctors who had the authority to grant or deny a patient's wish to die, and would, in essence, be places where one could "go to one's death."[15] This was an idea he had written about before, as we saw in the previous chapter.

Throughout this first wave of national and international publicity, Kevorkian ably deflected any criticism of his involvement onto the medical establishment. "Why should criticism be leveled at me?" he asked the *Today Show*'s Deborah Norville. "Level it at the profession that's shirking its responsibility."[16] One of the questions that Janet Adkins's suicide suddenly raised was, indeed, medical: What role, if any, should doctors play in helping their patients die? Then, too, there was the legal question of what constitutes assisted suicide and the philosophical question of when a life is no longer worth living. Americans were living longer than ever before, thanks in large part to rapid advancements in medical technology. But longer did not necessarily mean better. More and more older people felt, as Janet Adkins had, that their lives—characterized as they were by chronic disease or illness—were simply no longer worth living. One journalist summarized the changing mindset of older Americans this way: "The patients who once looked to their doctors only for cures are now asking for more. They want help in managing death."[17] It was becoming clear that there had never been a case quite like Janet Adkins's.

The varied reactions to Adkins's death are best understood in the cultural context of the time. The right to die was already on Americans' minds by the summer of 1990 because of an ongoing U.S. Supreme Court case. The question before the Court since the previous summer was whether the state of Missouri could intervene in the Cruzan family's decision to remove the food and water tubes from their thirty-two-year-old daughter Nancy, who had been in a persistent vegetative state (PVS) for seven years. Five years after a 1983 car accident left Nancy in a PVS, a Missouri circuit court judge gave her parents permission to remove the feeding tubes. The state appealed, and the Missouri Supreme Court overturned the circuit court's decision in November 1988. The Cruzans appealed to the U.S. Supreme Court, which agreed in July 1989 for the first time in history to hear a right-to-die case. The justices ruled that incompetent patients were unable to exercise their right to refuse medical treatment under the Due Process clause of the Fourteenth Amendment. Without any clear and convincing evidence of Nancy's wishes to withdraw the treatment, the Court upheld the Missouri Supreme Court's 1988 decision. Nancy Cruzan would continue to live. The case was eventually remanded, and on rehearing, the Missouri court gave great weight to convincing evidence that if she had executed a living will, Nancy would have rejected the feeding tube. Ultimately, the tube was clamped shut, and Nancy Cruzan was finally allowed to die in December 1990.[18]

Since the equally well-known Karen Ann Quinlan case of the late 1970s and early 1980s, public opinion had been slowly moving toward greater patient autonomy. Two relevant questions had been included in the National Opinion Research Center's General Social Survey since 1977. One asked, "Do you think a person has the right to end his or her own life if this person has an incurable disease?" By 1990, the percentage of respondents who answered "yes" was at an all-time high of 60.6 percent after climbing steadily; it had been just 39.3 percent in 1977. The other was specifically about physician-assisted suicide, and asked, "When a person has a disease that cannot be cured, do you think doctors should be allowed by law to end the patient's life by some painless means if the patient and his family request it?" Approval for this question had increased from 61.6 percent in 1977 to 72.4 percent in 1990.

A separate poll conducted by the Roper Organization on behalf of the Hemlock Society found that 64 percent of Americans favored medically assisted suicide.[19] Reflecting these trends in public opinion was Hemlock's membership which, in the five years leading up to Janet Adkins's suicide, had doubled to more than 30,000. Finally, more than half the lawyers questioned in a 1988 *American Bar Association Journal* survey said that giving lethal injections to terminally ill patients who request it should be legal.[20] In retrospect, it seems clear that by 1990, the time was ripe and the culture ready for an event that would spark the right-to-die movement. When Jack Kevorkian assisted in Janet Adkins's suicide in June of that year, he provided it.

The range of opinions reflected just how much confusion there was about the dilemmas it raised. Derek Humphry, a cofounder and the executive director of the Hemlock Society, the largest right-to-die organization in the country at the time with 34,000 members,[21] supported Dr. Kevorkian. He believed that "it's not death with dignity to have to travel 2,000 miles from home to die in the back of a camper,"[22] and took a page from Kevorkian's book by placing the blame squarely on the legal and medical institutions: It was "indecent what [Janet Adkins] was forced to do by antique laws and our head-in-the-sand medical establishment," he declared.[23] Kevorkian, from Humphry's perspective, was innocent of any wrongdoing; after all, he pointed out, Janet Adkins had "offered herself to this form of death." He continued: "The poor lady elected to fly all the way to Detroit, elected to go into the van and elected to push the button. That has to be suicide by any logical reckoning."[24] In fact, Kevorkian was not only innocent, according to Humphry, but deserved to be applauded for taking up the battle: "Most of the time the people involved in these cases can't bear the public eye, but Dr. Kevorkian is a fighter and he is trying to challenge the conservative wings of the medical and legal communities."[25]

Representatives from other right-to-die movement organizations saw things from a different angle from the Hemlock Society's leader. Rose Gasner, who had been the legal director for the Society for the Right to Die in the late 1980s, argued that "You can refuse treatment but, under the law, you can't say, 'Kill me.'"[26] That may have been the legal truth in some states, but the growing number of medical doctors who were assisting in their patients' suicides was quickly becoming a poorly kept secret. These doctors had simply been more covert than Kevorkian had been. "It's not uncommon for physicians of cancer patients to say, 'Here's some medication and make sure you don't take more than 22 pills because 22 pills will kill you,'" explained UCLA professor Judith Ross.[27] "It happens quite often," added Dean Kurtz of Florida State University's law school, "but usually by withholding medication or providing too much morphine."[28] One medical doctor even suggested that "many doctors admit privately that they have advised patients that they would die if they took a few extra pills and some have said that they injected an extra dose of morphine that ended life."[29]

In fact, the publication of a 1988 article in the *Journal of the American Medical Association* called "It's Over, Debbie," had ignited a small public outcry by alerting the country to what many doctors had been secretly doing for decades: helping their patients kill themselves. The anonymous author of the piece, a young medical doctor, described giving a lethal injection of morphine to a dying patient whom he did not know. Albert Johnson, the head of the medical history and ethics department at the University of Washington in Seattle, offered a stark warning about Janet Adkins's suicide: "What Dr. Kevorkian's case is is the real life version of the Debbie story, a shocking story."[30]

Many medical ethicists shared Professor Johnson's shock. Professor Ross of UCLA remarked dryly that "Killing patients is not a good activity for doctors to be engaged in."[31] "Even if society wants something like this done, and it's not clear that they do," she believed, "someone other than doctors should do it." After all, she continued, "If doctors do it, it sends a really problematic message to patients: 'Do you know what your doctor's up to?'"[32] Arthur Caplan, the director of the Center for Biomedical Ethics at the University of Minnesota, also found the circumstances of the Adkins case troubling, to say the least. Of Kevorkian, he simply said: "A person who promotes euthanasia and the right to die is not someone you want advising people on whether they should take their life."[33] Caplan would become one of Kevorkian's most vocal critics in the years ahead.

Other scholars saw a rapidly approaching sea-change: "This is a phenomenon that is going to be increasingly common," predicted Maxwell Mehlman of Case Western Reserve University. Alan Meisel, a law professor at the University of Pittsburgh, suggested that Kevorkian had single-handedly "brought the debate out of the woodwork." He believed that the debate over assisted suicide was "percolating just beneath the surface in hundreds of medical decisions yearly"; he also believed that Kevorkian might very well prove to be the first of "a whole new profession—thanatists," or facilitators of death, who would assume the job of assisting individuals who wished to kill themselves.[34]

This is precisely what Kevorkian had in mind. He agreed that doctors should not use his device. Instead, he envisioned obitoriums, or suicide clinics, where people could go to end their lives. The employees "should be salaried, not fee-for-service, so there's no profit motive," he argued. Asked whether he thought the Mercitron or obitoriums would encourage suicide, he replied that people already committed suicide every day: "They jump out of buildings, they blow their brains out, they drink lye. Is that better?" In fact, Kevorkian believed that the kind of "painless, dignified alternative" that he was proposing might actually keep people from killing themselves: "They do that because they panic and they want to do it because they might not be able to if they become incapacitated. If they knew they had an out for as long as they wanted maybe they would wait a little longer."[35]

The question at the forefront of many critics' minds was Janet Adkins's mental state in the days leading up to her death. "I don't automatically believe that [Janet Adkins] understood what she was doing," said William Winsdale, a philosopher, lawyer, and psychoanalyst at the University of Texas Medical School. "I would like to have had a videotape of all the conversations [Kevorkian] had with her and her family. I would want evidence."[36] Kathleen Nolan, an ethicist at the Hastings Center in New York, argued that Kevorkian could not have adequately evaluated Adkins's mental competence: "He acted unilaterally. He took all the responsibility for accurate diagnosis, prognosis, assessment of competence, assessment of the morality of the action. That leaves the patient vulnerable to mistakes at any one of those levels."[37] Kevorkian's reply to critics who questioned Janet's mental state was terse: "She knew enough to know what was coming and to know she didn't want it."[38] But this was akin to "playing God," some critics argued. The doctor's response was concise: "Well, everybody plays God. . . . Any intervention into a natural process in the human body is playing God."[39]

Kevorkian also quickly—and predictably—drew the ire of pro-life organizations. Comparing the Janet Adkins case to that of Nancy Cruzan, Mary Senander, the director of the International Anti-Euthanasia Task Force, flatly argued that there was no difference: "Either way, the intent and the result is a dead patient."[40] She made her organization's position very clear: "Homicides should be prosecuted, whether committed by thugs in dark alleys or doctors in bright rooms."[41] Mary Jo Kahler, the executive director of Human Life of Washington, added that "[Dr. Kevorkian] was the direct facilitator of [Janet Adkins's] death. He acquired the lethal drugs, he built the equipment used, he stuck the IV into her arm." At the time, Kahler's group was working to block Washington State's Initiative 119 which, if passed, would give certain patients the right to die. She used Kevorkian as an example of what could happen should the measure ever become law. "This is not the Wild West," she exclaimed, "and we do not promote the killing of vulnerable and sick people."[42]

Perhaps it was members of the medical community who offered the harshest rebukes of Kevorkian. "What he did is like veterinary medicine," suggested Dr. John Finn, the medical director of the Hospice of

Southeastern Michigan. "When you take your pet to the vet, he puts the pet to sleep. I think human beings are more complicated than that." For good measure, he added: "I think he should have his license revoked."[43] Dr. Melvin Kirschner, the cochair of the joint committee on medical ethics of the Los Angeles County Medical Association and the Los Angeles County Bar Association, shared Finn's perspective: "Kevorkian did this without any guidelines whatsoever. Physicians cannot just, willy-nilly, assist someone in killing themselves."[44] Both the Canadian Medical Association (CMA) and the American Medical Association (AMA) opposed active euthanasia, which includes physician-assisted suicide, and, therefore, Kevorkian's actions. "It's very demoralizing," said Dr. Robert Butler, the head of geriatrics at Manhattan's Mt. Sinai Hospital, "to hear of a 54-year-old giving up life when you're in your 80s and have heart disease and arthritis and some dementia and are still surviving, maybe working and taking care of your spouse."[45] The chairman of the AMA's board of trustees put it more plainly: "Under no circumstances should a physician intentionally cause death."[46] The medical associations, however, seemed increasingly out of touch with public opinion. As we saw earlier, public support for assisted suicide had increased steadily during the 1970s and 1980s. By 1990, a significant and growing majority of Americans were in favor of assisted suicide. Kevorkian's practice of it—a medical procedure—seemed palatable to many. One nursing home resident who was suffering from Parkinson's disease put it this way: "I'd pay somebody to take me out behind the barn and shoot me but this sounds a lot neater."[47]

Kevorkian's participation in Janet Adkins's death not only stirred up the debate over assisted suicide, but spurred legislative action in Michigan and beyond. Republican State Senator Fred Dillingham quickly introduced a bill making assisting in a suicide a felony. He feared that Michigan would quickly become "a haven, the place to go" for people who wished to kill themselves. The penalty for doing so, if Dillingham's bill passed, was up to four years in prison and a fine of up to $2,000.[48] On the West Coast, Washington Citizens for Death with Dignity sponsored Initiative 119, which would amend the state's 1979 Natural Death Act to allow a "terminally ill" adult to sign a directive that asks a physician to provide "aid in dying." It defined a "terminal condition" as one for which two physicians declare in writing that a patient has no more than six months to live, or is in an irreversible coma or persistent vegetative state. Initiative 119 quickly accumulated more than the required 150,000 signatures for it to go to the state legislature, and by the end of 1990, the legislature was considering passing the issue directly to the voters by putting it on the ballot the following fall.[49] It would appear on the ballot in 1991, as we will see in chapter 3.

Ironically, for one simple reason, Janet Adkins would not have been eligible to receive the legally administered dosage under the state's existing Natural Death Act or under the expanded rights called for by Initiative 119: She did not meet the legal definition of "terminally ill."[50] In fact, observers noticed that with Kevorkian attracting most of the media attention, there had been a tendency to forget about Adkins. For the remainder of the decade, patients' rights advocates would complain, often bitterly, that something important was being lost amid the public's and media's fascination with Dr. Kevorkian, who had already "become something of a national ghoul."[51] It was his patients themselves who were being lost, pushed aside and forgotten by a media monster that only grew hungrier as the decade wore on. As one journalist put it six months after Adkins's death, "[Kevorkian] is indeed a fascinating character. But in our continuing efforts to understand what makes him tick, in the search for the ethical underpinnings of this issue, we repeatedly overlook Janet Adkins."[52]

For his part, Dr. Kevorkian saw the issue in black-and-white terms. He believed he was duty-bound to transcend the law and ethics when the situation called for it. "The law and ethics flatly don't mean a thing to me," he declared, "when a patient is in front of me and needs help."[53] "People cry on the phone and say, 'Please help me,'" he said. "Why should I care what brainwashed ethicists and non-thinking physicians say?"[54] He continued to hold the medical establishment in low esteem, and to promote his role of an outsider to it: "The medical society is stuck in the Dark Ages," he charged. "I'm sure if they could, they would burn me at the stake."[55] Although it would not come to that exaggerated end, the relationship between Kevorkian and members of the mainstream medical community would remain acrimonious for the rest of the decade.

✿ ✿ ✿

On June 8, four days after Janet Adkins's death, Judge Alice Gilbert of the Oakland County Circuit Court issued two orders to Jack Kevorkian: stop using the Mercitron and do not take part in another person's suicide. The judge's decision was in response to Kevorkian's request for a partial injunction, rather than the full order argued for by prosecutors, that would allow him to continue using his machine under "a specific set of circumstances." The doctor had wanted time to set up a committee of specialists who would determine a permanent "death policy" for when to use the Mercitron: "Let me put together a small team, called the Untouchables," Kevorkian pleaded, invoking Eliot Ness's famous team of federal agents that finally brought down gangster Al Capone in 1932. "I guarantee," Kevorkian continued, "under my supervision, it would be incorruptible."[56] Judge Gilbert was not convinced.

To this point, Kevorkian had steadfastly refused to hire a lawyer. "To me, this law stuff doesn't mean a thing," he had said. "When I break a law, I'll get a lawyer."[57] On August 17, assistant Oakland County prosecutor Michael Modelski filed default papers after Kevorkian did not respond to the injunction. Judge Gilbert gave the doctor an additional twenty-one days to respond to the default papers before warning him that if he did not file the documents requested by the prosecutors, she would grant a permanent injunction against the use of the Mercitron.[58]

Realizing he did not possess the legal expertise he needed, Kevorkian finally agreed to hire a lawyer. By the following Tuesday, August 21, Attorney Geoffrey Fieger of Southfield, Michigan, had filed papers to dismiss the judge's motion holding Kevorkian in default for not responding to her temporary injunction. So began a long, intense, and very public relationship between Kevorkian and Fieger. Kevorkian's sister Margo had read about the then-unknown Fieger in the newspaper and initially contacted the brash, six-foot-five-inch lawyer to arrange a meeting with her brother. The two men immediately hit it off. The older brother of Doug Fieger, the lead singer of the rock band The Knack, Geoffrey would demonstrate a flair for dramatic public presentations that had been honed while earning undergraduate and graduate degrees in speech at the University of Michigan in the early 1970s.[59] It served him well during his years defending Jack Kevorkian.

By the end of August, state prosecutors had still not filed a criminal charge against Kevorkian. But they had begun putting together a case. "The whole theory of our case," Michael Modelski explained, "is that

Dr. Kevorkian has been on a crusade. Once Kevorkian found a guinea pig for his machine, he had to go ahead and use it. He put himself on the line."[60] By his own repeated admission, the doctor *was* on a crusade, but at that time, it was not an illegal crusade under Michigan statutes. And he had taken every precaution so as *not* to "put himself on the line." Nevertheless, prosecutors eventually found themselves with no choice but to indict him. "For me not to charge Dr. Kevorkian," insisted Oakland County Prosecutor Richard Thompson, would turn the county "into the suicide mecca of our nation."[61] Indeed, one of the results of such a long delay in charging Kevorkian was that a handful of terminally ill people and their relatives had traveled to Michigan under the mistaken assumption that assisted suicide was legal there.[62] Michigan had become, to use Thompson's term, a "magnet" for people wishing to get help in ending their lives.[63]

On Monday, December 3, six months after Janet Adkins's death, Thompson finally charged Kevorkian with first-degree murder.[64] "Dr. Kevorkian was the legal and primary cause of Mrs. Adkins's death," Thompson declared. "His only purpose in seeing her was to kill her. He cannot avoid culpability by the clever use of a switch."[65] Kevorkian had expected to be charged only with manslaughter. He continued to believe that he had not committed murder;[66] after all, he correctly pointed out, "In a murder case, the person who is killed does not want to die."[67] Murder in the first degree—killing with premeditation—was not a light charge for Thompson to bring against Kevorkian. If he were to be convicted, the doctor would face mandatory life imprisonment with no possibility of parole.[68] Thompson knew this, but charged Kevorkian anyway with committing the most serious kind of homicide.[69] Kevorkian quickly posted the $150,000 bail and was released.

He was matter-of-fact when he met the press. "I don't feel any different," he claimed. "When you haven't broken any law, you don't feel like a criminal."[70] For his part, Geoffrey Fieger, who was now Kevorkian's chief lawyer, was confident that the doctor would be acquitted. "Nobody has been convicted of what Dr. Kevorkian has been charged with in seventy years," he claimed, "and I don't think Michigan will step back into the Dark Ages." Fieger added, "It was [Janet Adkins's] decision. Nobody knows how much more time she had. Nobody's God. People have a right to decide their own destiny."[71] Already, Fieger's framing of the issue had become virtually indistinguishable from Kevorkian's. For example, Kevorkian had previously used a reference to the Dark Ages in describing the medical establishment.[72] Fieger's emphasis on the importance of individual decision making and rights was also consistent with the doctor's thirty-five-year-old message.

A preliminary hearing, which was required for all felony cases in Michigan, began on December 12; its purpose was to determine whether Kevorkian should stand trial. Among the first to testify were Detective Sergeant Haire of the Michigan State Police and Michael Podeszwik of the Medical Examiner's office, both of whom had been among the first on the scene of Janet Adkins's suicide, and Dr. Jacob Chason, a neuropathologist. Dr. Chason testified that he had seen only one brain among the more than 10,000 he had autopsied in his career that showed more deterioration from Alzheimer's disease than Adkins's. It was damaging testimony to the prosecution's case. The now confident Geoffrey Fieger, with what would prove to be characteristic flair for direct and colorful language, spoke to reporters during a recess. From his perspective, there was clearly very little evidence that Kevorkian should be put on trial. "There's zippo," he said. "There's less than nothing."[73] Fieger also announced that Kevorkian himself would not testify, which meant that the judge would hear only third-hand accounts of Adkins's death.

Each side planned to rely on past court decisions. The prosecution was going to invoke a 1920 Michigan case in which a man was convicted of first-degree murder for mixing poison and placing it within his suicidal wife's reach. She took the poison, and it killed her. The case was never overturned by a Michigan court. Across the aisle, the defense was going to cite a 1983 decision by a Michigan appellate court in the case of a young man who had been convicted of murder for his role in his friend's suicide. The two had been drinking together when he handed his friend a gun and urged him to shoot himself. Much to the young man's surprise, his friend pulled the trigger, and he himself was convicted of murder. The appeals court eventually overturned the conviction, and the state Supreme Court upheld the appellate decision.[74]

More important than invoking past precedents was the plan of the defense team—all of whom were representing Kevorkian *pro bono*—to show the forty-five-minute videotaped conversation that Kevorkian had had with Janet and Ron Adkins two days before her death.[75] On June 2, Kevorkian and the Adkinses had met in a Madison Heights motel room to discuss what was about to happen. Ever careful, Kevorkian said he

had "made the tape to document the thing, to document the procedure."[76] Prosecutors had used a search warrant to seize the tape from
Kevorkian a few months later, after he refused to surrender it voluntarily.

Before it was ever shown in the courtroom, the nature of the videotape's content was publicly contested by the two sides. Geoffrey Fieger
casually described it in this way: "Basically, the tape shows Janet Adkins
and her husband discussing what she intends to do and why. It shows
that she has decided she knows what's going to happen to her and that
is not for her." Richard Thompson had a different perspective: "I think
it is very damning to their position. I think any physician or professional
psychiatrist would be horrified at the decision that Dr. Kevorkian made
on the basis of that interview." Thompson added that the tape had been
made for eventual public consumption. "The tape obviously was made
for showing to the public after [Adkins's] death," he argued, "because at
the end, Dr. Kevorkian points to the camera and says, 'The public out
there wants to know why you did it.'" Finally, Thompson expressed his
belief that Janet was not fully cognizant of what she was doing or saying.
"Most of the tape is Dr. Kevorkian asking leading questions and putting
words in the mouth of Janet Adkins," he said. "Looking at that tape, you
will still have a question in your mind whether this was a fully voluntary
and knowing decision. . . . She looks confused in many instances."[77]

Upon viewing the tape, Clarkson District Judge Gerald McNally,
who presided over the hearing, disagreed with Thompson's assessment.
One of the most damaging pieces of evidence to the prosecution's case
was the following taped exchange:

Kevorkian: Janet, you know what you're asking me to do.

Janet: Yes.

Kevorkian: You realize that. You want help from me.

Janet: I do.

Kevorkian: You realize that I can make arrangements for everything,
and you would have to do it. That you would have to push the
button.

Janet: I understand.

Kevorkian: And you realize that you can stop at any time. You don't have to go on.

Janet: Right . . .

Kevorkian (to Ron): You understand, of course, that I prefer that she do change her mind and go on [living]. You understand that.

Ron: Yes.[78]

Another exchange between Kevorkian and Janet further strengthened the doctor's defense:

Kevorkian: Janet, are you aware of your decision and the implications of your decision?

Janet: Yes.

Kevorkian: What does it mean? Can you put it in plain words? What is it you want?

Janet: I would like to . . .

Kevorkian: Put it in simple English.

Janet: . . . self-deliver.

Kevorkian: Simpler yet. Simpler than that. Do you want to go on?

Janet: No. I don't want to go on.[79]

These portions of the videotape, among others, made it clear to Judge McNally that this was not a premeditated murder. On December 13, after just two days of testimony, evidence, and arguments, he cleared Kevorkian of the first-degree murder charge for his role in Janet Adkins's death. The judge called suicide a "private and personal matter," and said that Kevorkian had not committed any crime under Michigan laws. In Judge McNally's view, there was simply no evidence, let alone proof, that Kevorkian had planned and carried out Adkins's death. Indeed, the current state of Michigan law on assisted suicide was "at best murky," according to the judge.[80]

The next day, Richard Thompson bluntly stated his position: "I don't agree at all with Judge McNally's decision." He continued: "Dr. Kevorkian administered poison to Mrs. Adkins, contrary to Michigan's murder statute, which says that killing by the administration of poison is murder in the first degree." Perhaps realizing that Kevorkian had not actually "administered the poison" to Adkins, Thompson stated that he would not appeal the judge's verdict. Instead, he believed that "these profound issues should be decided by the legislative branch of government." He added: "Until the legislature enacts new law, my office will continue to examine each case individually on its own merits." Judge McNally had also emphasized the need for political action by insisting that the legislature needed to provide "direction and regulation" as soon as possible. In addition to assisted suicide's status as a legislative rather than a criminal issue, Thompson pointed out, there was no guarantee that the Michigan Supreme Court or the state's Court of Appeals would even hear the case. Third, and not least important, an appeal would be costly to taxpayers. He knew he simply could not convict Kevorkian of a crime under current laws; indeed, he agreed with the part of Judge McNally's ruling that noted the lack of a Michigan law making it a crime to assist a suicide.[81] Legislators needed to act if another similar case was to be avoided.

Geoffrey Fieger was outspoken in his reaction to Thompson's refusal to appeal the verdict. "I'm pleased that he's not going to waste further taxpayers' money on an appeal," Fieger said. "And I hope he'll drop the civil case as well. I hope he decides not to enforce morality through the prosecutor's office."[82] He struck the same note in commenting on Judge McNally's decision, calling it "a rejection of the prosecutor's attempt to make a moral issue into a legal issue, where clearly the law had not spoken."[83] Fieger would become almost as recognizable an actor in the Kevorkian saga over the next several years as the doctor himself. His comments after the dismissal of these first charges against his client were indicative of the kind of rhetoric that was to come. First, he indirectly blamed Thompson for wasting taxpayers' money by bringing a charge at all; siding with taxpaying citizens is rarely a losing strategy for those involved in a media war. More important was Fieger's last sentence, which warned Thompson about imposing his own morality on the citizens of Oakland County. Fieger positioned himself and his client as defenders of the common person's individual rights and autonomy against an overstepping government. In an early demonstration of his penchant for conjuring a dramatic image, Fieger remarked, "Jack Kevorkian no more committed murder than the reporter writing the story."[84]

For his part, Kevorkian felt "relieved and gratified by the judge's decision." Using the same rhetorical emphasis on reason over emotion that he had been using for decades, he added, "Actually, for the first time in this whole thing, I glimpsed a sense of rationality in the jurisprudence in this country. . . . I didn't think what I was doing would create such a tornado."[85] Years later, upon the occasion of Kevorkian's own death in 2011, his niece Ava Janus would confirm her famous uncle's naiveté. After assisting in Janet Adkins's suicide, he and his sister Margo, Ava's mother, simply "thought they were going to go out for coffee." The instant media attention "was not what my uncle expected," she said.[86]

Despite Geoffrey Fieger's wishes, and his filing of an emergency appeal that asked that the state's civil case against his client be postponed until after the criminal case was resolved, the civil case against Kevorkian would continue in 1991. This was not unexpected by either side. After all, there was still the matter of the temporary injunction that Thompson had obtained on June 7, three days after Janet's death, that barred Kevorkian from using the Mercitron again.[87] Since her death, the injunction had prevented subsequent assisted suicides, and Thompson wanted it to stay that way, at least until the state legislature had reached a decision on the issue.[88] The prosecutor wanted the state to make the temporary injunction permanent. After all, Kevorkian had tauntingly remarked in the days after Janet's death that it would take him only a couple of days to build another device, should the original be confiscated by authorities. "A high school student could do it," he had said. "As soon as a suitable case comes up, I'll make a new one and do it again."[89] He had also predicted that the next incarnation of the Mercitron would be "smaller, more sophisticated, smoother looking. About half a pound, very few moving parts. Can't go wrong."[90] Nevertheless, Fieger believed that making the injunction against the Mercitron permanent would be tantamount to "issuing injunctions against K-Mart for selling guns."[91]

By the time Judge McNally handed down his decision clearing Kevorkian of the murder charge, the doctor had changed his mind about tactics. Now, he said, he had no intention of assisting in other suicides. Instead, he wanted "to work with the authorities, work within the medical profession on a controlled basis to address this crucial issue and establish guidelines." One of Kevorkian's less outspoken lawyers, Michael Schwartz, explained why the doctor did not plan to use the Mercitron again: "Not because it's against the law to do so," he said, "but because the focus now ought to be on changing the law, rather than on the device."[92] Kevorkian appeared conciliatory at the end of 1990. "My point has been made," he stated in an interview. "I'm not on some kind of ego trip and I don't want to be accused of acting like the Lone Ranger or a loose cannon. I want to start working with the authorities—medical and legal—and have others join me to hammer out a system that is relatively foolproof with built-in safeguards and have laws put in place to enforce those safeguards."[93] It was the first of many challenges Kevorkian would issue to "the authorities."

"All I'm trying to do," Kevorkian had claimed back in June 1990, "is condense the time between the birth of this idea [of assisted suicide], and its wide acceptance."[94] The questions on many people's minds at the end of 1990 centered on what would happen if the authorities did not accept the doctor's challenge. Would he still try to pursue legislative change? Or would he assist in other suicides? For aside from the court injunction against using the Mercitron, which Kevorkian seemed ready to sidestep by simply building a new device, he could, for all intents and purposes, assist in suicides if he wished. As we will see in the chapters ahead, he did just that by taking advantage of his new position as the leader of the right-to-die movement, utilizing the media to frame the issue, and relying heavily on Geoffrey Fieger's legal acumen—even if he could no longer use the original version of the homemade "Rube Goldberg apparatus" that had set him down this path.

3

"A SERIAL MERCY KILLER ON OUR HANDS"

The Emergence of Dr. Death

"**B**oy, do I feel terrible." It was February 5, 1991, and Jack Kevorkian seemed momentarily lost in a rare public display of self-pity. He had just heard Oakland County Circuit Court Judge Alice Gilbert's scathing decision, which converted her eight-month-long temporary ban against using the Mercitron into a permanent one. She barred Kevorkian both from using his device again and from assisting in any more suicides. After his acquittal on murder charges not even two months earlier, Kevorkian was brought back down to earth by Judge Gilbert's ruling in the civil case. And Prosecutor Richard Thompson finally got his wish. [1]

It had been only a three-day hearing, but the drama was high. The prosecution's goal was straightforward: "to keep Dr. Kevorkian from going unchecked with no safeguards, from zapping people in the middle of his van out of nowhere." Michael Modelski, the assistant prosecutor, had a twofold attack plan: to demonstrate that Kevorkian had acted outside of mainstream medical practices and to prove that he still posed a threat, especially to ailing, vulnerable patients. Modelski wasted no time in making the first point. "Dr. Kevorkian's claimed powers fly in the face of the medical profession's own ethics, fly in the face of the code of medical conduct, and are totally outside the medical profession," he asserted. "What he claims he can do and what he has done in the Janet Adkins case is actually anti-medical."[2] It was not difficult to paint Kevorkian as an outsider to the medical establishment.

The second part of the prosecution's plan was not as easy to carry out. Modelski began by calling Dr. Murray Raskind to the stand. Raskind was a professor of psychiatry at the University of Washington, the director of the University's Alzheimer's Disease Research Center, and Janet Adkins's physician. He testified flatly that Janet was "not competent to decide whether to take her life." He also used his hour-long testimony to recount his strong objections to Kevorkian's plans for Janet. "I said this was the wrong person for a test case. She's not terminally ill. I said, 'As soon as you meet this person you'll see she doesn't meet the medical criteria.'" He pointed out that his patient had been in good spirits and physically fit. Raskind also stated that he had tried calling Janet repeatedly, but never got in touch with her. Soon after, he heard about what Kevorkian had helped her do. Throughout Raskind's testimony, Kevorkian only smiled and shook his head in disagreement.[3]

The defense team, led by Geoffrey Fieger, responded by pointing out an apparent contradiction raised by Raskind's observations. How, Fieger wondered, was it likely that Adkins would have had several more years before the onset of severe dementia but was incapable of making a rational choice to end her life? Raskind's testimony under cross-examination, however, was cool and calm, and Fieger was not able to achieve the effect he had wanted. So, in what had already become a typical ploy, he continued his line of argument outside the courthouse by appealing to reporters. "If she had such a great life ahead of her," Fieger asked them, "how was she mentally incompetent?"[4] He knew the case was lost.

Even though Kevorkian admitted to feeling "terrible" after Judge Gilbert handed down her ruling, he did not permit himself to wallow for more than a moment. After stating that he would abide by the judge's decision, he quickly added: "I can still speak out and promulgate the idea. There's still free speech, isn't there?"[5] There was more than a little sarcasm and defiance in his voice, as he rhetorically questioned the extent of his rights as an American citizen. In what would become a familiar tactic, he positioned himself as a moral man against an immoral profession. "Every doctor has become very defensive about this, and—what's the word—apologetic," Kevorkian complained. "And I'm not." He confidently elaborated on what he meant: "What I did [with Janet

Adkins] was ethical. It was between a patient and a doctor. The trouble today with the profession, not with individual doctors, is that it has confused sentiment with compassion. It has become maudlin and less compassionate." He insisted that he had simply practiced "tough love" with Adkins—in the same way that a parent would, and should if necessary, practice it with a child. "I loved that woman," he claimed, "and what I had to do was tough."[6]

Kevorkian was stunned by Judge Gilbert's ruling, and rightfully feeling terrible. The judge's verbal summary of her decision—to say nothing of the thirty-four-page ruling itself—was thorough and harsh. She accused Kevorkian of seeking public recognition by pointedly referring to his "bizarre behavior" and "unabashed disregard and disrespect for his profession." She questioned his moral sincerity: "His real goal is self-service, rather than patient service." And she even seemed to take a personal shot or two at the doctor: "The reasons why Dr. Kevorkian has been unable to find employment in any accredited hospital are made patently clear to the court."[7] These judgments of the man and his "mission" would reappear time and time again in the years ahead.

Geoffrey Fieger let loose with much more defiant comments than his client had. After promptly declaring his intention to appeal Judge Gilbert's decision, Fieger described the judge herself as "out of the Dark Ages." He also accused her of trying to use the power of the bench to impose her own moral position: "A judge in this state has no right to grant injunctions on moral issues," he said flatly. His opponent saw the moral aspect of the case differently. From Richard Thompson's perspective, the judge's decision "reiterates the interest of the state in preventing suicide and the sanctity of life." He added: "It returns some sanity to the issue."[8] This would not be the last time that Fieger and Thompson would go head to head in the media. Underlying all of their opposing rhetoric were appeals to the public's emotions. Interestingly, while each camp tried to frame the topic in ways that would garner public support, both appealed to the same emotions, only in different ways: outrage, fear, and indignation were predominant. And so, from Kevorkian and Fieger's side, came the picture of heartless, retrograde legal and medical establishments that insisted on using their organizational and political might to impose their moral virtues on the citizenry. They presented themselves as the vanguard against the moralistic imposition. Thompson, on the other hand, appealed to people's indignation about the act of assisting in another person's death. His invocation of the "sanctity of life" implied that he was out to defend humanity against the onslaught of rogue doctors and unfeeling medical technology.

The day after Judge Gilbert handed down her decision, Fieger leaked the news to the media that Kevorkian had been "counseling" a dentist who was dying of cancer and considering suicide. "The dentist," Fieger explained at a news conference on February 6, "has the facilities to obtain the drugs, but not the know-how to administer the drugs." The attorney made his client's role clear: "Specifically, Dr. Kevorkian explained to the patient in detail the mechanism involved with drug delivery, appropriate concentrations of agents in solutions, their preparation and the appropriate method of delivery."[9] At the time, no one paid too much attention to this admission.

By the end of October 1991, Kevorkian again entered the public spotlight by helping two women kill themselves—at the same time. The bodies of Sherry Miller, forty-three, and Marjorie Wantz, fifty-eight, were found in a cabin in the Bald Mountain Recreation Area, just under forty miles north of Detroit, on the night of Wednesday, October 23. Kevorkian himself had called the police just after 7:00 p.m. to tell them about the bodies.[10] Captain Glenn Watson of the Oakland County Sheriff's Department originally could only say that both women were "victims of some sort of contraption. I don't know what it is."[11] There were actually two contraptions. Geoffrey Fieger was quick to provide the details about one of them: "There's a mask that [Miller] placed over her face. She just breathed it and went to sleep."[12] Wantz used a device that was similar to the Mercitron. Fieger said little about his client's role, other than that Kevorkian had been "present" at the scene: "He provided the expertise. He provided the equipment but did not assist in the deaths at all." In fact, Kevorkian stood quietly by as the two women connected themselves to their respective "suicide machines."[13] Fieger explained, in an effort to frame the double assisted suicide in a more agreeable way, that Kevorkian "feels compelled as a human being to render compassionate treatment to patients who have no alternative."[14] "It's a humane, ethical, medical act," he added, and called Kevorkian "a modern-day hero" who would "make a dramatic impact on society as a whole."[15]

Kevorkian himself refused to cooperate with authorities—a marked departure from his approach following Janet Adkins's suicide. His silence not only delayed the police investigation, but made a confusing legal situation even more difficult. Captain Watson complained, "They've invoked their right to remain silent. Consequently, all the facts we're getting we have to get through our investigation."[16] He added that "Dr. Kevorkian refused to give a statement so we are going to look into it as a homicide," although he thought it was "highly unlikely" that the doctor would be charged with murder.[17]

The next day, Kevorkian was questioned by police but released. The day after that, state officials began threatening to revoke his medical license and to again charge him with murder. They also admitted that it would take at least several weeks before deciding whether to charge Kevorkian with a crime, in part because the toxicology reports would take that long to come in, but primarily because, as Captain Watson put it, "We don't really know if a crime has been committed and Michigan does not have a law against doctor-assisted suicides."[18] Even Richard Thompson, the Oakland County prosecutor who had failed to make a criminal case against Kevorkian for his role in Janet Adkins's death, weighed in: "Dr. Kevorkian is a free man, garnering the publicity he normally seeks." But, Thompson admitted, "We don't know what part he played, if any."[19]

The scene of the double assisted suicide was a one-room rented cabin in the picturesque, 4,600-acre park. "They had taken two bunkbeds apart and laid them side by side in the middle of the room," Watson said. Each woman lay in street clothes, covered in white sheets. Wantz, who had endured ten pelvic operations to alleviate "chronic pelvic pain" caused by papilloma virus, was connected to a device that was similar to the Mercitron. She was the first of the two women to die, with her husband by her side and two strings attached to her fingers. The first, which she consciously pulled, activated the anesthetic. Once her arm fell flat a couple of minutes later, she automatically pulled the second string, which sent the sodium thiopental pulsing through her body. She died at 5:05 p.m., just a few feet away from Miller, who was preparing for her own death. Kevorkian then asked Miller whether she still wanted to go through with the procedure, and she indicated that she did. Disabled by multiple sclerosis (MS), Miller was then fitted with a mask that was connected by a line to a tank of carbon monoxide. "I love you," she said to Sharon Welsh, her best friend. "I love you too," Welsh replied.[20] Soon after this brief exchange, at 6:15 p.m., Miller died. It was not immediately clear who had placed the mask on her face, although it did not much matter.[21]

According to Fieger, both women had pleaded for Kevorkian's services for two years.[22] For several months, in fact, Kevorkian had refused to help the women, but for different reasons: Miller's parents and teenaged children opposed her decision to kill herself, and Wantz's condition had not been proven to be beyond medical help.[23] During this time, each woman underwent a medical and psychological evaluation process, which involved Kevorkian consulting with their treating doctors and family members.[24] When Kevorkian finally decided to help them, he wanted both suicides to be committed together, since he could not be sure that he would be available to help the second woman after aiding the first one. "He was afraid he would betray one if he left the other," Fieger later explained. "He was fearful of being stopped and leaving one to suffer."[25]

No one could question the women's resolve. Sherry Miller had testified during the civil proceedings against Kevorkian in January 1991 that her life had not been worth living since the beginning of her twelve-year battle with MS. "I went from a cane to a walker to a wheelchair," the former secretary said. "Look at me. I can't walk. I can't write. It's hard for me to talk. I can't function as a human being." She implored the court: "You sit in this chair for a year, not being able to do anything and having to be made comfortable, and then tell me about the quality of my life." Looking down and weeping, she quietly asked and answered one question: "What can anybody do? Nothing. I want the right to die."[26] Marjorie Wantz had expressed a similar sentiment in a letter that she handed to her husband shortly before her death, and instructed him not to open until after she was gone. "I do not call this living," she wrote. "What is it like to go to a grocery store or go for a walk?" She also stated that she had begged Dr. Kevorkian for two years to help her end her life. "The last two years, I should say 13 months, have been pure hell. No doctor can help me anymore. If God won't come to me, I'm going to find God. I can't stand it any longer," she wrote.[27]

Six days after the twin suicides, Fieger released a videotape that seemed to support his and Kevorkian's version of the story. He also read a statement from Kevorkian that warned authorities of "slipping back into the dark age of ignorance and intolerance." The statement reiterated one of the doctor's long-standing wishes: "I ask that a blue-ribbon commission be convened to establish appropriate guidelines to regulate the right of people to decide their own destinies."[28] By this point, authorities had still not charged Kevorkian with a crime, even though he had clearly violated the ten-month-old court order, stemming from the Janet Adkins case, which barred him from assisting in any other suicides. Until his client was charged, Fieger stated, he would not issue any further statements or comments.[29]

The videotape released by Fieger was recorded at the home of Miller's parents, the day before Miller's and Wantz's deaths, and showed the two women "chatting amiably," as well as weeping and laughing as they explained to Kevorkian the extent of their suffering. "I thought about it for a long time, a long time. I have no qualms about my decision. I want to die and I know there's no turning back," Miller said in a faltering voice. "I could do it tonight."[30] Wantz stated that she had tried unsuccessfully three times to kill herself by inhaling carbon monoxide and twice by overdosing on sleeping medication. "I tried loading a gun, but I didn't know how," she admitted. "If you do it yourself, you don't know what you're doing. I wish I could have done it a year ago or two years ago. Three days seems like three months when you're hurting and going crazy."[31]

The tape also showed Kevorkian asking both women, and their families, several times whether they had second thoughts. Gary Miller admitted, "I hate to see my sister kill herself. But I think she has the right to say that she has had enough. I couldn't put the needle in her hand. I couldn't hold a pillow over her head. But I'm not going to step in and stop her."[32] Kevorkian also spent about twenty minutes on the hour-long tape describing the device he would use to inject a lethal dose of drugs into the women's bloodstreams—although Miller, whose veins proved too delicate for Kevorkian's needle, ultimately inhaled carbon monoxide instead.

Some representatives of the Hemlock Society were quick to describe Kevorkian's motives as "purely humanitarian" and to claim that the doctor "has done the nation a service."[33] But Cheryl Smith, a lawyer for Hemlock, pointed out the potential for coerced assisted suicides. She said that the double suicide underscored the need for new laws. "This type of ad hoc assistance in suicide for the dying," she believed, "is wide open to abuse because there are no ground rules and no criteria."[34] The leaders of right-to-life groups and some Michigan legislators continued to oppose Kevorkian. "It appears that one man has received a deadly immunity to do as he pleases with the lives of seriously depressed and ailing people," declared Barbara Listing of Right to Life of Michigan, who was evidently under the misguided impression that Wantz or Miller, or perhaps both women, suffered from clinical depression. She called on the state's legislators to quickly pass a law banning physician-assisted suicide before Kevorkian opened a "chain of suicide clinics, in effect making him a death mogul."[35] State Senator Fred Dillingham was sympathetic to Listing's argument. "My feeling is we need to punch Kevorkian's lights out right now," he said. "He's proven himself to be a danger."[36] The senator continued: "Here in this state, he is referred to as Dr. Death. We're looking at somebody who wants to be Dr. God. It's a very scary concept. He violated a court order, violated medical ethics, then turns around and broadens it to the chronically ill. It makes me wonder what's next if we don't get him checked in this state."[37]

Some academics also continued to denounce Kevorkian. "Kevorkian continues to show the dark . . . side of the active euthanasia movement," pronounced Arthur Caplan, a bioethicist and the director of the Center for Biomedical Ethics at the University of Minnesota, as well as a chief opponent of Kevorkian who had testified against him during the Adkins case.[38] "He is a man with a cause, and the cause is immoral, unethical, and very dangerous."[39] Even in the face of Miller's and Wantz's expressed wishes, Caplan claimed that "these two deaths will give the nation a collective pause, because these two deaths are so difficult to defend."[40] He continued: "What we've got on our hands now is a serial mercy killer. . . . I think we should jail him."[41] Caplan, as we have seen, had opposed Kevorkian's actions from the beginning. At the time of Adkins's death, he had stated his position unequivocally: "I think Kevorkian basically did the equivalent of pointing the gun. The only thing he failed to do was pull the trigger."[42]

The members of Michigan's Board of Medicine agreed with Senator Dillingham about the need to "check" Kevorkian. On November 21, almost a month to the day after Miller's and Wantz's deaths, they unanimously voted to suspend Kevorkian's medical license indefinitely, which meant that he could no longer prescribe, obtain, or administer drugs. The board's members also hoped that Kevorkian would now be vulnerable to a criminal charge of practicing medicine without a license if he tried to assist in another suicide. One board member, expressing a belief that was shared by her colleagues, said of Kevorkian: "He's clearly intentionally prepared to violate the public health code." Frank Kelley, Michigan's attorney general, made the board's position clear: "Under our system, people are not allowed to take the law into their own hands." Michael Schwartz, one of Kevorkian's lawyers, countered that a license was not necessary to help people commit suicide: "Dr. Kevorkian can do anything that any unlicensed human being can do if asked for advice."[43] Geoffrey Fieger promptly filed a formal appeal of the board's decision.

Three weeks earlier, on November 1, Kevorkian had addressed, via telephone from Michigan, the participants at a conference sponsored by *Free Inquiry*, a magazine published by the Council for Secular Humanism. "I will not follow the example of those immoral Nazi doctors, which the rest of the doctors in this country seem to be doing," Kevorkian's voice boomed over the conference loudspeakers. Arguing that doctors in Nazi Germany should have refused orders to torture and conduct experiments on their victims, Kevorkian suggested that "our civilization is equally culpable because we have equally immoral laws which, on the contrary, force doctors not to do what they should be doing."[44] By equating U.S. doctors with those in Nazi Germany, Kevorkian was drawing a clear distinction between his virtues and other physicians' vices. And by blaming the situation on "immoral laws," rather than on the decisions made by individual doctors, he was able to garner even more public support. After all, it was not the fault of doctors, the majority of whom were trusted by Americans, but of a legal abstraction.

Despite Kevorkian's blanket dismissal of the medical profession, many doctors themselves were ambivalent about their rogue colleague. The *Medical Tribune*, a New York–based weekly (now biweekly) newspaper for physicians, asked doctors to comment on the Janet Adkins case. Nearly half (45 percent) of the 250 who did so approved of Kevorkian's role.[45] The *Tribune*'s Editor summarized the tone of the responses:

> We got unbelievable letters, such as the Michigan doctor who said: "I disapprove of what he did, but when I get a little older I'll probably be calling on Dr. Kevorkian." We got letters revealing that doctors themselves, who were anonymous, had been involved in these things.

We got letters that went to great lengths and took religious themes, letters that revealed a lot of doubt in doctors' minds about when and how they should be doing this. And if you look at the bylaws of the American Medical Association you'll see that it's very confusing, because doctors are under a social contract to keep people alive and at the same time to remit suffering. Try that little Solomonic thing.[46]

Despite the AMA's official stance against physician-assisted suicide, its members held a range of personal opinions.

The debate over the ethics and morality of Kevorkian's assistance in Miller's and Wantz's suicides took place in the days leading up to a November 5, 1991 vote in Washington State to legalize assisted suicide and euthanasia. Initiative 119, as we saw in the last chapter, specified that physicians could only assist in the suicides of people who had been judged terminally ill and had less than six months to live. Both sides in the debate invoked Kevorkian. The right-to-die group Citizens for Death with Dignity, for example, backed the measure by arguing that Kevorkian's assistance in Adkins's death "underscore[d] the fact [that] there are currently no specific laws to govern this type of activity." Those who opposed the measure, like the Reverend John Paris, a professor of medical ethics at Holy Cross College, warned that "what [Kevorkian is] doing is precisely what will happen with the passage of Initiative 119."[47]

Ultimately, Initiative 119 was rejected by voters, 54 percent to 46 percent. Many in the right-to-die movement blamed Kevorkian, and his role in Miller's and Wantz's deaths, for the narrow defeat. Derek Humphry, president of the national Hemlock Society and author of the 1991 best-selling suicide manual *Final Exit*, provided his version of events soon after. "Hemlock heard that Dr. Kevorkian was planning to help two people to die just before that vote [on Initiative 119]," he wrote, "and we sent emissaries to ask him not to do it. We believed—rightly as it turned out—that his actions might confuse a section of the electorate. Dr. Kevorkian said he would not, but he did. Exit polls showed he helped to shift some of our marginal supporters to vote for the other side."[48] For Humphry, the trouble was that the Miller and Wantz cases were not as "clear cut" as the Janet Adkins case had been, and some voters had become concerned enough about the potential for abuse to vote against the measure. He lamented that Kevorkian had "muddied the waters" after "the Hemlock movement" had spent ten years trying to convince the medical establishment of the importance of helping the terminally ill. Humphry began distancing himself and his organization from Kevorkian. "His name is being linked with ours; our campaigns are seen by some—particularly our detractors—as the same," the Hemlock president complained.[49]

Other prominent figures in the right-to-die movement also began criticizing Kevorkian in 1991. One of them was Dr. Timothy Quill, who had revealed in an article in that year's March issue of the *New England Journal of Medicine* that he had prescribed an overdose of barbiturates to a forty-five-year-old longtime patient named Diane who was dying of leukemia, knowing full well that she would use them to end her life. When asked how his action differed from Kevorkian's, Quill provided a succinct answer—even if the first part of it was inaccurate: "He met his patient only the evening before. My involvement was part of an ongoing relationship. And I wasn't there when she did it."[50] Quill disapproved of two particular aspects of Kevorkian's first case then: the lack of an "ongoing relationship" between Kevorkian and Janet Adkins, and Kevorkian's presence at her death.

Quill had decided, with the permission of Diane's family, to publicize his actions because of his mixed feelings about Kevorkian's behavior. "It focused on machines, and making it a mechanized, sterilized process was not right," Quill said. "He did not know the person well; that was so far away from anything I could do." Instead, Quill discussed with Diane and her family options for both treatment and suicide. He asked her to speak to a psychologist, which she did. He also advised her to seek counsel from the Hemlock Society. When Diane decided that she wanted to die, Quill believed it was a reasonable choice made by a mentally competent patient. After Diane, he never again assisted in a suicide. The soft-spoken, bespectacled Quill, a practicing physician in New York and a current AMA member, stood in stark contrast to the man nicknamed Dr. Death. The difference between their cases, according to one Kevorkian critic, was "like night and day."[51]

By December, the board of Californians Against Human Suffering (CAHS) joined the anti-Kevorkian chorus. In an open letter, it condemned the doctor's behavior "in the strongest possible terms" and, speaking directly to Kevorkian, it "urgently request[ed] that you cease and desist from assisting any more suicides." The letter continued: "Let men and women decide the issue by examining their own conscience [*sic*] free of the fears you invoke with your unaccountable actions. You cast too dark a shadow on what many see as a ray of hope."[52] The group was in the midst of its efforts to put the right to die before voters in the 1992 election. Its campaign was trying to distance itself from Kevorkian by pointing out a few aspects of his cases. First, at least two of the women he helped die had not been terminally ill. Second, his "patients" had not been his patients at all; he barely knew them, Finally, none of them had filled out any kind of advance directive, a document that describes ahead of time the kind of end-of-life care a person wishes should that person become unable to make medical decisions. All three of these aspects were addressed by the group's proposed legislative measure. Like Derek Humphry, CAHS representatives also argued that Kevorkian's actions contributed to the defeat of Initiative 119 in Washington State.[53]

On December 18, Oakland County Medical Examiner Dr. Ljubisa Dragovic ruled that Sherry Miller and Marjorie Wantz did not commit suicide—rather, they were victims of homicide. "Suicide," Dr. Dragovic wrote in his report, "is reserved for self-inflicted death. In this situation, all the evidence indicates these deaths were brought about by another person."[54] From Geoffrey Fieger's perspective, the finding was "false and fraudulent" since "everybody knows they committed suicide." He also suggested that the medical examiner's decision "was prompted by political pressure." Fieger elaborated, with typically defiant gusto: "There is no basis in fact or medicine for Ljubisa J. Dragovic to describe the deaths as the result of homicide, other than his secret agreement to act as a willing accomplice of prosecutor Richard Thompson's self-righteous crusade to drag the people of Michigan into the Dark Ages." Dr. Dragovic quickly shot back, calling Fieger and his client "off the wall." For his part, Kevorkian tried to arouse public sympathy for his two recent clients: "All that counts to me," he said matter-of-factly, "is the welfare of the patient. That's all that matters."[55]

The day after Dr. Dragovic's decision, Richard Thompson asked a grand jury to decide whether Kevorkian should face murder charges for his most recent efforts. The jury's work would be difficult, since the witnesses to Wantz's and Miller's suicides "have refused to cooperate and give statements to the sheriff's investigators," as Thompson put it. Still, "I'm not going to allow Oakland County to become the suicide mecca of the nation," he insisted, using the same analogy he had used the year before in the wake of Janet Adkins's death. Fieger's initial response, delivered at a morning news conference with Kevorkian sitting quietly by, was his bluntest yet: He dismissed Thompson as a "buffoon." After also calling Thompson an "arch-Machiavellian manipulator" and accusing him of "living 2,000 years behind the times," he asked: "Who was murdered here?" After all, even "the families and friends of the alleged victims" do not believe the two women were murdered, Fieger argued. As a result, he predicted, Kevorkian would again be cleared if Thompson charged him with murder. Fieger accused Thompson of the same motive that he had one year earlier: "The prosecutor of Oakland County is sworn to uphold the law, not take on a personal vendetta because of his own peculiar political or religious beliefs." Behind Fieger as he spoke to reporters was a well-placed prop: a picture of Thompson with a big, red clown's nose.[56] Naturally, Thompson was not amused. He continued to participate in the drama that was purposely being played out in front of the news cameras, stating to reporters: "Kevorkian, through his attorney, is attempting to turn these serious proceedings into a media circus. There seems to be no limit to the extent Dr. Kevorkian and his sidekick will go to promote their views and distract public attention from the profound issues involved here."[57]

By the end of January 1992, Kevorkian began promoting one view in particular, both in print and in the press: the need for a national network of "obitiatrists"—suicide specialists. During a January interview, he summarized his forthcoming eighty-one-page article in the February issue of the *American Journal of Forensic Psychiatry*. "You can't let [obitiatry] be done by every doctor or it certainly would be abused," he admitted, in his typically pragmatic fashion. He also pointed out that "no doctor is going to get rich doing this. They have to be very compassionate and very carefully selected." Thirteen doctors were asked to react to Kevorkian's plan. Predictably, their opinions were mixed. "The bottom line is Dr. Kevorkian has gone too far, too fast," flatly argued one doctor in Arizona. Others were more ambivalent, like the New York psychiatrist who wondered whether Kevorkian was "a hero, a villain, a pioneer or a misunderstood eccentric genius." Suggesting that Kevorkian had bipolar disorder, he added: "Or is he merely suffering from a serious lithium deficiency?" Other doctors seemed more supportive of Kevorkian's plan. "Veterinarians do this routinely for animals," argued a Navy psychiatrist. "Should the physicians of humans do less?" Kevorkian himself also tried to appeal to people's collective sense of humanity by making essentially the same argument: "The only reason I'm doing this is it's the correct action to take. There are suffering humans out there. Why would you let a human suffer?"[58]

During the first week of February 1992, Kevorkian was arrested on murder charges while taking a walk near his home in Royal Oak. The grand jury that Richard Thompson had convened had indicted Kevorkian a couple of days earlier on two counts of murder—the degree of which was unspecified—and one count of delivery of a controlled substance; the indictments were not announced, however, until after Kevorkian's arrest. Thompson had requested a high bond, which Judge Richard Kuhn promptly rejected by setting the amount at $5,000 for each count. Kevorkian quickly posted the bond and was released.[59]

After Kevorkian's release, Don Rubin, a freelance journalist, leaked a story to the press about the fate of his friend, Dr. Gary Sloan. Rubin claimed that the forty-four-year-old terminally ill dentist had been communicating with Kevorkian by telephone and mail for almost two years. Sloan ultimately sought Kevorkian's advice about how to kill himself. Ever obliging to potential "clients," Kevorkian mailed instructions to Sloan about how to build a device similar to the Mercitron, which Sloan subsequently used to kill himself in the house he shared with Rubin on March 4, 1991—almost a year prior to Kevorkian's latest arrest. Colon cancer had been entered as the official cause of death, no autopsy had been performed, and Sloan's body had been cremated. Rubin also claimed that it had taken Sloan twenty minutes to die, which was fourteen minutes longer than Kevorkian had said it would take; sarcastically, Rubin noted that it had been "as good a death as you can expect" under the circumstances. Rubin had decided to come forward—and his timing, in retrospect, seemed quite purposeful—"to warn others of what he called Dr. Kevorkian's cavalier attitude toward helping people kill themselves." With regret in his voice, he said: "We had no other choice. I wish we had someone else. [Kevorkian's] turning this into a circus." Geoffrey Fieger, not surprisingly, was quick and uncompromising in his response. "Dr. Kevorkian sent [Sloan] graphics printed in a newspaper of the machine itself," he pointed out. "Dr. Kevorkian offered to counsel the man if he would come to Michigan and bring his medical records. The dentist didn't want to do that."[60]

As we saw above, it was actually on February 6, 1991, the day after Judge Gilbert had banned Kevorkian from using the Mercitron, that Fieger had announced that his client was counseling a California dentist, whom he would not name, about how to kill himself. At the time, no one paid much attention to the claim. Once Rubin leaked the story to the media one year later, Fieger suggested that he had made his announcement in order to test the judge's injunction. Rubin countered that Kevorkian's disclosure had upset Sloan at the time.[61] Regardless of which side was being more truthful, the matter quickly—and somewhat surprisingly—disappeared from the headlines.

Kevorkian's preliminary hearing regarding the Wantz and Miller assisted suicides ended on February 17, with Fieger confidently predicting that the charges would be dropped.[62] Not even two weeks later, the judge ruled that Kevorkian should stand trial on murder charges, with the maximum punishment being life imprisonment without parole. On March 12, Oakland County Circuit Judge David Breck allowed the prosecution and defense six weeks to respond to procedural motions made by each side, but he did not set a trial date or indicate when he would rule on the motions.[63]

Perhaps impatient with the uncertainty, Fieger, who was in San Francisco for a symposium of the American College of Forensic Psychiatry, issued a warning during an interview with the *San Francisco Chronicle*: "I say to you, Dr. Kevorkian is going to do it again." He continued: "Dr. Kevorkian will not be stopped or intimidated by the criminal charges. He believes what he is doing is right, and he will continue to do it." Fieger also alluded to the open secret that some doctors had helped their patients die: "Dr. Kevorkian is doing this because he wants the medical profession to come forward and deal with the issue in the open, not in the shadows as they do now."[64]

The symposium, at which Fieger was asked to give a speech about Kevorkian's concept of "medicide," was contentious. For his part, Fieger questioned what he perceived as society's double standard. On one hand, he pointed out, medical professionals had the power to withdraw feeding tubes from patients who were in a persistent vegetative state, which effectively starved them to death over a period of two to three weeks. On the other hand, the law made no room for lethal injections for these same patients.[65] Fieger was distinguishing between what has traditionally been called "passive" and "active" euthanasia. The only, but crucial, difference between the two was the nature of the doctor's role—passively allowing a patient to die by disconnecting a feeding tube versus actively bringing about a patient's death by way of a lethal injection.

Members of the audience were quick to pounce. Some asked how a doctor could determine without any doubt that someone was going to die. Others questioned the rationality of anyone who wanted to end his or her life. One physician put it bluntly: "I didn't go to medical school to kill people." By the end, though, the tide seemed to turn. California psychiatrist John Ravin pointed out that "society considers it a sign of compassion to put a sick animal out of its misery." He then asked the seventy-member audience how many people supported a sick person's right to receive assistance in suicide. The majority of the people in the room raised their hands.[66]

Geoffrey Fieger's prediction at the beginning of April that his client would "do it again" soon proved accurate. On May 15, Kevorkian was present at the suicide of a fifty-two-year-old, seriously—but not terminally—ill woman named Susan Williams.[67] Police found her lying face up in bed, with a gas mask over her face, which was attached by a hose to a tank of carbon monoxide. Williams had severe multiple sclerosis, which had left her legally blind and incapacitated. Also present at Williams's suicide were Kevorkian's sister, Margo, and members of her family. Dr. Kevorkian's precise role, however, was unclear; so unclear, in fact, that Lieutenant Daniel Zalewski of the Clawson Police Department admitted that "We don't know whether a suicide occurred or a homicide."[68] The confusion was due in large part to Kevorkian's refusal to make public statements except through Fieger. And Fieger kept changing the story.

Here is how it unfolded. After Kevorkian left Williams's suburban Detroit home on Friday morning, Fieger said that the doctor had helped her kill herself to end her suffering from multiple sclerosis. At a press conference several hours later, Fieger backtracked, saying "that all he had meant was that Dr. Kevorkian had counseled Mrs. Williams and was present when she took her own life by placing over her face a mask attached to the carbon-monoxide canister." Fieger was clear: Kevorkian did not actively participate in the suicide. In fact, Fieger stated that he did not even know who had provided the carbon-monoxide canister to Williams—even though he did know that his client was present and that he had used the same procedure with Sherry Miller not even seven months earlier. "He did not assist [Williams] because she did it herself," Fieger said. "She put the mask on. She turned on the gas." In other words, Kevorkian had counseled Williams but "was only a bystander in her death."[69]

Several hours after Fieger's initial clarification, he revised the story again. During a Friday night interview with WJBK, a Detroit television station, Fieger claimed that he had since learned that Kevorkian had brought the canister to Williams. By Sunday, Fieger was forced to go on the defense, insisting that providing the canister did not qualify as "actively" assisting in Williams's death: "[Dr. Kevorkian] brought the canister. Anybody can buy that. He didn't go out and get it. Somebody gave it to him. He provided nothing sinister."[70] The fact of the matter, according to Fieger, was that his client "hates to see suffering." He added: "[Kevorkian]'s not going to stop . . . doing the right thing." In fact, Fieger warned, "If they put him in jail, he will starve himself to death."[71]

But Michigan governor John Engler wanted to put a stop to Kevorkian's crusade. Before Michigan "become[s] known as the suicide state," as he put it, he asked that a bill before the State Legislature be speeded up. The bill would forbid anyone from helping another person commit suicide. Governor Engler was well aware that despite Kevorkian's four assisted suicides, which now dated back over two years, his state still did not have a law against the act.[72] Other observers were less sanguine about the potential of any new law to stop the crusading doctor. University of Minnesota bioethicist Arthur Caplan, for example, believed that Kevorkian "thinks of himself as someone who is not going to be bound by law or social convention." He could not help but add that he found Kevorkian's brazenness "deeply disturbing because the stakes are as large as they ever get—that is, life and death."[73]

On May 17, Fieger released videotapes that had been recorded just before Williams's suicide. On one of them, Kevorkian tells Williams's sisters that she would need help putting on the face mask. The tapes also clearly presented Williams's side of the situation: "I want to die. I'm tired of sitting and watching the day go in and out. . . . I just want to die."[74] From Kevorkian's and Fieger's perspective, the videotapes provided ample evidence of Kevorkian's passive role. But not everyone who saw the tapes was convinced. Dr. Dragovic, the medical examiner

who had denounced both Kevorkian and Fieger after the double suicide of Sherry Miller and Marjorie Wantz, was particularly outspoken.
"I was appalled. They made a mockery of a death scene. They were
serving pizza. They were watching television. It was like a party. It was
grotesque. . . . It was a three-ring circus."[75]

Dragovic's colleague, Dr. Kanu Virani, who was the chief deputy
medical examiner of Oakland County, believed that the tapes clearly
showed that Kevorkian played an active role in Williams's suicide. The
tapes were so clear to Dr. Virani, in fact, that he ruled the death a
homicide rather than a suicide—a decision that was, as he put it, "par-
tially dependent on the demonstration" of Williams's weak and feeble
condition on the tapes. "There is definitely active participation by another person, or maybe more than one person," he said during an interview after issuing his ruling. "That's why it is not a suicide. In forensic
pathology, if a person takes her or his life entirely by her or himself, it's
suicide. If someone actively participated in the procedure, that's homicide, not suicide."[76]

Judge David Breck disagreed. On July 22, he rejected the first-
degree murder charges brought against Kevorkian for the deaths of
Sherry Miller and Marjorie Wantz, fully nine months after the double
suicide. In fact, the judge appeared to condone Kevorkian's behavior,
asserting that "some people suffered such pain [that] their lives could
not be enhanced by medical treatment and should be given the chance
to have a doctor help them end their lives." At the same time, he
required Kevorkian to wait for legislators to write laws making physician-assisted suicide a legal practice before assisting in another one.
Characteristically pragmatic, Kevorkian paid no attention to the order.
"If the case were extreme, I would not just stand there waiting for a law
to be written," he said. "This is a medical service. It always was."[77] To
Kevorkian, a needy patient always trumped legal debates.

Two months later, he provided his medical service again. At the end
of September, he helped fifty-two-year-old Lois Hawes, who had terminal lung cancer, kill herself. She had contacted Kevorkian two weeks
earlier, and informed him that her cancer had spread to her brain; she
had been given three months to live when she was diagnosed in April.
Geoffrey Fieger explained during a press conference that his client had
decided to help Hawes after studying her medical records and an oncol-
ogy report, as well as receiving a psychiatrist's decision that she was

mentally competent. Representing Kevorkian's fifth assisted suicide, Hawes opted for the same technique that Kevorkian had used with Sherry Miller and Susan Williams: inhaling carbon monoxide from a canister that was attached to a mask placed over her face. "Please give me the gas," were the last words she spoke, according to Fieger, in the presence of two of her sons, two of her sisters, and a niece. Kevorkian's lawyer casually added that he did not expect any charges to be filed against his client. Richard Thompson, who predicted that the ruling on Miller's and Wantz's deaths "would make Michigan the only state in our nation that legalized active euthanasia," took Hawes's death to mean that Kevorkian was once again "thumbing his nose" at the authorities.[78]

Kevorkian seized his latest moment in the public spotlight to begin campaigning for two of his old ideas: removing (and then auctioning) transplantable organs from assisted suicide patients, and performing medical experiments on prisoners condemned to death. Speaking at a National Press Club luncheon at the end of October, Kevorkian insisted that "There is more life to what I'm doing than death." He added that he wished he and other like-minded medical professionals could be free to "use death and the dying process for good, for human betterment."[79] Kevorkian also announced that he was currently counseling five patients who wished to avail themselves of his services—one with arthritis, one with cancer, one with emphysema, and two with Lou Gehrig's disease—and was receiving inquiries from two or three others every day.[80]

"We need an auction market for organs," Kevorkian argued, which "would eliminate the scarcity [of donated organs]." His reasoning: "The rich would buy them, freeing the donated ones to go to the poor." Kevorkian told the audience that prison officials, politicians, and medical professionals blocked the efforts of inmates who had agreed to donate their organs and volunteer for experiments. Regarding the former, six inmates had specifically told Kevorkian they wished to participate. "These six men could save thirty to thirty-five human beings who are going to die automatically," Kevorkian reasoned. He also outlined his thinking about the latter: "We would do experiments on this human being that we can't do on humans today, and try to learn something. The person would never wake up." As he had done in his 1985 article in the *Journal of the National Medical Association*, Kevorkian argued for offering inmates a choice between a conventional execution and a death that would involve being anaesthetized for experimentation and never waking up.[81]

The doctor also struck a defiant tone at the National Press Club luncheon. In addition to promising to continue participating in assisted suicides, he spoke directly to politicians: "You pass any law against assisted suicide and euthanasia and I will disobey it. I state it openly because it is immoral medically."[82] Kevorkian was more confident than ever in the righteousness of his position and his actions. After assisting in five suicides, he was also more confident than ever that he could get away with disobeying any subsequent laws.

Kevorkian's defiance continued. On December 15, almost two months after his speech at the National Press Club and just hours before Michigan Governor John Engler signed a law which temporarily made assisted suicide illegal in Michigan, Kevorkian helped his seventh and eighth patients—both women, like the previous six—kill themselves.[83] Marguerite Tate and Marcella Lawrence had both appeared with the doctor at a December 3 news conference protesting the bill, which at that point had just cleared the legislature. Tate, Lawrence, Kevorkian, and other critics of it argued that it would effectively make criminals of compassionate doctors who removed feeding tubes from dying patients. They also accused the Michigan legislature of rushing to pass a "shaky" bill just to stop Kevorkian.[84]

"'The pain I have, I wish they (lawmakers) could have for just one night,' sixty-seven-year-old Marcella Lawrence said that day. 'If I was up on the 13th floor right now, I would jump.'" She was suffering from heart disease, emphysema, and arthritis in her back. Marguerite Tate, who was three years older than Lawrence, had Lou Gehrig's disease. Unable to speak, she could communicate only by typing on a keyboard. Tate "was depressed that she couldn't do anything," her next-door neighbor of fourteen years said. Chief John Dalton of the Auburn Hills, Michigan, police department said officers responding to the scene of the double suicide at Tate's home had found Lawrence on the bed in a bedroom, and Tate in a reclining chair in her living room. Both women had masks over their faces, which were attached to canisters of carbon monoxide.[85]

Governor Engler signed the legislation later that day, imposing a fifteen-month ban on assisted suicide to begin on March 30, 1993. During the ban, a commission would study the subject and make a recommendation to the state legislature for a more permanent solution. Politicians would then have six months to act before the law's penalties lapsed. The penalties included felony charges for anyone convicted of helping in a suicide, punishable by up to four years in prison and a $2,000 fine. Engler also took the opportunity to denounce Kevorkian's latest actions as "murder," and to vow to prosecute the doctor if he helped anyone die after the law took effect. "I want to sign it today as a protest to what Mr. Kevorkian has done," he said. Engler continued: "The methods of Mr. Jack Kevorkian, and I stress 'Mr.' since his license to practice medicine has been suspended [in Michigan], are wrong because he has deliberately flouted the law and taken it upon himself to be his own judge, jury, and executioner in Michigan." He added: "No one should have that right. In Michigan, that will not stand." Michigan state Senator Douglas Carl, who voted for the law, also chimed in: "We can't have somebody marching around preying on depressed people who think they may be hopelessly ill. We can't have somebody going around indiscriminately snuffing out people's lives." Explaining that "Dr. Kevorkian told me that he is held to a higher standard," Geoffrey Fieger announced that the new law would not stop his client from assisting in suicides.[86]

Toward the end of the year, Dr. Thomas Payne, the head of the Michigan State Medical Society, expressed his concern that all eight of Kevorkian's patients thus far were women. "I don't know if he's picking on people who are more defenseless, but it's an alarming trend," he said. News stories began drawing attention to the pattern. The first was a December 20, 1992, *Los Angeles Times* article, which included a comment from a faculty member at Boston University's medical school. "If someone is going around killing women," George Annas said, "all about the same age, it's only the fact that he has an MD that lets him get away with it." The headline of a December 31, 1992, article in the *Toronto Star* also pointed to the trend.[87] It represented the first time that a journalist specifically questioned the fact that all of Kevorkian's patients to that point had been women. "The disparity [between men and women] raises questions about whether Kevorkian is taking advantage of vulnerable people at a vulnerable point, or whether there is something in women that propels them to appeal to a high-profile male stranger at this most private and profound moment in their lives," the author suggested.[88]

Rita Marker of the International Anti-Euthanasia Task Force, who would become an outspoken critic of Kevorkian, had made the argument over the summer, after Susan Williams's death, that Kevorkian was purposely targeting women. After calling him a "medical serial killer," she had said, "He's grandstanding on the bodies of dead women."[89] At that point, the doctor himself had offered his own explanation for the emerging pattern, asserting that "women are far more realistic about facing death and have the guts to do it." Kevorkian's lawyers attempted to brush aside the latest concerns about all of his patients being women by pointing to the fact that he had counseled both male and female patients. Still, Geoffrey Fieger was forced to acknowledge that "we've noticed this [disparity], too, and we're as confounded as you." He suggested that it was merely a coincidence.[90] Perhaps not as coincidentally, Kevorkian's next two patients—and, extending into May 1995, ten of the next fifteen—would be men.

4

"WE'RE SOME FRIENDS OF DR. KEVORKIAN'S"

Pushing for the Right to Die

By the beginning of 1993, state legislators' fears of Jack Kevorkian reached a peak. On January 7, the doctor mentioned that he might travel to Ohio to assist in suicides. He had been contacted by several Ohioans who wished to end their lives, and he knew that neither suicide nor assisted suicide was illegal in the state.[1] In fact, a 1987 state supreme court ruling had differentiated between assisted suicide and other types of crimes like murder and manslaughter.[2] Bordering as it does his home state of Michigan, Ohio seemed the most logical next choice for Kevorkian, especially since Governor Engler's recent signing of a bill that temporarily made assisted suicide illegal in Michigan. As he had done in Michigan, he would offer his talents to Ohioans free of charge as "a compassionate service." He called on the state's medical establishment to join him. "This is a medical problem," Kevorkian continued to argue. "I want Ohio's medical associations to work with me so we can set the guidelines in these cases."[3]

Ohio state officials and religious leaders immediately reacted to Kevorkian's tentative plans—even though he had not said when he would come to the state or identified the Ohioans who had contacted him. Attorney General Lee Fisher admitted that there were no laws in Ohio against suicide or assisted suicide. But, he threatened, local prosecutors were free to seek charges of assault, manslaughter, or even murder, depending on the specifics of each case. Elizabeth Balraj, the Cuyahoga County Coroner, emphasized that any assisted suicide in her county would be thoroughly investigated. "I'm against [assisted suicide]," she stated flatly.[4] Tim Pond of the Catholic Conference of Ohio claimed that the legislative arm of the Church was actively building support for a law against assisted suicide: "You can expect a bill in the legislature very soon," he promised.[5] But it was Ohio Senator Robert Nettle who was the most confrontational toward Kevorkian. After calling the state's laws vague, he challenged Kevorkian directly: "I want to make it clear to all the Dr. Kevorkians that Ohio is ready to deal with this issue. He may want to rethink any future travel plans."[6]

Kevorkian responded by speaking directly to Ohioans: "I would hope that the Ohio Legislature holds off [on enacting a law against assisted suicide] until your state's medical association addresses this issue."[7] Not even a week after Kevorkian announced his travel plans, one of Nettle's colleagues, Senator Grace Drake, sponsored an emergency bill making it a first-degree felony to help or advise someone to plan, attempt, or commit suicide in Ohio. It also made forcing, coercing, or threatening anyone into suicide or attempted suicide a first-degree felony. At the time, the possible prison sentence for first-degree felonies in the state was four to twenty-five years. State Representative Dale Van Vyven promptly introduced a similar proposal in the House.[8] The emergency clause in Drake's bill provided that if the legislation were approved by the General Assembly, it would become effective as soon as it was signed by the governor rather than the customary ninety days later.[9]

As it turned out, all of the back-and-forth in the media was for nothing. Eight days after announcing his imminent trip to Ohio, Kevorkian canceled it. And he did so very publicly, citing the efforts of "hysterical" Ohio legislators to stop him. "I'm not coming to Ohio in that irrational, beehive atmosphere," he continued. "Your prosecutors are waiting like sharks to arrest and imprison me just because they want to, even though they don't have a law to do it." Of Senator Drake's emergency bill, he said, "They want to pass an immoral law that keeps terminally ill people from getting the help they want. This is fanaticism, an inquisition." He added: "Your legislators don't care about suffering patients. Based on some dogma in their heads, they are in support of a proposed immoral law that would perpetuate human suffering." Of the senator herself, Kevorkian turned nasty. Drake was "cruel and barbaric" and "a despicable human being." In case there was any doubt about the strength of his conviction, he added, "You can print that."[10]

The hullabaloo at the beginning of 1993 foreshadowed what was to come for the rest of the year. It would be the most dramatic year yet for Kevorkian, complete with jail time, a hunger strike, appearances in court, significantly more defiant rhetoric and stage-worthy antics—and more dead bodies. The immediate legislative action in Ohio, which came as a direct result of Kevorkian's announced trip there, was an indication of his growing stature. Kevorkian was, by this point, seen as the face of the right-to-die movement. In just a few months, he would grace the cover of *Time* magazine alongside the headline "Doctor Death."

Kevorkian's first patient of the new year was also his first male patient. On January 20, Jack Miller inhaled carbon monoxide to end the pain caused by metastatic bone cancer. Two weeks later, Kevorkian helped Stanley Ball and Mary Biernat kill themselves, with their children present, at Ball's home on the shores of Lake Michigan, again with carbon monoxide. Both had been suffering from cancer—pancreatic in the case of the eighty-two-year-old Ball, and of the breast for Biernat, who was seventy-three. Ball was also legally blind and jaundiced from his cancer.[11] "The patients were in extreme pain," Geoffrey Fieger explained, "and . . . near death. The message they both left is they have the right to decide their own lives and deaths without the interference of government." Four days after the double suicide—Kevorkian's third thus far—the doctor assisted in the suicide of Elaine Goldbaum, who had multiple sclerosis. "I can no longer continue living like this," Goldbaum had written in a December 28, 1992 letter to Kevorkian that Fieger read at a press conference after her death. "The loss of dignity is atrocious. I have no control over my urination and need to wear diapers twenty-four hours a day." With Goldbaum's death, Kevorkian had suddenly helped as many people die in two months (six) as he had helped in the previous two and a half years combined. His opponents, such as Rita Marker of the International Anti-Euthanasia Task Force, were worried that at this accelerated pace, people would quickly become desensitized to the practice. "I think it's going to become news if there isn't a victim every week," she predicted.[12]

Michigan's new law temporarily banning assisted suicide was passed at the end of 1992, but it would not take effect until March 30, 1993.

Given that Kevorkian had already helped six people die during the waiting period, it was not surprising that opponents of assisted suicide began calling after Elaine Goldbaum's death for an immediate ban. Michigan State Representative Ken Sikkema responded that emergency legislation would be introduced in the second week of February in the Senate, and that he "would do everything in his power" to get the House to pass it. Geoffrey Fieger responded by accusing state legislators of being controlled by a "right-wing fanatic religious minority."[13] Sikkema's legislation did not pass and Fieger claimed that Kevorkian would continue aiding suicides, even after the ban went into effect, because the law represented "a violation of his code to help suffering patients." Fieger asked, "Why should he stop unless people stop dying or suffering? Only unrighteous oppression will make him stop." Anticipating the accusation to come, Fieger made a point of saying that Kevorkian "won't speed helping someone who's not appropriate." Leelanau County Prosecutor G. Thomas Aylsworth was helpless, at least until the ban was due to go into effect. "My hands are tied," he shrugged.[14]

The day after Valentine's Day, Kevorkian helped Hugh Gale inhale a fatal dose of carbon monoxide. Gale, a seventy-year-old retired security guard who had been suffering for a decade from emphysema and congestive heart disease, had not left his home in almost three years. He died with his wife at his side.[15] Just four days later, on February 19, Kevorkian assisted in the suicides of his fourteenth and fifteenth patients, both of whom traveled to Michigan from California homes. Kevorkian's audacity prompted California officials to threaten to suspend Kevorkian's medical license, which he had received in 1957. A deputy state attorney general in San Diego said, "The medical board has concerns that [Kevorkian's] California medical license is going to be a vehicle to start to injure people in this state," despite the facts that these were the doctor's first two patients from California and that he lived halfway across the country. The executive director of the California Medical Board added, "This man is no angel of mercy. He is unfit to practice." Kevorkian was indifferent to the threat. "The license is immaterial to me," he said, "as long as I can help suffering humans."[16]

It was not just Ohio, Michigan, and California officials who were opposed to Kevorkian; right-to-life groups also continued to criticize him. "The clock is running," warned Edward Rivet of Michigan Right to Life. "The sooner we can provide a mechanism for stopping him, the better." At least one right-to-die group also began to express concerns about Kevorkian. Patrick Hill, an ethicist for Choice in Dying, lamented that "Kevorkian has polarized the issue long before it has to be polarized. This is closing the door on discussion. The way he's behaving calls into question the legitimate rights of dying patients."[17]

Two groups, however, appeared to support Kevorkian: the American Civil Liberties Union (ACLU) and, surprisingly, the Wayne County Medical Society. The key phrase is "appeared to" since neither group expressed explicit approval of the doctor's actions. Instead, both were critical of a proposed immediate ban on doctors assisting in their patients' deaths. "Some physicians fear if life support is withdrawn from a patient," said Michael Thomas of the Wayne County Medical Society, "the death could be called a doctor assisted suicide." A Michigan House committee had approved the new ban the day after Hugh Gale's suicide, but neither the full House nor the Republican-controlled Senate had taken up the bill yet. The cochair of the state's Judiciary Committee expressed his belief that implementing the ban earlier than March 30—the effective date of the ban Governor Engler had signed into law in December 1992—would risk it being ruled unconstitutional.[18] Nevertheless, the governor promised to sign this ban too, if and when it reached his desk.[19]

As right-to-life groups demonized him and state legislators scrambled to stop him, Kevorkian continued assisting in suicides. On February 18, he helped two cancer patients in their forties, Jonathon Grenz and Martha Ruwart, kill themselves. Local authorities used the same language as the prosecutor in Leelanau County had used after Elaine Goldbaum's death. Officer William Himmelspach, who responded to two of Kevorkian's earlier assisted suicides in Waterford Township, claimed "our hands are tied" even while the doctor is "going on a rampage." He continued: "We're getting so many [assisted suicides] now we just go in and do our job."[20] It suddenly seemed that no one would be able to stop Kevorkian, at least until the state law went into effect on March 30.

An old nemesis, however, was determined to do so. After the Grenz-Ruwart double suicide, Oakland County Prosecutor Richard Thompson reappeared on the public scene in a dramatic way: At the end of February, he ordered the first search of Kevorkian's home. He and Macomb County Prosecutor Carl Marlinga informed reporters that an activist from Operation Rescue, a pro-life organization that also targeted abortion clinics, had recovered a document entitled "Final Action" in the garbage of longtime Kevorkian associate Neal Nicol. The document, a copy of Kevorkian's description of the last few minutes of Hugh Gale's life, persuaded the prosecutors to investigate Gale's assisted suicide as a homicide. According to Thompson, investigators found "a doctored final action sheet where the language that has the phrase 'take it off' has been whited out and they have concocted language to fit into that space."[21] Signed by Kevorkian, Gale's wife, and two other witnesses, the document read that on two separate occasions during the procedure, Gale had become agitated and said "Take [the mask] off!" Immediately after saying it the second time, he became unconscious. From Thompson's perspective, the case was clear: "The fact that this document . . . with [Gale] asking [that] the mask be taken off and the [use of the] mask was continued, takes it out of the realm of assisted suicide and puts it into the realm of attempted homicide."[22] The document was enough to justify a search warrant. Fieger dismissed the entire scene: "A bunch of right-wing Christian nuts again called Dr. Kevorkian a murderer. It's laughable." Even Marlinga did not seem optimistic: "Even assuming we could prove that Mr. Gale was asking that the mask be removed . . . that still doesn't mean we could move to a homicide charge without analyzing what Dr. Kevorkian's legal obligations were in that situation."[23]

The story from Gale's wife, Cheryl, who was present at his death, corroborated Fieger's and Kevorkian's version of the events. According to Cheryl, her husband had asked once to have the mask removed—he had begun to feel hot under the tent that had been put around him to enclose the gas flow—but he later put it back on.[24] She also said the document in question simply contained a typing error. The original version had Gale asking Kevorkian twice to remove the mask from his face. The first time, Kevorkian did so; the second time, he did not. Fieger's explanation—which Cheryl confirmed—was that Kevorkian had mistakenly typed "Take it off" twice in the original draft of the report, and it was quickly corrected in the final version.[25]

Kevorkian's Royal Oak apartment and Nicol's Waterford home were searched on February 25. On the same day, Governor Engler signed a new bill that immediately banned assisted suicide.[26] Earlier that day, in response to the facts that Kevorkian had already assisted in seven suicides since the governor had signed the previous bill and that it was still more than a month before the state law would take effect, the Michigan House and Senate had voted to make the ban effective immediately. The votes were ninety-two to ten and twenty-eight to six, respectively. Senate approval had come just ninety minutes after approval by the House. Michigan legislators had finally acted, quickly and decisively, to try to stop the doctor. "We can't have somebody marching around preying on depressed people who think they may be hopelessly ill," said state Senator Douglas Carl. "We can't have somebody going around indiscriminately snuffing out people's lives."[27]

Kevorkian's small apartment above a beauty salon became the scene of another media spectacle two days after the searches: a demonstration by about thirty abortion opponents who had made opposing assisted suicide part of their cause. In fact, Reverend Patrick Mahoney, a national leader of Operation Rescue and one of the organizers of the demonstration, tied the two debates together by claiming that "this is the *Roe v. Wade* of assisted suicide." Though the doctor himself was not home at the time of the protest, about seventy-five of his supporters showed up to effectively drown out Reverend Mahoney's activists— mainly by pacing the sidewalk and carrying signs that read "My Life. My Death. My Choice" and the like. Fairly quickly, they took over the sidewalk altogether.[28]

The consequences of Kevorkian's activism had literally begun to hit home. Perhaps partly for that reason, Geoffrey Fieger announced on March 1 that Kevorkian would not assist in another suicide until a court ruled on an attempt to block Michigan's new law. The ACLU had filed a suit earlier that day on behalf of two cancer patients and eight health care professionals, arguing that the state ban violated the right to privacy and the right to due process that are guaranteed by both the Michigan and the U.S. constitutions. "The state has no business dictating . . . an intensely private decision," said a representative of the Michigan ACLU. The patients' language was fiery and metaphoric: Teresa Hobbins, a forty-two-year-old with the blood disease multiple myeloma, said: "This cruel and merciless law, like the terminal disease I have, violates me." Nevertheless, Kevorkian agreed to wait. When asked how long he would stay silent, Kevorkian only said, "I have to abide by my attorney's advice not to comment." His lawyer was a bit more forthcoming: "He's not going to wait forever," Geoffrey Fieger said. "Jack will not make them suffer endlessly."[29]

On March 6, Carl Marlinga, the Michigan county prosecutor, declared that he would not file criminal charges against Kevorkian for the doctor's part in Hugh Gale's suicide—as long as the only evidence that the authorities could produce was the note found in Neal Nicol's trash. Appearing on the Michigan public television show *Off the Record*, Marlinga said that the document might support a manslaughter charge but that it would be flimsy evidence in favor of a murder charge. Marlinga would, however, "order a coroner's inquest to compel testimony from witnesses to the death," which could result in Kevorkian facing charges.[30]

Despite state officials' opposition to Kevorkian, polls showed widespread public support of him. One of the doctor's more visible supporters was thirty-three-year-old Dawn Haselhuhn, a stay-at-home mother from suburban Detroit who formed a grassroots citizens' group of 420 members called "Friends of Dr. Kevorkian." She said, "Dr. Kevorkian is a great man; he is a hero. The people want Kevorkian. They want [the legalization of assisted suicide]."[31] Since childhood, Haselhuhn had battled a severe case of diabetes, which her doctors said would kill her before her forty-fifth birthday; she also went to church regularly and believed in God. But, she told an interviewer, "I got so tired of seeing the pro-lifers on the news, demonstrating in front of Jack's apartment, that I decided to get something together. . . . A TV guy stuck a microphone in my face and asked what my group was called. All I could think to say was, 'We're some friends of Dr. Kevorkian's.'"[32]

On March 10, Kevorkian told ABC's Barbara Walters that he planned to assist in another suicide: "It will be soon," he said, despite Michigan's new law banning the practice. The doctor was undecided, however, about whom he might help: "There are two or three candidates right now. Every day more candidates show up." Walters appeared sympathetic to Kevorkian's cause; in fact, she went as far as trying on the mask that his patients used to kill themselves, which produced a series of pictures that ABC scrambled to recall. In the end, Kevorkian threatened to go on a hunger strike if he was imprisoned. "I will stop eating," he declared. "In effect, the state will assist my suicide."[33]

The specter of prison did not seem to daunt Kevorkian. Asked during an interview with *Newsweek* magazine whether jail "scare[d]" him, he answered, "Well, I've been there twice and I wasn't frightened. When you walk down the aisle with holding cells on each side, and someone spots you and then there's suddenly an uproar of cheers, and hands come through the bars to shake your hand, would you worry? That happened both times."[34]

The doctor did seem daunted, however—or at least troubled—by his perceived role as an angel of mercy. Describing his mood during the fifteen assisted suicides in which he had thus far participated, he said, "It's tough on me. You've got to steel yourself. Every doctor does. If a doctor didn't do that, he couldn't function. Medicine is a real tragic profession in most cases. You steel yourself and you cannot empathize too much, although I do. Several times tears have come into my eyes. These are not happy moments. The ending of a human life can never be a good moment." In typical fashion, he blamed politicians and physicians for putting him in this position. "Of course you can't legislate this," he argued. "Every case is unique. This cannot be legislated. That's what's wrong with all these silly initiatives. No other medical practice has law controlling it. It's the medical profession's fault that this is happening." When asked if his decision to assist in a suicide would be influenced by the law, he stated, "I will help a suffering human being at the right time when the patient's condition warrants it, despite anything else. That's what a doctor should do." He continued: "I have never cared about anything but the welfare of the patient in front of me. I don't care about the law. I don't care about injunctions. I don't care about legislators."[35]

Kevorkian's approach had always been more black and white than gray. When asked about the process by which he screened out patients, he explained: "People who call up and say, I'm diabetic, I've got heart disease, you know they can go on. That's not terminal, that's not critical. Many psychiatric cases, and you know they are in agony. Some people have told me from the age of 4 to 35, they've never wanted to live. These cases don't qualify. I don't even consider them." And again: "In cancer cases, it's obvious. In many cases, we have just one major session and then a brief session just before. It's obvious, they're dying. In cases of multiple sclerosis or Lou Gehrig's disease, we followed one woman for a year and a quarter, with five or six sessions. You can see in these sessions how she deteriorates. It's a medical problem that doctors have got to evaluate." The doctor was equally clear about his relationship with the people he decided to help. "Yes," he admitted, "I make patients suffer [by making them wait]. But they do it for me because they trust me and they know the option is there. They know they're not going to die in extreme agony. I keep them going as long as possible." Kevorkian used Sherry Miller as an example, claiming she "wrote HELP, exclamation point. [She used b]ig letters when she first wrote 'help.' She already was so bad she couldn't do it herself. She kept saying, 'I waited too long, I can't do it myself.'"[36]

Defending his consultation process, Kevorkian said, "[My patients] contact me by phone or letter. If they can't write, a relative will do it for them. I ask them to enclose medical documentation of their problem. Then I evaluate the records myself. I go over them with my assistant, who's a medical technologist and has some medical expertise, for some more input. We go to the patient's house, with the patient's friends and relatives there, whoever the patient wants, with my two assistants. We will have a videotaped discussion, and all this is summarized in writing." When asked about the mindset of each of his patients, Kevorkian took the opportunity to discount the religious aspect: "Not one of them fears death, not one. I've had all kinds of religions, and not one wanted a religious consultation. Religion is totally irrelevant to what they want."[37]

Soon after the broadcast of Barbara Walters's interview with Kevorkian, an inquest into Hugh Gale's death—a procedure before a six-member jury to determine whether a death is accidental, suicide, or homicide—was abruptly canceled.[38] Carl Marlinga subsequently announced that he would not file criminal charges against Kevorkian in the case. "Those present at the time of [Gale's] death did nothing more than provide the means for him to accomplish a result that he desired," the prosecutor wrote. Nonetheless, on April 28, Kevorkian had his California medical license suspended. In delivering the ruling, Judge Alan Meth asserted matter-of-factly that medical doctors "do not assist people in committing suicide."[39] California Deputy Attorney General Thomas Lazar stated triumphantly, "He is now Mr. Kevorkian, and no longer Dr. Kevorkian." One of Kevorkian's longtime opponents, medical ethicist Arthur Caplan, saw the tide turning: "From all around the country, a clear message is being sent to Dr. Kevorkian . . . that this is not the way to proceed."[40] The unlicensed doctor was now—at least in theory—prevented from practicing medicine anywhere in the United States.[41]

Yet on May 17, Kevorkian helped Ronald Mansur kill himself. Mansur had been battling terminal bone and lung cancer for two years, and became Kevorkian's sixteenth patient after inhaling carbon monoxide through a gas mask at his real estate office in Detroit. Kevorkian's participation was in direct defiance of the new Michigan law banning doctor-assisted suicide for fifteen months and of the revocation of his medical license. For those reasons, it was immediately seen as a test case. Kevorkian faced up to four years in prison and a $2,000 fine for what amounted to a felony under the state's law.[42] He knew the potential consequences, and perhaps that was why there was no suicide message, no videotaped interview, no handwritten notes, and no relatives present.[43] Observers wondered how the authorities would respond.

The initial rhetoric from each side was predictable. "Dr. Kevorkian proceeds at his own risk or own peril in Wayne County," warned assistant prosecutor George Ward in a radio interview. Kevorkian's participation in Mansur's death was "a very calculated ploy," according to the International Anti-Euthanasia Task Force's Rita Marker. "He has generally been quite careful to see to it to get the most possible [media] coverage," she asserted, "and I think he has done it again." Geoffrey Fieger invoked his usual arguments about the importance of civil liberty and individualism: "Knowing Jack, he cares about suffering people and believes suffering people have the right to decide their own destinies." Fieger also took the opportunity to declare his opinion that charging Kevorkian would be a mistake because "the authorities have absolutely no proof he's broken the law whatsoever." He continued: "There's no way they can find any jury that will convict him. It's not a crime to be present when someone commits suicide." Fieger's argument had proven correct thus far. To this point, Kevorkian had beaten three murder charges and escaped any wrongdoing in Hugh Gale's suicide.[44]

On May 21, four days after Kevorkian assisted in his sixteenth suicide, Wayne County Circuit Court Judge Cynthia Stephens overturned the state's ban on doctor-assisted suicide. Judge Stephens took the same position as the ACLU; namely, that the ban violated people's right to control their lives.[45] "This court cannot envisage," she ruled, "a more fundamental right than the right of self determination."[46] Officially, Judge Stephens struck down the bill on technical grounds: She believed that it was unconstitutionally added on to a bill that set up a special commission to study assisted suicide in Michigan. Michigan Attorney General Frank Kelley quickly filed an appeal challenging Judge Stephens's ruling. If his request for an emergency stay of the judge's decision was granted, prosecutors could again charge people with a felony for assisting in a suicide.[47] Nearly three weeks later, on June 22, the Court of Appeals voted two to one to hear arguments in the case as soon as possible, and blocked Judge Stephens's order to overturn the ban on assisted suicide. Assisted suicide again became a felony in Michigan.[48]

Kevorkian kept a fairly low profile during the summer of 1993, spending time playing ping-pong at the home of one of his lawyers, among other activities. Other right-to-die movement leaders, however, were not as quiet. Hemlock Society cofounder Derek Humphry, who had begun distancing himself from Kevorkian as early as the spring of 1992, now felt the need to do so more publicly. On June 2, the *New York Times* published a letter to the editor written by Humphry in response to a May 17 article that had referred to Kevorkian as "a long-time member of the Hemlock Society."[49] Humphry wished to correct the misinformation. "[Kevorkian] is not and never has been associated with Hemlock or any other group campaigning for the legal right to choose to die," he wrote. But Humphry's letter was intended to do more than that. Erroneously claiming that Kevorkian's medical education was "slender," he sought to marginalize the doctor from the right-to-die movement. "Dr. Kevorkian is a loner, the loose cannon of the euthanasia movement," Humphry asserted. He blamed Kevorkian and his "media blitz" for provoking "a backlash in eight states" which were now trying to strengthen their laws against assisted suicide. The letter made clear Humphry's belief that Kevorkian was a liability to the movement.[50] Dr. Timothy Quill agreed, telling *Newsweek* magazine a couple of months earlier that Dr. Kevorkian "has caused as much harm to the movement for meeting the needs of dying people as he has helped." Quill, as we saw in chapter 3, had begun criticizing Kevorkian's relationships with his patients as early as 1991. "Suicide is the sole basis for the relationship he has with his patients," Quill told *Newsweek*, "and that is frightening."[51]

On August 4, Kevorkian publicly demonstrated his indifference, both toward other right-to-die movement leaders' criticism and toward the judicial wrangling, by assisting in his seventeenth suicide. In so doing, he seemed to be daring prosecutors to charge him. "I assisted Thomas Hyde in a merciful death," he announced, "there's no doubt about it." Hyde, a thirty-year-old landscape architect suffering from Lou Gehrig's disease, inhaled a lethal dose of carbon monoxide from a tube and mask that Kevorkian, by his own admission, provided and applied to Hyde's face in the back of his van. Kevorkian pleaded not guilty during an August 18 court appearance, and was released on $100,000 bond to appear again later in the month.[52]

Geoffrey Fieger echoed what he had argued many times before, telling reporters that Kevorkian had been charged with "an offense already declared unconstitutional, struck down and stayed by the Court of Appeals." Kevorkian himself vowed to continue assisting in suicides. "I will always do so when a patient needs me," he promised. On the other side was a new opponent for Kevorkian and Fieger: John O'Hair, the mild-mannered, strongly principled Wayne County prosecutor. "Euthanasia," to O'Hair's mind, was "just a euphemism for first-degree murder." While insisting that the rule of law be enforced, O'Hair also believed that assisted suicide "is a profound social and moral question which must be decisively and forthrightly addressed in Michigan." He confessed to being frustrated by politicians' inaction. "There is no other state that has had this experience," he said. "That's why I feel it's so important that our Legislature make a decision." Fieger had a great deal of respect for O'Hair. "I don't really consider him an adversary," the usually combative attorney admitted. "He seems to be a seriously kind and compassionate man."[53]

In many ways, the shy and self-effacing O'Hair was the opposite of Fieger's and Kevorkian's longtime nemesis, Oakland County prosecutor Richard Thompson. "I think part of the role of the modern-day prosecutor," O'Hair asserted, "is to make our justice system a better system, not just to formulate charges and administer the office." He made a surprising announcement at an August 17 news conference: He would, of course, pursue charges against Kevorkian, but he would also propose a bill to legalize physician-assisted suicide in Michigan. He also said that he would not seek a prison term for Kevorkian—who faced up to four years or a $2,000 fine—unless the doctor took part in another assisted suicide before the Hyde case was decided.[54]

Most surprising was O'Hair's evident admiration for Kevorkian. He called the doctor "a very courageous person" and described Kevorkian's willingness to assist in others' suicides as "his method of bringing this issue to the forefront." Still, he made it clear that "I am not defending Kevorkian. I am strongly committed to upholding this law. I'm an advocate of life. I do not condone suicide or assisted suicide." He added his belief, however, that "there is a very narrow set of circumstances that would constitute an exception to the rule." In fact, the sixty-three-year-old O'Hair confessed that he personally would not have "a moment's hesitation" in seeking a doctor's help to end his own life.[55] But the matter transcended personal opinions. "The issue should not be myself or Kevorkian," the prosecutor believed. "The issue should be whether or not under well-defined circumstances a terminally ill person may seek the assistance of a licensed physician in ending their life."[56] O'Hair's nuanced position disturbed some of Kevorkian's harsher critics. "To suggest we will convict [Kevorkian] but not send him to jail as long as he promises to be good is not realistic," argued Ed Rivet of Right to Life of Michigan. Rita Marker was more direct: "I think O'Hair without a label clearly identifying him could be mistaken for the defense attorney."[57]

Kevorkian's preliminary hearing in the Thomas Hyde case began on August 27. Fieger immediately moved that the charges against his client be dropped because the state law was unconstitutional. "Although Dr. Kevorkian and I do wish a trial," he told reporters later that day, "we are not so selfish to believe or understand that this issue revolves solely around Dr. Kevorkian or his guilt or innocence. It is far more important for the people of the state of Michigan that the law is struck down." He added that a trial would be "more spectacular than important" if the judge did not strike down the law. He continued, adding his usual dramatic flair: "If Dr. Kevorkian is convicted, then God help any other medical professional who wants to help anybody. He'll be squashed like a fly."[58]

"I want to end this, I want to die," Hyde had told Kevorkian during a thirty-minute videotaped conversation the two men had on July 1, just over a month before Hyde's suicide. The defense played the tape in front of the packed courtroom on the first day of Kevorkian's preliminary hearing, right after Fieger's motion to dismiss the suit. It showed the doctor presenting Hyde with a contract and affirming that Hyde had freely sought his help in order to end his pain and suffering. "You have to understand," Kevorkian could be seen telling Hyde, "you are in control, no one else—not even so-called laws." Ultimately, Kevorkian asked, "Is it your choice absolutely?" Hyde replied, after struggling to bring his hands to his chest, "Mine, mine." Hyde sobbed as he proceeded to scrawl his name on the contract and other documents, and he and his partner, Heidi Fernandez, cried together as they hugged. Fernandez said on the tape, "Tom is suffering so. He wants to be free—to be free of this body. His soul will be free." Present in the courtroom on the day the tape was shown, Fernandez choked back sobs as she spoke to reporters: "I'm here to show support for Jack. I'm here for Tom. He's here in spirit."[59]

Fieger's argument, coupled with the videotape, convinced District Court Judge Willie Lipscomb to postpone his decision on whether Kevorkian should stand trial until he could hear arguments on the law's constitutionality. From the doctor's perspective, the matter was simple: The medical community could erase the controversy over assisted suicide by sanctioning it. "To blame is organized medicine," he claimed. "They're the cause of all this, because all they need say is, 'This is a legitimate service,' which means no layman can do it without punishment, like any other medical service."[60] After the day's proceedings had ended, Kevorkian asked reporters a rhetorical question: "Did anyone doubt that this procedure was meticulously carried out or is that a loose cannon on the tape?"[61]

Judge Lipscomb was not convinced of the law's unconstitutionality. He ordered Kevorkian on September 9 to stand trial for his role in Thomas Hyde's suicide, but allowed him to remain free on $100,000 bond. This would be the first jury trial for Kevorkian, but it would not deter him from his mission. The very night the judge handed down his decision, Kevorkian assisted Donald O'Keefe, a seventy-three-year-old Ford Motor Company worker with bone cancer in inhaling carbon monoxide. According to Fieger, O'Keefe had signed a thank you note for Kevorkian, which stated, "It's a nicer world because of thoughtful people like you." Fieger also raised the idea of a hunger strike if Kevorkian were sent to jail: "He will not eat and will not be force fed. Dr. Kevorkian will not survive very long in prison." He added: "God help us all if the prosecutors anywhere can put us in jail for a doctor rendering that kind of compassion." Kevorkian himself taunted the authorities. "Locking me up is the only way to stop me," he stated during an interview.[62]

Laura Lopus, a twenty-nine-year-old nurse at Henry Ford Hospital in Detroit, hoped it would not come to that. "I don't know a single person I work with who is opposed to what Dr. Kevorkian does," she said. Lopus, who was a member of both the Friends of Dr. Kevorkian and the Hemlock Society, had watched her father die of cancer. "I'm a Catholic, but my God isn't a torturer," she argued. "The thing that people need to know is that Dr. Kevorkian is not soliciting business. People contact him, and he turns most of them down. We are just so glad that there is a Dr. Kevorkian out there."[63]

On September 14, Kevorkian was charged—for the second time—with violating the state ban on assisted suicide for his role in O'Keefe's death. John O'Hair referred to Kevorkian's behavior as "reckless lawlessness" during a press conference. He continued: "All indications are that more deaths will follow unless he somehow is brought into check. If jailing is what is necessary, then jailing is what it must be." To show he was serious, O'Hair asked Judge Richard Manning for an unusually large cash bond of $250,000. Fieger argued that a quarter-million dollars was a "vindictively, absurdly high amount" and countered with his own absurd bond recommendation: $1. The judge set the bond at $10,000 and, more importantly, set as one of the conditions that Kevorkian "not engage in any activity which will in any way be a violation of the assisted suicide statute." The prosecution knew a conviction was a long shot since only Kevorkian had been present at O'Keefe's suicide and he had refused to discuss his role. Still, they pressed charges, at least in part because under Michigan law doing so would make it easier to ask for a higher bond in a subsequent case. And, given Kevorkian's record over the past two years, they had good reason to believe there would be a subsequent case.[64]

Ten days after Kevorkian was charged in the O'Keefe case, Judge Thomas Jackson of Detroit Recorders' Court—a state court with limited jurisdiction—set a February 15, 1994 trial date for the doctor. "I want you to warn your client," he advised Kevorkian's lawyer, Michael Schwartz, "that I order him to obey all laws." He added that Kevorkian could be put in prison if he assisted in any more suicides. "This law is immoral," Kevorkian declared to reporters outside the courtroom. Invoking the war-crime trials after World War II, during which the Allied judges argued that the Germans should have been disobeyed, Kevorkian added: "The Nuremberg tribunal said there is a duty to disobey such laws, and I believe in following the Nuremberg tribunal." Kevork-ian and his principal lawyer would stick with the Nazi Germany motif. On October 12, Redford Township District Judge Karen Khalil ordered Kevorkian for the second time to stand trial over the death of Donald O'Keefe. Geoffrey Fieger immediately appealed to the public: "They want to put him in jail without a trial—the way the Nazis would do it," he told reporters.[65]

And then, on the morning of October 22, Kevorkian took part in his nineteenth assisted suicide. In so doing, he pressed even harder on the authorities. Merian Frederick, a seventy-two-year-old woman with Lou Gehrig's disease, died in Kevorkian's 1920s Royal Oak apartment build-ing, which was scheduled for demolition in December. Also present at Frederick's death were her son and his wife, as well as a pastor from the First Unitarian Universalist Church in Ann Arbor. Importantly, this was the first time that Kevorkian had assisted in a suicide in his own apart-ment building. For that reason alone, it carried symbolic, if not legal, importance. It also posed a direct challenge to the authorities by mak-ing it clear that he planned to continue ignoring the warnings of judges and prosecutors to stop. As Kevorkian's previous patients had done, Frederick herself pulled the clip off the facemask, starting the flow of carbon monoxide that killed her.[66]

Dr. Dragovic, the medical examiner who had ruled as homicides all eleven of the deaths assisted by Kevorkian in Oakland County, sneered when he heard the news of Frederick's death that "this symbolic thing of pulling the clip [off the facemask] is just for the birds." He ruled Frederick's death another homicide, primarily because "suicide is the killing of the self." The distinction was crucial—and political. Dragovic's position was that without Kevorkian providing the canister, the gas, and "the arrangement of the equipment . . . there would be no death." Richard Padzieski of the Wayne County prosecutor's office was even more direct. "We cannot let this continue to make a mockery of the law, whether you like the law or not," he said. Kevorkian, on the other hand, argued that since people activated the flow of carbon monoxide them-selves, they committed suicide. Michael Schwartz predicted that "if the finding of homicide leads to a charge of murder, that case will end as have the other murder cases against Dr. Kevorkian—dismissed."[67]

In an interview over breakfast at a Southfield pancake house soon after being questioned by the police about Frederick's death, Kevorkian said he expected to go to jail. "This is what I have wanted for two and a half years," Kevorkian said. "They charged me before, but they didn't put me in jail. I'm going now." Again he threatened a hunger strike, saying: "There's nothing in life worth dying for. But I'd rather die this way than die of any excruciating disease." To emphasize his client's point, Fieger nodded toward Kevorkian's breakfast of a single scrambled egg, ham, toast, and coffee. "You may well be looking at his last meal. Jack's going to jail. He will not post bond." Kevorkian was trying to force a showdown. "The gauntlet is down," Fieger said. "It is ending now. Either this immoral law ends or Dr. Kevorkian's life does."[68]

On November 5, Dr. Kevorkian got his wish. He was sent to a 10' × 10' isolated prison cell after refusing to pay the required 10 percent of his $20,000 bail in order to remain free. "He does not wish to purchase his freedom," Fieger announced. Kevorkian also refused to eat or drink anything but juice, water, and vitamins. To eat, according to Kevorkian, "would be to cooperate in my own enslavement." Fieger made it very clear that his client "would refuse to co-operate with authorities and would resist any attempts to move him or feed him as long as he remained in custody." His words and tone were ominous: "I don't think Jack will live to see another court date. We're just doing the death watch." Kevorkian's opponents were not amused. "Now he's attempting to portray himself as a martyr for a cause," Rita Marker retorted. The next day, several hundred supporters marched outside the Detroit jail, demanding that Kevorkian be released. They held placards that read, "Stay Out of My Life, and Death," and chanted "Free Jack Now!" Perhaps responding to the protesters, Wayne County Sheriff Robert Ficano claimed that he would seek a court order, if necessary, to force-feed Kevorkian.[69]

Just a few days later, on November 9, Kevorkian was unexpectedly bailed out by a Michigan lawyer who opposed assisted suicide and had never met its most famous proponent. John DeMoss, who posted $2,000 in cash for the $20,000 bond, said he "just felt it was time for this charade to end." He acted on a belief that Kevorkian was "trying to hold the whole legal system up to ridicule." Describing Kevorkian's supporters, he said, "I think they've reduced the issue of suicide and assisted suicide to a hysterical bunch of rhetoric that has no meaning." But, he continued, "If I can get him out of jail and get those people to stop protesting in front of the jail and saying 'free Jack' and so forth, then I think my $2,000 is well-spent." Appearing unshaven, Kevorkian was disappointed. "My purpose has been thwarted and nothing really is going to change," he lamented. He predicted almost optimistically that he would be sent to jail in Oakland County soon for Merian Frederick's death. And, after eating a piece of apple pie—a symbolic act staged by Fieger—he vowed to undertake another hunger strike if he was again sent to jail.[70]

He continued to do his best to make sure that happened. Just two weeks after being bailed out, Kevorkian was present at the suicide of Ali Khalili, an Illinois physician suffering from multiple myeloma. It was the second suicide in a row to take place in Kevorkian's apartment building—in the vacant unit across from Kevorkian's apartment in which Merian Frederick had died—and the fourth since Michigan's ban was passed in February. Khalili was also Kevorkian's first patient who was a doctor. The Khalili case was unique in yet another way. For the first time, media accounts read that Kevorkian had "attended" a suicide, rather than "assisted" or "participated" in it. The language did not matter to John O'Hair, who suggested that Kevorkian was flouting the law. "We've had 20 [deaths]. We don't need 40 to tell us he isn't going to stop," the prosecutor said. "I don't think we can tolerate that lawlessness . . . and let him get away with it," the prosecutor said. Attorney John DeMoss, when asked whether he regretted having bailed out Kevorkian, said he felt "a mixture of sadness and guilt, and besides, I'm getting mad as hell." Kevorkian's lawyers continued to make the case that he was a crusader on behalf of individual rights. "In order to kill the message, they try to kill the messenger," countered Michael Schwartz. "When we look at this in retrospect, we will look at Jack Kevorkian as a civil rights leader, a pioneer who has sought to bring forth help for the suffering and relief for those in pain."[71]

Both sides were increasingly tense. On the night of Sunday, November 28, tensions boiled over in what the *New York Times* called "a bizarre drama." Believing another assisted suicide was about to take place, police forced their way into Kevorkian's home. They had seen "a white male being physically supported by two women" enter the apartment. It turned out that one of the women was Kevorkian's sister, Margo. The other was Dawn Haselhuhn of Friends of Dr. Kevorkian. The man was her fiancé, whom she had brought to meet the famous doctor. "One of the police stuck his foot in the door," Dawn recounted, "and Jack asked if he had a warrant. He said, 'I know we don't have a warrant to be here, but we're not leaving.'" The officers later denied entering the apartment. But that did not stop Kevorkian from filing a $5 million suit against Richard Thompson and the Royal Oak Police Department. [72]

Kevorkian's prediction about being sent to jail for Merian Frederick's death turned out to be correct. On November 30, he was charged for the third time in assisting in a suicide for his role in Frederick's death. He continued to say that he would refuse to post bail and would refuse to eat. Asked if he was concerned about the prospect of Kevorkian undertaking a hunger strike, Richard Thompson smiled and said, "I believe in free choice." Kevorkian continued to emphasize the medical, rather than the political or legal, side of the issue. "The only people qualified to regulate this are medical men," he asserted. "This is solely a medical matter, and my priority is, and always will be, the patient who needs this service." After waiting for several hours in Fieger's office for the warrant to be issued, Kevorkian lost his patience and walked out. Confusion ensued, and a spokesperson for the Oakland County prosecutor's office said the doctor was "now consider[ed] a fugitive." From the Caribbean, where he was on vacation, Geoffrey Fieger called the comment "ridiculous," and assured everyone that his office would "present Dr. Kevorkian in court tomorrow morning at 9 A.M." The doctor turned himself in later in the day. [73]

Dr. Kevorkian was indeed presented in court the next day, and promptly sent to prison—for the second time in the same month—on charges of violating Michigan's law against assisted suicide. Once again, Kevorkian planned a hunger strike. Michael Schwartz indicated that he would not eat "until he is released or, unfortunately, until he is dead." Speaking more generally, Schwartz said, "He will not buy his freedom or cooperate with those who are enforcing an immoral law which is about to be declared unconstitutional." When Judge Daniel Sawicki ordered Kevorkian to pay a cash bond of $50,000, the doctor answered "Go to hell" under his breath. "You call this a civilized society?" he exclaimed as he was led away by police. "Why don't they make [bond] a million? I won't pay for my own freedom." When a reporter asked afterward if he was upset about his high bond, he quipped, "No, I shouldn't come this cheap. It should have been a million." Kevorkian had been on edge both before and throughout the bond hearing. He refused to be fingerprinted at his arraignment. And, in an outburst during the hearing, he pointed at a Royal Oak detective and shouted, "You're a liar, Tom Poff, a liar!" He spent much of the proceedings laughing silently at the judge and angrily whispering in Schwartz's ear to counter the prosecution's accusations.[74]

Kevorkian's refusal to eat while in jail quickly became its own debate.[75] One week into his fast, the doctor was "considerably weaker," according to Fieger, but refusing to undergo a physical examination. "We are now, as much as I hate to say it," the attorney said, "beginning the death watch." Oakland County Sheriff John Nichols, for one, was not worried. "As far as I'm concerned, if he doesn't want to eat, he doesn't have to eat," he shrugged. The sheriff's comment pointed to the question at the heart of the growing debate; namely, whether authorities had the right to force-feed a prisoner. By the middle of December, less than two weeks into his hunger strike, Kevorkian again made national news when he was taken to the emergency room at North Oakland Medical Center after complaining of chest pains. Fieger claimed that his five-foot-eight-inch client's weight had dropped from 128 to 115 pounds during his stay at Oakland County Jail—a 10 percent loss, his lawyer was quick to point out. After a twenty-four-hour stay in the hospital, Kevorkian was sent back to jail.[76]

On the same day that Kevorkian was admitted to the hospital, courts in Michigan's two largest counties handed down conflicting rulings. Judge Richard Kaufman of Wayne County Circuit Court struck down Michigan's nine-month-old ban on assisted suicide on the grounds that it was unconstitutional and dismissed the charges against Kevorkian for his role in Donald O'Keefe's death. Geoffrey Fieger had warned that his client "will die in jail unless Judge Kaufman grants the reprieve."[77] Prosecutors immediately challenged the forty-one-page ruling, petitioning the state appellate court to stay Judge Kaufman's decision and asking the state supreme court to rule as soon as possible on the constitutionality of the assisted suicide law. Earlier the same day, Judge Daniel Sawicki in Oakland County ordered Kevorkian to stand trial for his role in the suicide of Merian Frederick. Fieger pleaded with Sawicki to reduce his client's bond from $50,000 to a symbolic $100. He said that if the judge did so, Kevorkian would promise not to assist in any more suicides until an appellate court ruled on the constitutionality of the state law. Sawicki refused. Fieger was furious after the decision. "This is purely an outrageous personal vendetta on the part of Richard Thompson," he accused. "We have got to save the life of Dr. Kevorkian, who is being held in jail under an unconstitutional law." Fieger criticized Judge Sawicki, too, accusing him of being "out to kill Kevorkian." He promised to file motions with Oakland County Circuit Judge Jessica Cooper to reduce the bail amount and to rule that Judge Kaufman's decision applied statewide, thus voiding all charges against his client.[78]

Kevorkian was released from jail a week before Christmas, after refusing solid food during his seventeen-day jail term. His release was contingent upon a promise. "I must and will pledge that I will not participate in the practice of what I call 'medicide'—the physician-aided termination of human suffering—until the matter is finally resolved by higher courts of this state or of [sic] a vote of the public," he recited to Judge Jessica Cooper. Kevorkian attended the hearing in a wheelchair; Fieger claimed his client was too weak to stand. Immediately afterward, Kevorkian was taken to Detroit's Sinai Hospital, where he requested a bowl of lentil soup. Judge Cooper evidently felt sorry for Kevorkian. She reduced his bail to $100 and, over objections from the prosecution, stated that the doctor should "be able to have his holidays with his family." Still, Kevorkian found himself, upon his release, wearing an electronic tether and "effectively under house arrest," according to the judge. The device allowed court officials to monitor his compliance with a judge's order to stay within forty-five meters of his apartment. Richard Thompson was skeptical about the usefulness of the device in this particular case, suggesting that "tethering Kevorkian to his home, where the recent suicides have occurred, is like tethering an alcoholic to a bar."[79]

By the end of 1993, Kevorkian had helped twenty people kill themselves.[80] He had become, in the words of one columnist, "death's ecstatic minion."[81] An essay in *The Economist* referred to him as "death's dissident."[82] And, of course, he had been immortalized as "Doctor Death" by *Time* magazine back in May. Regardless of the labels applied to him, Kevorkian was thinking of a different approach by the end of the year. "What I am going to do now instead," he claimed, "is carry on a whistle-stop campaign, city to city, to get this guaranteed by a vote of the people as a fundamental right."[83] Geoffrey Fieger, too, stated that his famous client would henceforth devote his energy to leading a campaign to legalize assisted suicide. The doctor suddenly seemed to be more interested in passing a state constitutional amendment than in assisting suicides.[84] He gave every indication of moving away from engaging in direct action techniques and toward agitating for legislative change.[85]

Nevertheless, the new year brought more legal ramifications stemming from his previous assisted suicides. On January 4, Richard Thompson charged him with assisting in sixty-one-year-old Dr. Ali Khalili's November 1993 death. "Continued defiance and disregard of the law passed by the duly elected representatives of the people cannot be condoned and must be resisted," Thompson declared. Seeing it as his public duty to charge and prosecute Kevorkian, he continued: "I make no apologies for enforcing the law." Geoffrey Fieger responded with an insulting warning letter to Thompson: "Your arrest of Dr. Kevorkian would be even stupider than the stupidest thing you have ever done in your life (and, believe me, you have done some unbelievably stupid things)." At the time that Thompson charged Kevorkian, the doctor was already under house arrest and wearing an electronic ankle bracelet for his role in Merian Frederick's October 1993 death.[86]

Simultaneously, a three-judge panel of the Michigan Court of Appeals was considering the constitutionality of the state's ban on assisted suicide. Two of the three cases they heard involved Kevorkian. In point of fact, the state legislature had adopted the ban specifically to stop Kevorkian. Promising a speedy decision, Judge E. Thomas Fitzgerald said, "This is perhaps the first court in this country that has had to make the decision that we had to make. We will try to get you a decision as quickly as possible, doing the best we can."[87] Three county judges had already ruled it unconstitutional, two on technical grounds that prohibit one bill from having two separate objectives.[88] The most recent to do so was Jessica Cooper who, at the end of January, dismissed two of the three remaining assisted suicide charges against Kevorkian. In so doing, she freed him from house arrest.[89] The only outstanding case was that of Thomas Hyde, who had died in Kevorkian's van nearly six months earlier. Both the prosecution and the defense agreed to suspend a trial in that case until a decision was reached by the Michigan Court of Appeals.[90]

Kevorkian began trying to make good on his promise to effect legislative change. On January 30, he began a ballot drive for a state constitutional amendment to legalize doctor-assisted suicide by urging about

700 churchgoers—in a speech between services at St. Paul's Presbyterian Church in the western Detroit suburb of Livonia—to join him. He would need to collect 256,700 signatures by July 1 to place the referendum on the November 1994 state ballot. "It's almost an insult to put this on the ballot . . . because that right [to assisted suicide] exists," declared Kevorkian. The proposed amendment read: "The right of competent adults, who are incapacitated by incurable medical conditions, to voluntarily request and receive medical assistance with respect to whether or not their lives continue, shall not be restrained or abridged."[91]

Attended by John Pridonoff, the executive director of the Hemlock Society, and Ron Adkins, the husband of Kevorkian's first patient and by now the Oregon president of Hemlock, the church event had been organized by Pastor Thomas Egglebeen, who invited Kevorkian to speak. The pastor set the tone of the program by offering his perspective on the belief of many Christians that suicide is a mortal sin. "It's a hoax. . . . It's just not true," he told those gathered. "There are six or seven incidents in Scripture where a suicide is reported and it's treated kindly and tragically. In no way at all is the person condemned."[92] Geoffrey Fieger also offered some brief opening remarks, which sought to frame the matter more broadly: "This is not about suicide. This is about the right to decide for yourselves whether to seek a soft landing when you have decided you have endured as much suffering as you can." He concluded with the warning that some religious groups would "spare no expense" to defeat the amendment. Lynn Mills, a spokesperson for the anti-abortion group Operation Rescue, responded during an interview afterward. "It's nice to agree with Geoffrey on something," she said sarcastically. "Michigan Right to Life is known as one of the best organized and best funded in the country."[93]

"What this is all about is the right not to have to suffer," Kevorkian told the audience. "This is really a right that already exists, and we already have, but which we have to put in writing because of human irrationality. Every reasonable adult is going to have to realize that if he votes 'no' on this, he is throwing his right away." The doctor was confident and engaging, and had gained back much of the weight he had lost during his recent hunger strike. The captive audience gave him a standing ovation, but not before a few hecklers had broken in during both Kevorkian's and Fieger's remarks. Two people holding Bibles over their heads interrupted the program, and one of them yelled, "This church has been cursed today!" Another called out, "You have allowed a wolf into the sanctuary." One attendee held a sign that read *kookicide*. Both of the latter were ejected from the church. A bolder antagonist confronted Kevorkian directly. "Did you skip medical school the day they told you that doctors were supposed to keep people alive?" he asked. Kevorkian's response was delivered with a cold stare: "Do you want to give up your right to decide whether you should suffer or not?" The young man, after a pause, said no. "There," Kevorkian answered. "That's the question that should have been asked."[94]

Less than two months after this event, Kevorkian announced that he would assist in the suicide of a woman in her seventies suffering "crippling pain" from severe rheumatoid arthritis unless she got stronger painkillers. His deadline was three weeks from the time of his announcement: April 19, to be exact, which was the day he was scheduled to stand trial on charges of violating Michigan's assisted suicide ban. The woman's doctor quickly offered to prescribe a morphine patch, and a handful of other doctors contacted Geoffrey Fieger with offers to help her. Predictably, the reactions to the doctor's announcement caused a furor. Calling it a "publicity stunt," Rita Marker said, "I think Kevorkian and his lawyer are heartless enough to use this woman. It was so crass, so calculated." The patient herself, when asked if she was considering suicide, replied on videotape: "I think that would be the best thing for me." She had lost her legs and one eye to arthritis already, and described suffering from debilitating pain. "She wants somebody who will give her stronger medication to make the rest of her life more comfortable," Fieger said. Kevorkian had counseled the woman for two years, during which time doctors had refused to prescribe stronger painkillers because they were afraid she would become addicted. "Dr. Kevorkian has encouraged her to continue to live," claimed Fieger. "However, he cannot provide any other alternative other than [assisted suicide] at this point."[95]

As his trial date neared, Kevorkian seemed conflicted. Three months earlier, he had promised that he would not assist any more suicides. Soon after, he had pledged to try to change the law, rather than break it, by starting a drive for a ballot initiative to make assisted suicide legal in Michigan. That effort was showing signs of success; by late March, Fieger claimed that they had collected almost half of the necessary signatures.[96] Yet here was Kevorkian, threatening to help another person kill herself. He also began to publicly question his previous tactics, such as staging hunger strikes and demanding that no one post bail to release him from jail: "I realized the hunger strike probably wasn't a good idea," he admitted. "Looking back it might have been a mistake if I had died."[97]

5

"A GAME OF CAT AND MOUSE"
Kevorkian on Trial

The long-awaited and highly anticipated first trial of Jack Kevorkian began in Detroit on April 21, 1994, nearly four years after he participated in the first of his twenty assisted suicides. If convicted, the doctor faced up to four years in prison and a $2,000 fine. Geoffrey Fieger's opening statement equated the right to die with other human rights, which by now was a familiar way of framing the subject. "Thomas Hyde was dying surely, terribly and painfully," he began. "Dr. Kevorkian's intention was to end his suffering." To everyone's surprise, Fieger then began mounting a technical defense. He claimed that the case should be dismissed because it was being tried in the wrong jurisdiction. "Thomas Hyde did not die in the city of Detroit and the county of Wayne on Belle Isle," Fieger told the jury. "His suicide took place in Royal Oak [in Oakland County], Michigan at Dr. Kevorkian's home, and [prosecutors] never even bothered to check," Fieger told the jury. He explained that after Hyde's suicide, Kevorkian drove the body to Belle Isle because he feared mistreatment at the hands of the Oakland County police. Outside the courtroom after the day's proceedings, Fieger told reporters he would seek a dismissal of the charges after the prosecution presented its case. Once the jury was sworn in and the charges were dismissed, Fieger asserted, the legal doctrine of double jeopardy would prevent prosecutors from subsequently trying his client on the same charge in Oakland County. Kevorkian himself showed little interest in the proceedings. He spent most of the second day in court studying a book on the Japanese language, looking up from time to time to listen to what was being said.[1]

Wayne County Assistant Prosecutor Timothy Kenny informed the jury that Hyde did not, in fact, die in Royal Oak. Evidence was provided by Detroit police officer Anita Banks, who testified that she saw Kevorkian's van parked on Belle Isle around 8:00 a.m., just about ninety minutes before police pulled him over and learned of the assisted suicide. Despite this testimony, the first day belonged to Fieger, thanks in large part to his being allowed to show the jury a videotape of Hyde, along with his partner Heidi Fernandez and Kevorkian, discussing Hyde's condition a month before he died. The video showed Kevorkian asking Hyde what he wanted. It took him almost a minute to choke out his answer: "I want to end this. I want to die." The tape ended with Hyde crying on Fernandez's shoulder and Fernandez saying, "I've watched him suffer too long." Several jurors were visibly moved by what they saw.[2]

True to his word, Fieger rested his case on Monday, April 25, and immediately petitioned to have the case dismissed. He and Timothy Kenny took turns attempting to convince Judge Thomas Jackson of their respective positions. Citing a Michigan law that allowed the attorney general to choose the county in which to try a case if it was uncertain where the crime occurred, Kenny presented an order from Michigan Attorney General Frank Kelley, which stated that Wayne County was where the matter should be "prosecuted and punished." Despite Fieger's objection that the order from the attorney general was secretly obtained overnight and presented improperly to the court, and his accusation that the prosecution and the attorney general were "ganging up" on his client, the judge did not think a dismissal was warranted. He denied Fieger's motion and ordered the trial to continue. Judge Jackson also, however, refused to allow the jury to hear the attorney general's decision and left it to the jury to determine the location of the crime. Jackson warned the jurors that they would have to acquit Kevorkian unless they could find beyond a reasonable doubt that Hyde had died in Wayne County.[3]

Two days later Kevorkian took the stand for the first time, appearing relaxed in a sport shirt, blue sweater, and white windbreaker. Fieger planned to exploit a loophole in Michigan's assisted suicide law by arguing that his client had acted to ease Thomas Hyde's pain, which was allowed under the law, rather than to kill him. To that end, Kevorkian testified that he had acted to protect Hyde's "autonomy" and denied that he had expected Hyde would be killed by inhaling carbon monoxide. When Kenny attempted during cross-examination to get Kevorkian to admit that he knew the carbon monoxide would cause Hyde to die, the doctor said, "I had a fairly good idea that he would die." Again, in response to a similar question from Kenny, Kevorkian simply stated: "I surmised he would die—that's a guess." Kenny asked, "Were you startled, sir, after 20 minutes [of inhalation] to find out that he was dead?" Kevorkian replied that he was not: "I didn't expect he might survive. My expectation was that his suffering would end. It's as simple as that." Later, Kevorkian added: "I did not want Mr. Hyde to die, just as a surgeon doesn't want to cut off a leg [to stop a spreading disease]. I wanted to help him end his suffering with the only means known and available to me."[4]

During his testimony, Kevorkian also detailed the circumstances of Hyde's death. He explained that his longtime assistant, Neal Nicol, had picked up Hyde at his house early on the morning of August 4 and driven him more than twenty miles to Royal Oak, where they met Kevorkian in an alley. They helped Hyde into Kevorkian's Volkswagen van, and the doctor drove to a parking lot behind his nearby apartment and performed the assisted suicide there. Kevorkian stated that it was only then that he drove to Belle Isle, in a deliberate attempt to mislead authorities about the place of death. "It was to protect my physical person that I decided to do that," he explained, claiming that the Wayne County authorities had treated him well in the past but that those in Oakland County had "strong-armed" him before. His original plan, he explained, was to perform the procedure in Belle Isle but he changed his mind out of fear that his "clunker" of a van would break down or that he would be discovered while carrying out the procedure.[5]

The existing state law against assisted suicide stated that it did not apply to a procedure "if the intent is to relieve pain and discomfort and not to cause death, even if the procedure may hasten or increase the risk of death." Kenny argued that the clause in the law was meant to apply only to medication, not to carbon monoxide. But when he pressed Dr. Stanley Levy, a Detroit internist, to state that carbon monoxide was not a recognized medicine, he got nowhere. Levy said, "I think the procedure was a heroic effort on Dr. Kevorkian's part to control pain and suffering which was otherwise out of control." All Kenny could get Kevorkian himself to admit to was placing a mask over Hyde's face and giving him a string to pull that would release the flow of carbon monoxide into his lungs. The defense's plan was working.[6]

As a result, Kenny, like previous prosecutors of Kevorkian, was almost forced to resort to painting the doctor "as a lonely medical outlaw who has feuded with colleagues, advocated bizarre experiments and harbored a lifelong, morbid fascination with death." Kevorkian himself took the opportunity to showcase some of his favorite rhetorical devices—and even cracked jokes—during his three hours on the stand. He spoke contemptuously about the medical establishment and the "socially criminal" American Medical Association. "When your conscience says that [a] law is immoral, don't follow it," Kevorkian stated, comparing himself to Gandhi and asserting that he never intended to obey Michigan's law against assisted suicide since similar laws "have been passed throughout history, mainly in the dark ages."[7]

Fieger, recognizing the need to stick to his game plan, emphasized in his closing statement Kevorkian's "kindness and compassion" toward Thomas Hyde and reiterated that his client had only tried to ease Hyde's pain and end his suffering. "Can it be that we become criminals when we want to end our suffering, that compassionate people who say, 'Yes, you have that right,' are criminals to be sent to prison?" he asked the jury. Fieger was growing more animated: "Have we lost all sanity? My God, are we human? Is it possible that the prosecutor today, in this courtroom, at 2:25, said that Thomas Hyde was condemned to die the most horrible death anyone could imagine? You are going to stand up and say, 'No, no more, never again, no more prosecutions, no more persecution.'" Fieger portrayed his client as a defender of basic human rights and dignity, invoking Margaret Sanger (who was arrested in 1916 for promoting birth control), the civil rights movement, and the past persecution of Catholics, Jews, and gypsies. "What kind of people would we be," he asked the jury, "that we would treat Thomas Hyde worse than our pets, worse than a dog or cat, lying there begging for mercy with no hope of survival? The right of Thomas Hyde to make a choice, to be a free American, cannot be taken away." Heidi Fernandez, who had testified earlier in the day and sat in the front row during closing arguments, began to cry during Fieger's dramatic conclusion.[8]

Kenny was not so moved. In his cooler argument style, he closed by attempting to persuade the jury to narrow its focus to the law: "The wisdom of the assisted suicide statute is not on trial," he explained. "What is before you is the issue of whether Jack Kevorkian assisted Thomas Hyde in committing suicide." Kenny spent roughly half of his closing argument on the matter of the location of Hyde's death, emphasizing the contradiction between Fieger's claim during a press conference shortly after the suicide that Hyde had died on Belle Isle and his claim during the trial that the death had occurred at Kevorkian's house. "First they said they brought this down to Detroit so the city of Detroit could resolve this important issue," he said to the jury. "Now they're saying, 'Wait a minute, this should be dismissed because it didn't happen here.' Is Dr. Kevorkian going to Belle Isle just to make a report to authorities? It doesn't make sense."[9]

Kenny also sought to distinguish between the doctor's motives and his intent in arguing that even if Kevorkian had been motivated by a desire to relieve Hyde's pain, his intent in providing carbon monoxide was to cause the man's death. To make his point, Kenny held up the large, metal carbon monoxide canister that was used in Hyde's death, and asked the jury, "What was Jack Kevorkian's intent with regard to this canister, which was filled with carbon monoxide? Do you think Dr. Kevorkian thought he would take two whiffs, pull off the mask and then he'd drive him home, saying, 'Hope you feel better'?" After the trial, Kevorkian grew "testy" with reporters, as one put it. "I expect to end up in jail," he said. "This isn't a real trial, it's a farce. I want a conviction, because a conviction on an unconstitutional law would be a double black eye to this rotten system."[10]

In the end, Fieger's defense worked. On May 2, Dr. Kevorkian was acquitted in the case of Thomas Hyde. The jury had equated Kevorkian's role in Hyde's suicide with the prescription of experimental medication for terminal patients—in other words, with a step to relieve suffering and not necessarily to kill. Obviously frustrated, Kenny described Michigan's law, which was set to expire in less than six months, as "fraught with ambiguities," and expressed his belief that it would have to be rewritten if anyone expected a conviction in future assisted suicides.[11]

A strong indication of legislators' and prosecutors' uncertainty about how to handle Kevorkian came a week after the acquittal. On May 10, the Michigan Court of Appeals handed down two two-to-one majority rulings. The first was that the state's ban on assisted suicide was invalid on technical grounds and, thus, unconstitutional. Two of the three judges ruled that because the ban was included in a bill that set up a commission to study death and dying, it violated the provision in Michigan's constitution that a bill must cover only one subject. The appellate court's second ruling was more surprising. Declaring that there was no constitutional right to suicide or to assisted suicide, the judges ordered murder charges to be reinstated against Kevorkian in the double suicide of Marjorie Wantz and Sherry Miller. Judge Thomas Fitzgerald wrote in the majority opinion, "Liberty and justice will not cease to exist if a right to commit suicide is not recognized." As we saw in chapter 3, Kevorkian assisted in the deaths of Wantz and Miller in a cabin in the Bald Mountain Recreation Area in 1991, two years before Michigan's law went into effect. The original murder charges against Kevorkian were dismissed in July 1992 on the grounds that the state had no law against aiding in someone else's suicide. Now, with the appellate court's new ruling, Oakland County Prosecutor Richard Thompson once again found himself with only murder charges to try to stop Kevorkian.[12]

While Michigan was struggling to enforce its current law, another state struck down its own. Nearly 2,000 miles away on the day after Kevorkian's acquittal, U.S. District Judge Barbara Rothstein struck down Washington State's 140-year-old ban on assisted suicide. Her reasoning was that the law violated the 14th Amendment by restricting a person's liberty. "There is no more profoundly personal decision," she ruled, "nor one which is closer to the heart of personal liberty than the choice which a terminally ill person makes to end his or her suffering and hasten an inevitable death." Columnists like Charles Krauthammer, who mockingly described Rothstein's decision as "distinguished . . . not just by its illogic but by its hubris," and Terry Eastland, who called the decision "a breathtaking display of judicial activism," were outraged, especially in light of the failure of Initiative 119 in Washington State less than three years earlier. Other commentators, like Ellen Goodman, predicted that assisted suicide would soon make its way to the U.S. Supreme Court. Conservatives and liberals alike began equating the controversy over assisted suicide with the cultural debate over abortion.[13] All understood that it was Kevorkian who was driving it.

The day before the verdict in his favor, Kevorkian had received a political piece of good news: The Michigan chapter of the American Civil Liberties Union had come out in support of his drive to put a constitutional amendment on the November ballot. The ACLU's board of directors urged its 9,000 members and ten Michigan branches to join Kevorkian's effort.[14] Between Kevorkian's acquittal and Judge Rothstein's ruling in Washington, the time seemed ripe to begin building public support for a constitutional amendment. Indeed, public support for suicide as a right for terminal patients reached an all-time high in 1994: nearly two-thirds (64.2 percent) of Americans believed that a person with an incurable disease had the right to end his or her own life. In addition, 70.7 percent of Americans believed that doctors should be allowed by law to end a terminal patient's life if the patient and his or her family request it. The tide seemed to be turning in favor of Jack Kevorkian and assisted suicide.

✿ ✿ ✿

"I'm announcing my possible candidacy," Jack Kevorkian told reporters in Lansing at the end of May 1994. The doctor vowed that his top priority, if elected governor of Michigan, would be to "put an end to the corruption" in the state legislature, a body he called "an inquisition, a tool of the religious right." He added, "There'll be a lot of vetoes." Kevorkian's announcement appeared to stem directly from his activism: "My administration would have the most honest people around. I'm not a political animal, but when you meddle with my rights, I get interested." He would need to collect over 25,000 registered voters' signatures in less than two months in order to get on the ballot as an independent candidate.[15]

Kevorkian's name did not appear on the ballot that November. But his political savvy had grown over the past few years. With the help of Geoffrey Fieger, he had learned how to use the media to draw attention, to shape and then dominate the public discourse, and to use personal and emotional appeals to make his case and to counter his critics. So, when it was reported a couple weeks after his acquittal that he had tried to stage an exhibition of Adolf Hitler's paintings to raise money for charity in the mid-1980s, he was able to quickly and successfully counter. "The idea a few friends and I were working on was to put together a show of art by all the wartime leaders who painted, to entertain people and to raise money for charity," he clarified. Hitler was one of those World War II leaders, as were Dwight D. Eisenhower and Winston Churchill. During the interview, Kevorkian calmly displayed a sheaf of correspondence dated 1984 and 1985 from the Eisenhower Presidential Library and from the British National Trust. "We were going to mix them up and have people try to guess who painted what, make it kind of a game," he explained. "Unfortunately, the whole thing fell through, because we couldn't get use of the Churchill and Eisenhower paintings. They offered to sell us slides, but not to use the actual works." In addition, Houston businessman Billy Price, who owned a large private collection of Hitler's work, declined Kevorkian's request to allow part of it to be included in a public exhibition. Kevorkian's plan had been to donate the proceeds to the Michigan Holocaust Memorial Center. "Wouldn't that have been ironic," he said, "to use Hitler's paintings to raise money for a Holocaust memorial." For his part, Fieger volunteered that he intended to auction three of Kevorkian's own paintings to raise money for the ACLU-supported petition drive to get a proposal on assisted suicide on the November ballot.[16] With that, the simplistic stories claiming that Kevorkian wanted to sponsor an exhibition of Hitler's paintings—stories with provocative headlines like "Kevorkian and Hitler Art"—immediately disappeared.

While Kevorkian was winning the public relations battle, he remained the target of Michigan's judiciary and legislature. At the beginning of June, the state supreme court issued an order temporarily reinstating the law banning assisted suicide. The order also revived the commission that had been created to make recommendations to the state legislature about how to treat assisted suicide. The commission planned to complete its report within a week. Since the order established that the assisted-suicide law would expire six months after the committee issued its final report, the supreme court's order to reinstate the ban also had the effect of guaranteeing that there would be no law against assisted suicide by the end of 1994. Even the commission's recommendations were not expected to amount to much. At its last meeting on April 25—before it was disbanded when the Michigan Court of Appeals voided the assisted-suicide law on technical grounds on May 10—its members had voted nine to seven to recommend decriminalizing assisted suicide. But six members, more than a quarter of the commission, had abstained or been absent. Because of the ongoing legal messiness, one reporter called it "anyone's guess as to what law-enforcement officials might do if Dr. Kevorkian or another physician assisted in another suicide."[17] Kevorkian himself ventured his own prediction: "There's no doubt there's an awful lot of unnecessary suffering that will go on while this issue is being corrupted in the courts and Legislature."[18] The fact remained, however, that assisted suicide was once again illegal in Michigan.

The beginning of the summer found Geoffrey Fieger continuing the public relations goodwill tour. Speaking in Cleveland at the end of June to 250 people at a luncheon sponsored by the Cuyahoga County Bar Association, he called Kevorkian "one of my best friends." He continued, "He's a caring doctor and a very bright guy. He's also got a wonderful sense of humor." After four years of working together, he saw the real Dr. Kevorkian as "a skilled physician, a charming and intelligent man who follows baseball, likes the ladies and tells a good joke." He was not "the crackpot or evil-doer the media have portrayed him as." Rather, the doctor "is a board-certified pathologist, well-read and reflective, who just happens to look at the world a little bit differently than his colleagues."[19]

The second half of 1994 began with political and personal setbacks for Kevorkian and his cause. The former came at the beginning of July, when the doctor was forced to admit that he was now "pretty sure we won't qualify for the ballot." The drive to put a measure on assisted suicide before Michigan voters fell short by about 50,000 signatures. Still, Kevorkian looked ahead with optimism. "We'll shoot for November 1996," he promised. "That's a Presidential year. There will be a lot of voters." For a few months, Kevorkian had been blaming unusually bad winter weather for hampering the early part of the signature drive, which had begun in January. One of his lawyers, Michael Schwartz, said "the effort was also hurt by Dr. Kevorkian's trial" over the death of Thomas Hyde, even though the defendant was acquitted. Schwartz, like Fieger, made sure to present the ongoing political struggle as a dichotomy: tyrannical government infringing on individual liberty. "People favor the right to choose for themselves," he asserted. "They do not want the government to forbid them from ending their suffering."[20]

Kevorkian's personal loss came at the end of the summer. On September 11, his younger sister and confidante Margaret Janus succumbed to a heart attack at the age of sixty-eight. Margo, as she was called, had played an enormous role in her brother's activism, keeping all the patient records and videotaping the sessions between Kevorkian and his clients. She had been present at the first fifteen assisted suicides, and later helped to organize meetings of the patients' survivors. More recently, she had worked on the campaign to put an assisted suicide measure on the ballot. "She was my record-keeper, my videographer and my chronicler," said Kevorkian. "She was also my supporter when I had no other supporters."[21] Margo's daughter, Ava, would eventually become Kevorkian's sole heir.

By the beginning of October, just four months after the Michigan Supreme Court reinstated the ban on assisted suicide, the law was being challenged in the state's highest court. The ACLU of Michigan had taken up the cause by filing an appeal on behalf of two cancer patients and a handful of medical professionals. One of the patients, forty-four-year-old Teresa Hobbins, said, "I have the ultimate price to pay, so I should be able to choose. I'm competent. I've made the decision. I'm not going to let that disease kill me the way it can." The other patient, Ken Shapiro, compared assisted suicide to abortion in asking, "How can you have *Roe vs. Wade* as the law of the land, entailing a third entity and have abortion legal, when this involves just one individual, who, no matter what is done, is going to die? How can one be legal and not the other?" Kevorkian's old nemesis Richard Thompson argued in a brief that legalizing assisted suicide "will inevitably lead to the killing of the most vulnerable and voiceless in our society, the elderly, the mentally and physically handicapped, and our children who are retarded or chronically ill."[22] The justices' decision in the case would not come for two months.

In the meantime, Oregon made history by becoming the first state in the United States to legalize assisted suicide. Measure 16 on the November 8, 1994 state ballot read: "Shall law allow terminally ill adult patients voluntary informed choice to obtain physician's prescription for drugs to end life?" With 51.3 percent of voters answering "yes," Oregon's Death With Dignity Act (DWDA) was established. It was a watershed for the right-to-die movement. Attempts to repeal the act by the Oregon Legislature in 1997 and the George W. Bush administration in 2005 were blocked by Oregon voters and the U.S. Supreme Court, respectively. Those defeats, coupled with consistent statistics from the

Oregon Health Authority's mandatory annual reports demonstrating that DWDA opponents' fears that people would flock to Oregon to kill themselves were unfounded, spurred similar votes in other states (between 1998 and 2013, 752 DWDA patients died by ingesting a lethal dose of medication). At the time of this writing, assisted suicide is legal in four states in addition to Oregon: Washington State (as of 2008), Montana (2009), Vermont (2013), and New Mexico (2014).[23]

Less than three weeks after the historic vote in Oregon, Kevorkian assisted in his twenty-first suicide. Suffering from severe rheumatoid arthritis, a colon disease, and advanced osteoporosis, seventy-two-year-old Margaret Garrish inhaled carbon monoxide at her home in Royal Oak. Both her husband of fifty years and her son were present at her death. Garrish "was in a pitiful condition, a deplorable condition," according to one of her neighbors. Her health problems had crippled her hands and caused her to lose both legs and one eye. "She was in a lot of pain," said another neighbor. "She couldn't hold anything, she couldn't take care of herself." A third said, "I don't consider it a tragedy. Obviously it was well thought out and planned." A friend of the deceased put it succinctly: "If you can't use your hands, you have no legs and you lost an eye, if all you have left is your brain, it would be pretty hard to just lie there." Dr. Kevorkian left a signed document at the scene titled "Certificate of Medicide."[24]

It was Kevorkian's first assisted suicide in just over a year, and it came just one day after Michigan's temporary ban on assisted suicide came to an end. While the timing struck his critics as suspicious, Michael Schwartz insisted it was coincidental. Rita Marker accused Kevorkian of making his clients "feel that their importance could be assured by being dead." She added, "Kevorkian should be locked up to protect vulnerable people. These are planned serial killings. Serial killers don't stop." The coroner ruled Garrish's death a homicide.[25]

Within days, two doctors came forward to claim that Kevorkian had refused to allow them to treat Garrish's pain. Dr. Pavan Grover of Houston and Dr. John Nelson of Traverse City, Michigan, said they wrote and called Kevorkian and his lawyers with offers of help after hearing Garrish's appeal, aired on news shows around the country back in March, in which she said she wanted either pain relief or "a way out" of her suffering. They said they never received a response. Kevorkian shot back, suggesting that the doctors were primarily looking for publicity: "The woman's family didn't want to bother with them, and we had no need to contact them because the woman's own family doctor came forward and gave her morphine patches after she first said she couldn't stand the pain." He asked rhetorically, "What were they going to do, anyway, medicate her into a coma?"[26]

The year ended on a low note for Kevorkian and assisted suicide advocates across Michigan. In December, the state supreme court ruled that the ban on assisted suicide was indeed constitutional: "The right to commit suicide is neither implicit in the concept of ordered liberty nor deeply rooted in this nation's history and tradition," the justices wrote. In addition, they distinguished between killing oneself and being killed by another, and thus concluded that assisting suicide "is its own species of crime." Rejecting the state's long-standing definition of murder as "the act of intentionally providing the means by which a person commits suicide," the justices wrote that a person can only be charged with murder in a case "where there is probable cause to believe that death was the direct and natural result of [the person's] act. Where a defendant merely is involved in the events leading up to the death, such as providing the means, the proper charge is assisting in a suicide."[27]

The court also ruled that a person could be prosecuted for assisted suicide even in the absence of a law against the act (the failure of the Michigan House and Senate to agree on whether assisted suicide should be put to voters had killed the effort to enact a new state ban on the practice). The justices cited a section of Michigan law that said that anyone who commits an offense for which there was no stated penalty could be found guilty of a "common-law" felony and punished by a maximum of five years in prison and a $10,000 fine. The supreme court essentially ruled that assisted suicide was, and always had been, a felony in Michigan.[28]

The unusual ruling meant that the two dismissed Oakland County murder charges against Dr. Kevorkian would have to be reexamined by a trial court. The doctor now faced possible charges in seventeen different suicides in all. Richard Thompson declared a win. "I don't care how they want to argue it," he said, "this is a total victory for the prosecution and a total defeat for Dr. Kevorkian." He was confident that "it can be shown very clearly that [Kevorkian] met the court's test for murder."[29]

Kevorkian answered during a press conference in Geoffrey Fieger's office, vowing that he would continue to fight for "a fundamental human right—the right not to suffer—that cannot be taken away by any law." He continued by differentiating his morals from the interests of the state: "What happens to me now therefore will be a perfect sign of where your society stands and what it is." Criticizing Michigan's political and judicial authorities, he added: "This is a perfect, clear manifestation of the existence of the Inquisition in this state, no different from the medieval one. That may sound melodramatic," he admitted, "but it is true." Kevorkian also framed the court's ruling as an infringement of people's rights: "What happens to me personally is not relevant, and I don't care. I know what's right. My fundamental right not to suffer cannot be abrogated by any opinion, any fiat, any decree of anyone."[30]

Calling the decision "an outrage," Fieger was champing at the bit to defend his client in court. "If that's what they want, so be it," he declared. "Let's go to trial." Fieger estimated it would cost taxpayers tens of millions of dollars to repeatedly prosecute Kevorkian. He added: "You can't just go and make up a law nobody ever heard of and call it a common-law felony. Under the Ninth Amendment, I thought any rights not specifically given to the states are reserved to the people. In the meantime, I hope they charge us with murders in every one of the cases. I am ready to take on twenty-one murder trials, starting tomorrow." Fieger predicted that "no jury will ever convict Dr. Kevorkian; they couldn't even convict him of assisted suicide." Acknowledging that possibility, Wayne County Prosecutor John O'Hair offered that he was "going to sit on [the ruling] for a while." It was a wise decision, for Fieger's prediction turned out to be correct.[31]

⚙ ⚙ ⚙

The new year started well for the sixty-six-year-old Kevorkian, with prosecutors announcing that he would not be charged in the February 1993 double suicide of Stanley Ball and Mary Biernat. "Attempting to reinterview witnesses nearly two years following the alleged crime has proven to be difficult and futile," lamented lead prosecutor Tom Aylsworth in the middle of January. Perhaps feeling emboldened, Kevorkian announced that he would continue to help people commit suicide. "If someone needs it, I'll do it," he threatened, adding that he would petition the U.S. Supreme Court to overturn Michigan's ban on assisted suicide.[32]

March of 1995 brought the first ruling by a federal appeals court on assisted suicide. In a two-to-one decision, the U.S. Court of Appeals for the Ninth Circuit upheld a Washington law against the practice in ruling that a claim of a right to physician-assisted suicide had no basis in the "traditions of our nation" and was "antithetical to the defense of human life that has been a chief responsibility of our constitutional government." The decision overturned a lower court's finding that the law was unconstitutional. According to the *New York Times*, Judge John Noonan, who wrote the ruling, was "an anti-abortion legal theoretician and Catholic scholar before his appointment to the bench by President Ronald Reagan in 1986." Noonan was joined by Judge Diarmuid O'Scannlain, who wrote that the right to privacy did not include "the right to have a second person collaborate in your death." The lone dissenter, Judge Eugene Wright, argued that the state law violated "the right to die with dignity." The suit had been brought by the right-to-die organization Compassion in Dying, which had joined with three terminally ill patients (all of whom were now deceased) and a group of doctors. Its vice president, John Lee, said it would file an appeal. He added that the ruling showed the court's "lack of concern and compassion for the terminally ill who are suffering from intractable pain." The members of Americans United for Life, which represented a group of Washington legislators, had a different perspective. "What would be helpful in this area," said one of its lawyers, "is if people stopped looking at the law as a solution to a medical problem."[33]

The bad news continued for Kevorkian. In April 1995, the U.S. Supreme Court rejected his argument that there is a constitutional right to assisted suicide and, in so doing, opened the door for Michigan prosecutors to go after him for any and all of the twenty-one suicides he had been involved in since 1990.[34] The appeal had stated that "it is not the ending of life, but rather the ending of suffering, which is the genuine issue." The court turned down the case without commenting on it.[35]

In his typical fashion, Kevorkian fought back. On Monday, May 8, exactly two weeks after the court's decision, he presided over a twenty-second suicide. It was his first since the Michigan Supreme Court had ruled assisted suicide a common-law felony the previous December.

The Reverend John Evans, a seventy-eight-year-old Unitarian minister with pulmonary fibrosis, killed himself in his Royal Oak home early that morning. The local police were called to the home by Evans's wife, the Reverend Jan Evans-Tiller, just after 7:00 a.m.[36] Evans-Tiller, the minister of religious education at a Unitarian church in Detroit, offered the following in a statement released by Fieger: "My husband was a courageous man who had the courage to do what is right. Dr. Kevorkian is such a person also." Kevorkian's lawyer took the argument a step further: "Rev[erend] Evans and his family had a right to decide at the end of his life how much suffering he had to undergo. They reject such attempts by those in government who would make them suffer." Fieger announced that his client continued to stand ready to take on the law in the name of compassion and in the defense of an individual's right to die. "If somebody wants to try and intimidate [Kevorkian]," he warned, "they picked the wrong guy."[37] Fieger continued to spin a narrative about Kevorkian as a brave, compassionate defender of individual rights against the legal and political systems: "[Dr. Kevorkian]'s not going to be persecuted or intimidated into making people suffer."[38]

A spokeswoman for Operation Rescue in Michigan, a group that opposed assisted suicide, framed the doctor as more coldly calculating than warmly compassionate: "The only reason he hasn't killed somebody since Thanksgiving," asserted Lynn Mills, "is that he was waiting on the supreme court. They looked for an open window and a slow news day."[39] The fact that Evans and his wife were members of the clergy provided an interesting twist in this particular case, for Evans "sought to make his suicide a statement in [the right-to-die] debate" by allowing the release after his death of a letter he had written—but never sent—to several Unitarian Universalist churches:

> I am making this request of several local Unitarian Universalist churches, hoping to receive an affirmative reply while time remains and my sickness moves its course. I have terminal pulmonary fibrosis.
>
> UU churches have supported freedom of belief, opinion and speech. Now there is another freedom in need of support: freedom to choose the time, manner, and place of one's death. Unlike other issues or "causes" common in our churches, the right to die is not only a principle to be supported in general or somewhere else—it is here, now.

The finality of this act has a religious quality to it that William James called "solemn, serious, and tender." This, as well as the vindictive behavior shown by civil authorities in such matters, makes the occasion one of sanctuary.

Without disturbing your schedule for use of your building, will you let me rent space, or a room, for my physician-assisted suicide? No special preparation would be required.

For some 20 years, as a minister, I served churches in the Unitarian Universalist Association. Now I need to ask if the movement that I have called "home" has a place for me.[40]

In 1988, the First Unitarian Universalist Church had become one of the few denominations to pass a resolution allowing "terminally ill patients to select the time of their own death."[41] Now one of its own ministers had acted on it.

Just four days after assisting the suicide of John Evans, Kevorkian's oldest patient to that point, the doctor helped his youngest patient yet to kill himself. The death of twenty-seven-year-old Nicholas Loving, who had Lou Gehrig's disease, was different from Kevorkian's previous twenty-two assisted suicides in another way. The body was left in Kevorkian's van in a parking lot near the office of the Oakland County Prosecutor. When asked whether this was a gesture of contempt for the authorities, Geoffrey Fieger invoked pragmatism, concern for the public, and compassion for Loving's family: "Not at all. We just wanted to make it easy for the law-enforcement authorities and help them save the taxpayers money. We also wanted to spare the family scenes of the body bag being shown on TV."[42] Loving had died on a couch and his body had been moved into the van. Kevorkian's tactics were changing—and becoming bolder.

As with John Evans, an anonymous phone call to the medical examiner's office had alerted the authorities to Loving's death. Dr. Dragovic, the Oakland County medical examiner, called the situation "awfully bizarre." Although other coroners in the state had ruled the deaths of Kevorkian's patients suicides, Dragovic had ruled all of Kevorkian's assisted suicides in Oakland County—including, now, Nick Loving's—homicides. His reasoning in this latest case was that the young man "had not been physically capable of making all the preparations for his suicide."[43]

Rita Marker of the International Anti-Euthanasia Task Force had been arguing for five years that the doctor was committing homicides. She was aghast at the circumstances of Loving's death. "Here is the macabre and the ludicrous combined in the actions of Jack Kevorkian," she suggested. "It gives new meaning to 'in your face.' It's the sort of thing you see a child do." Oakland County Sheriff John Nichols agreed, accusing Kevorkian of "playing a game of cat and mouse." Republican Governor John Engler also weighed in: "It's wrong," he said, "but I have virtually no hope that [Kevorkian] will stop."

Both Fieger and Kevorkian understood well the loopholes in existing law—so well that Fieger publicly expressed defiance in response to Governor Engler's comments: "I speak for Dr. Kevorkian: there is no law. Read my lips, Governor Engler." They also understood that public support for Kevorkian was hovering around 60 percent. Fans paid as much as $400 for the doctor's autograph, and the author of the *Encyclopedia of Pop Culture* claimed that "Kevorkian is at least as well liked as Roseanne," a popular television actress at the time, because of his principles.[44]

Even if the assessments of Kevorkian's opponents were accurate, the reality was that convicting him of a crime would once again be difficult. "It's important to keep in mind that all we have is a body in a van," pointed out Richard Thompson. "It is very important for the public to understand that mere presence in a room where a suicide occurs is not a crime. You have to be able to prove he assisted in some specific way."[45] In addition to the continuing legal murkiness, Kevorkian's cause benefitted enormously from the support of his patients' families. Nick's mother, Carol, who had brought her son from Phoenix to Michigan for his suicide, said, "Dr. Kevorkian gave something to my son the medical professional refused. He gave my son control over his own destiny." She continued, "I spent 18 months as caregiver to my son and witnessed every moment of his agony. The good doctor's intervention was a blessing."[46] The fact of the matter was that in five years, not a single member of any of his patients' families had come forward, either before or after their loved one's suicide, to oppose the act or Kevorkian's part in it. "That's why these cases are difficult," admitted Wayne County Prosecutor John O'Hair. "There's no admissions or confessions."

On the same day as Nicholas Loving's suicide, the Michigan Court of Appeals upheld the five-year-old injunction—handed down after Kevorkian's first assisted suicide in 1990—ordering the doctor not to assist in any more deaths. The injunction had never been tested as Kevorkian appealed it and prosecutors used other tactics (for example, criminal charges) against him. Using what one *New York Times* article referred to as "unusually harsh language," the three-judge panel found that Kevorkian's "words and actions amount to an advertisement for criminal and unethical conduct." The judges continued: "Defendant has made clear that he stands ready to assist people in ending their lives. Defendant has made clear that neither the actions of the Legislature, the executive, nor the judiciary will sway him from his course. We will see." Michael Modelski, once an assistant prosecutor for Oakland County but now in private practice, interpreted the ruling to mean that Kevorkian could be immediately jailed for contempt of court if he assisted in another suicide. Geoffrey Fieger dismissed the threat as "crazy."

In June 1995, Kevorkian took another step in furthering his mission by opening his first obitorium, a clinic at which he would carry out assisted suicides. It was a short-lived venture. Kevorkian leased the building, a former hardware store in Groveland Township, Michigan, on a $500 month-to-month basis. The first patient to die at the new Margo Janus Mercy Clinic, named for Kevorkian's sister, was sixty-year-old Erika Garcellano, who had Lou Gehrig's disease and had been living in a nursing home in Kansas City. Her two sons and her best friend had accompanied her from Missouri and were present at her death. The next day, the owner of the building gave Kevorkian a month to vacate. "I'm looking at the pressure from authorities, from the media," the landlord said.[47]

Kevorkian's vision was for obitoriums to be affiliated with hospices and to provide for a procedure in addition to assisted suicide; namely, the removal of organs for transplant. As we saw in chapter 1, Kevorkian's interest in harvesting organs from condemned criminals dated back to the 1950s. Prisoners continued to write to him even now, forty years later, to offer their organs. One such person was Larry Grant Lonchar, an inmate on Georgia's death row. Lonchar had been convicted of three murders in 1986 and was scheduled to be electrocuted on June 23, 1995. He wrote to Kevorkian a few weeks beforehand to ask the doctor to recommend methods of execution that would not damage his organs. Lonchar wanted to donate a kidney to the detective who helped link him to the three killings. Deputy Attorney General Mike

Hobbs rejected the possibility outright: "The state has no discretion over how the death penalty is imposed. As far as the state is concerned in this particular case, we expect the death penalty to be administered in accordance with the law, and that's by electrocution." Lonchar's attorney was flabbergasted: "If someone knows they are going to be executed, why not do it in a way that would permit six people's lives to be saved? This is nuts."[48]

The debate over Lonchar's request came in the wake of the highly publicized liver transplant that retired major league baseball legend Mickey Mantle had just undergone. Mantle's ordeal had generated a great deal of publicity on the shortage of organs for transplant. Lonchar pointed to that publicity as one of the reasons for his decision to become a donor. "Why can't Death Row inmates, once their appeals are denied, be given the option of dying by execution or donating our organs?" he asked in a letter to the *Atlanta-Journal Constitution*. "Either way we are dead, so it's not like we are avoiding our death sentences. The most important fact is other people could live." Kevorkian agreed. "We're talking about saving at least three lives and maybe six," he said. "What's going to be gained by frying this guy?" He suggested that lethal injection would allow two kidneys and a liver to be harvested immediately after Lonchar's death. Harkening back to his decades-old interest in allowing condemned criminals the choice to be experimented on, Kevorkian also pointed out that if Lonchar were anesthetized and had his organs removed before he died, then his lungs and heart could also be saved.[49]

Ultimately, Lonchar's request was denied. A last-minute appeal did, however, stay his execution until the following year. In November 1996, he was put to death by electrocution. None of his organs was harvested. "It's insanity," Kevorkian concluded. "[Organ donation] is so rational, it scares people."[50]

* * *

Around 5:30 in the morning on August 21, 1995, a security guard at William Beaumont Hospital in Royal Oak noticed a car in a parking lot reserved for doctors outside of the emergency room. What had caught the guard's attention were the fogged windows and the temporary license plate taped to the rear window of the Renault Alliance. He did not think too much of it, however, and continued his rounds. When he checked again a little while later, he discovered, to his horror, a woman's body in the backseat covered with a sheet. It was Dr. Kevorkian's twenty-fifth patient.[51]

Hospital staff pronounced Esther Cohan dead at 7:20 a.m. The forty-six-year-old former executive secretary had been living in Skokie, Illinois, with her sister Judy. She was diagnosed with multiple sclerosis in 1981, but in the past year, the progressive disease had become unbearable. "As half my body has been dead for the past 14 months, I and I alone have decided to put the rest of my body at peace and my entire body out of the uncontrollable pain," she had written in a letter dated July 10, 1995. Judy read from it and from a second letter, dated August 9, at a press conference: "things went from bad to worse and I was nothing more than a bed veg, [so] I knew it was time to say, 'See ya.' . . . I know the people who care understand, and that's all that matters."[52]

Leaving Cohan's body at the hospital was a calculated move by Kevorkian. On one hand, Geoffrey Fieger said that it was done "in order to spare the family the tabloid media circus of the body bag scene on TV." On the other, he declared, "A hospital is now involved. We are hoping that physicians at William Beaumont Hospital recognize that this is an issue that physicians need to become involved in." According to one newspaper, Fieger also hinted that Beaumont had been purposely chosen because one of the hospital's practicing surgeons had been heavily involved in the decision to suspend Kevorkian's medical license in 1991. The same newspaper pointed out that Kevorkian's last four assisted suicides "seemed designed to provoke a legal showdown." That judgment was correct. Fieger himself declared after Esther Cohan's death that he and his client were "involved in a social struggle, aimed at changing society, hopefully for the better." Accordingly, Kevorkian's tactics had begun to change—and become more provocative—with John Evans's death three months earlier. Even so, prosecutors had not yet filed charges in any of the four assisted suicides that Kevorkian had attended so far in 1995.[53]

At the end of August, Fieger was back in court to argue for the dismissal of the murder charges that had been brought against his client for the 1991 deaths of Marjorie Wantz and Sherry Miller. "Dr. Kevorkian has been absurdly charged with murdering people who voluntarily committed suicide in front of friends and family," he announced to the media. "A murder charge cannot possibly stand." In fact, the judge who would preside over the hearing, David Breck, had dismissed these same murder charges in 1992. Still, in the wake of the December 1994 decision by the state Supreme Court that ruled assisted suicide a common-law felony, Oakland County assistant prosecutor Gregory Townsend simply said before the hearing, "I would expect the judge to follow the law." Fieger countered by suggesting that assisted suicide was only illegal, "if at all, in those cases in which a person persuaded another to commit suicide. Most of the time, Jack tries to talk them out of it."[54]

Kevorkian refused to even attend the hearing. "It's all a farce, and I don't care for these legal games," he said dismissively. "This is not illegal, no matter what they say, and the common people know it and support me." Judge Breck disagreed. Although he dismissed the murder charges on the grounds that there was no proof that the doctor had committed a direct act that caused Wantz's and Miller's deaths, he cited the state supreme court's ruling in ordering that Kevorkian be tried on charges of assisted suicide. Fieger objected. "It will be virtually impossible for Dr. Kevorkian to defend himself," he argued, "because we'll essentially be making up the elements of this crime. Those have never been addressed by any court." If convicted, Kevorkian faced up to five years in prison and a fine of $13,500.[55]

Kevorkian seemed unfazed by Judge Breck's decision. On November 8, another body was found in a car—this time, outside the morgue. Kevorkian's twenty-sixth patient was Patricia Cashman, a fifty-eight-year-old cancer patient who ran a travel agency in San Marcos, California. Geoffrey Fieger informed the media that the woman had suffered from breast cancer for three years; the cancer had spread throughout her body, and she had recently lost the ability to walk. The original autopsy was once again performed by Dr. Dragovic, whose findings contradicted Fieger's statement: Dragovic found no visible signs of cancer other than a mastectomy scar. After disputing the results, a microscopic examination was performed. The exam proved Fieger correct when cancerous cells were detected in Cashman's spine. Kevorkian's lawyer and the medical examiner did agree on one thing, however: Cashman had taken her life by both inhaling carbon monoxide and using a version of Kevorkian's Mercitron. Dragovic declared carbon monoxide poisoning the cause of death, but noted the presence of drugs in Cashman's system and signs of a fresh injection on her body.[56]

While Cashman's suicide would be the last that Kevorkian would attend in 1995, the doctor stayed busy during the last two months of the year. The day before Halloween, he announced the formation of Physicians for Mercy. The group, originally composed of seven medical professionals, would be dedicated to promoting terminally ill patients' right to die. Dr. Mohammed El Nachef, a kidney specialist from Flint, Michigan, was perhaps the clearest about the purpose of the body: "This is not a support group of Dr. Kevorkian," he said during a press conference. "This is a professional organization that will look into the issue from scratch." It was the first organized support Kevorkian had enjoyed from members of the medical profession. He said he would consider himself bound by the group's guidelines.[57]

By the beginning of December, the group had proposed ten guidelines to regulate the practice of assisted suicide. Under the proposed system, a competent adult who desired medical help in dying would first need to consult a "qualified obitiatrist," or doctor who helps people die. At the time, Kevorkian claimed to be the only practicing obitiatrist—a term he invented. He envisioned the position this way: "Ideally, it would be a salaried job for a retired physician who wants to benefit mankind. No one should get rich doing this." The obitiatrist would then refer the patient to at least two different medical professionals: a psychiatrist and a specialist in the patient's disease. The patient would be referred to a pain management specialist as well if pain was one of the symptoms of the condition. According to the guidelines, the consulting doctors could approve physician-assisted suicide only if they agreed that the patient was mentally competent and had a terminal condition, "that the agony cannot be relieved or controlled, and/or that the side effects of pain management and medical therapy are intolerable for the patient." Once they agreed and endorsed an assisted suicide, the obitiatrist would perform the "final action." Dr. William Kimbrough, an Ann Arbor psychiatrist and the spokesperson for the group, said: "This took a lot of time, effort and verbiage, but we are now in unanimous agreement on these [guidelines]." The goal was to have them accepted by the medical profession. Kevorkian softened his earlier position by saying that he would do his best to follow them, "provided there is cooperation from other physicians in their specialties; if they don't cooperate, I will have to act as I have in the past."[58]

In addition to *obitiatrist*, Kevorkian coined the term *patholysis* to replace physician-assisted suicide. "We want to get away from all the negative connotations," he said. "I will no longer use the term 'assisted suicide' for what I do. From now on, it's 'patholysis.'" The term meant "to relieve suffering." Both Kevorkian and Geoffrey Fieger remained conscious of the power of language to shape social reality. It was not just their introduction of medical-sounding terms to replace common words. It was their purposeful choice, made several months earlier, to stop saying that the doctor had "performed" an assisted suicide or "assisted" in a suicide. Instead, they had been saying that he "attended" a suicide, and that was the term that news stories had begun using. The semantic changes were meant, in large part, to emphasize that this was "a medical matter—solely," as Kevorkian put it. They also had the effect of describing Kevorkian's role in suicides as more passive than active.[59]

The initial reaction from the local medical community to the work of Physicians for Mercy was mixed. Dr. W. Peter McCabe, the president-elect of the Michigan State Medical Society (a state affiliate of the AMA), stated that the members of the society "feel that to attempt to regulate this would be a step down the slippery slope of involuntary euthanasia"—the unilateral killing of patients by doctors. Dr. Howard Brody of the society's bioethics committee was not so sure. In fact, he thought the proposed guidelines represented "something of a step forward." He continued, referring to Kevorkian specifically: "In the past he has been a lone ranger, acting as his own medical expert in all specialties. But while more doctors are better, I don't think our society is ready to just say, 'Fine—turn this all over to the medical profession.' I think we need to have some sort of oversight mechanism that performs some sort of regulating function."[60]

The disagreements pointed to the continuing lack of consensus within the medical community. Once again, it was the "lone ranger" who was the most sure of his convictions.

6

"I PREFER JAIL TO BAIL"

Forcing a Showdown

As the year 1996 dawned, Jack Kevorkian faced two criminal trials. One, scheduled for February 20, was to be for the deaths of Merian Frederick and Dr. Ali Khalili in 1993; Kevorkian would be tried under the state law banning assisted suicide, which was by this point expired. The other, slated to begin April 1, was for the 1991 deaths of Marjorie Wantz and Sherry Miller; his prosecution in those cases would be carried out under the Michigan Supreme Court's December 1994 ruling that assisting in a suicide was a common-law felony. Kevorkian would spend much of the first half of the year in legal proceedings. [1]

Before those began, however, he would assist in his twenty-seventh suicide. The robed body of forty-eight-year-old Linda Henslee, a former computer programmer from Wisconsin who had multiple sclerosis, was left in Kevorkian's Volkswagen camper outside the medical examiner's office in Pontiac at the end of January. Henslee's two daughters were with her when she died in an undisclosed location in Oakland County. An anonymous call to the medical examiner's office at 5:45 a.m. encouraged someone to check the van. "She had pain all over and huge, open ulcers," Geoffrey Fieger later explained. "Dr. Kevorkian had tried to encourage her to continue to go on for a while longer, but she was unwilling." Fieger refused to say anything specific about Kevorkian's role in her death, other than that his client had been counseling her for "many months." While Fieger continued, as he had done over the previous five years, to describe Kevorkian's patients as leading unbearable lives, and the doctor himself as a long-standing advisor to each of them, prosecutors continued to emphasize Kevorkian's brazen disregard for authority. Gregory Townsend, an assistant prosecutor in Oakland County, stated that "nobody is above the law, and Dr. Kevorkian is flouting it."[2]

✽ ✽ ✽

The second trial of Jack Kevorkian, for the deaths of Merian Frederick and Ali Khalili, began on February 20, 1996. "These trials are as much about personal freedom as any in our history," Geoffrey Fieger declared about what was ahead for his client. Emphasizing his familiar themes of individual rights, patient autonomy, and rationality, he continued: "They are not about the right to die. They are about whether we have the right to decide for ourselves that enough suffering is enough, and whether a physician can help a rational, competent adult seek a soft landing." Kevorkian's attorney also appealed, if only indirectly, to the public by implying that politicians and prosecutors were wasting tax dollars by going after his client. "If these juries fail to convict Dr. Kevorkian," he commented, "no one will risk the taxpayers' wrath by charging him again." For Gregory Townsend, however, the trial was strictly about the law. "[Kevorkian] has violated the statute, period," he said, adding that all he needed for a conviction is "an open-minded jury who will follow the law."[3]

The trial opened with each side painting its own picture of the defendant. John Skrzynski, an Oakland County assistant prosecutor, waved Kevorkian's 1991 book *Prescription—Medicide* in front of the jury. "He has spoken through his writings. His aim is not only to help suffering people," Skrzynski warned, "but is the first step in a larger plan to perform medical experimentation on live human beings." Calling Kevorkian a "ghoulish character," he said he would demonstrate the doctor's "vested interest in people wanting to kill themselves." Kevorkian stuck his fingers in his ears while Skrzynski spoke. Fieger, on the other hand, knowing full well why Kevorkian had been acquitted in the Thomas Hyde case in 1994, asserted that his client's sole intent in helping Frederick and Khalili commit suicide was to relieve their pain and suffering. The expired state law under which Kevorkian was being tried did not apply if a person's intent was "to relieve pain or discomfort and not to cause death, even if the medication or procedure may hasten or increase the risk of death," as the statute read. "Do you think there is ever a law that could be passed forcing people to suffer?" Fieger asked the jury.[4]

Just three days into the trial, however, Fieger's plan to portray his client as a compassionate doctor who was simply relieving his patients' suffering hit a snag. The Michigan Court of Appeals, on a petition from the prosecution, ruled that prosecutors only had to prove one of two facts: either that Kevorkian provided the means for Frederick and Khalili to kill themselves or that he intentionally participated in an act that allowed them to commit suicide. Judge Jessica Cooper was forced to revise the instructions she had previously given to the jury in order to reflect the new appellate ruling.[5]

Dr. Khalili's wife, Sandra, took the stand as a witness for the prosecution when testimony resumed. Ultimately, she would prove to be a stronger witness for the defense. During her testimony, both an hour-long videotape and letters from her husband were introduced as evidence. One segment of the videotape showed Dr. Khalili making a statement. "I want to live quite bad," he said, "but my suffering is awful, and there's no answer to the pain." He then signed a request to have Kevorkian help him die. "You see, at the present time I don't believe there is any option," he continued. "I think that's the best way." Sandra confirmed her husband's judgment. "My husband did not want to end his life, but he saw this as his only option left," she said. She also verified the extent of her husband's pain, testifying that she "did not know a person could endure such pain" and that it often took hours to get her husband out of bed and to the hospital for radiation treatments. Even so, she said she was "absolutely and totally shocked" when her husband told her that he had arranged to see Dr. Kevorkian. He gave her the name of the hotel where he would be staying in case she decided to join him. She waited a few hours after he left, and then followed him to Michigan. Kevorkian's sister Margo videotaped their session with Kevorkian and Neal Nicol. The videotape showed Kevorkian asking Sandra how she felt. "Well, it hurts me," she answered, "because I am going to miss him." Pausing, she added, "I know, I know, it's the right thing." The jury also watched Kevorkian ask Khalili on the videotape why he did not kill himself without assistance, since he could have procured the necessary drugs. "Well, yeah, that's a good question," the doctor answered. "Maybe I prefer that it be done by a professional person with the least chance of failure."[6]

When Kevorkian took the stand during the second week of his trial, he portrayed himself as exactly that type of "professional." His testimony sought to convince the jury that he was a compassionate, reasonable, patient physician whose only purpose was to relieve his patients' suffering. Kevorkian testified that before cases ever reach that stage he does everything he can to discourage potential patients from suicide. "I'm delighted when I don't hear from them again," he stated. "It is my unwavering policy to constantly question a patient and constantly advise them, to the point of nagging, suggesting that they do not proceed." Each of the patients that Kevorkian does decide to help is reminded by the doctor that "you can take the mask off at the last minute." When asked if he wanted to see his patients die, he answered, "No. My desire would be to see a patient pull the clip and take off the mask." He was clear about his intentions. The "only intent that I have," he said, is "that their suffering is ended."[7]

Kevorkian's second day on the stand produced more carefully worded responses. The doctor testified, for example, upon being shown the consent form for "medically assisted suicide" signed by Khalili, that "by signing this, my understanding was that he wanted to end his torment, end his torture." Did that mean that he wanted Khalili to die? asked John Skrzynski. "My intent was never to end his life," Kevorkian answered coolly. "My intent was to help the man fulfill his wish to end his suffering." But, Skrzynski insisted, Kevorkian knew that the carbon monoxide was always fatal. The doctor replied, "I don't prescribe carbon monoxide in a lethal dose; the patient does. Everything is always the patient's choice."[8] As careful as Kevorkian was trying to be during his testimony, he did slip up on one occasion. The doctor surprised Geoffrey Fieger by suddenly comparing his own intent to that of an executioner. "When an executioner pulls the switch on the electric chair, is his wish to kill a human being?" Kevorkian asked rhetorically. "Or to fulfill his duty to . . . implement justice and uphold the law?" Fieger, not wanting the poorly chosen comparison to color jurors' opinions of the doctor's intent, quickly asked his client whether he actually felt like an executioner. "Not at all," Kevorkian answered.[9]

Fieger returned to emphasizing Kevorkian's humaneness in his closing argument. "We are about to make history," he declared. "Not so much for Dr. Kevorkian . . . but for the fact that no prosecutor can ever attempt to convince free Americans that any law says kindness and compassion is a crime." Skrzynski's closing argument focused on the supposedly kind, compassionate doctor's intent. Pointing to the carbon monoxide canisters, he said, "This stuff is not medicine. It's a toxin. It kills." Four of the alternate jurors were dismissed after closing arguments. Two told reporters afterward that they would have voted to acquit Kevorkian.[10]

The sitting jurors unanimously did just that the very next day, after nine hours of deliberation and three votes. When the verdict was announced, Kevorkian's supporters in the courtroom cheered; the doctor turned and waved to quiet them down. John Skrzynski believed the prosecution had proven its case but that the verdict had gone in favor of Kevorkian because "it's difficult to get the jury to focus on facts rather than their emotions." Organizations that opposed the right to die were quick to weigh in on the verdict. A spokesperson for the American Life League charged that "Society has taken a step toward that point when human beings will cease to be human simply because they are in pain, dying or unwanted. This kind of compassion leads to the gas chamber." The Catholic Conference in Michigan called for a stronger law against assisted suicide.[11]

"It's been a tremendous stroke in favor of rationality," Kevorkian proclaimed afterward. "This is not a victory for me but for the very essence of human existence, and let me give you a promise, what I do will always be for human welfare. I will not abuse it." He believed that in rendering an acquittal, the jury had "restored the dignity and the memory of the patients involved." Speaking directly to his peers who had acquitted him, he offered the following: "I'd like to tell the jury the magnitude of what they accomplished there. It is not even a right that we're talking about. It is an inherent essence of human existence." His attorney agreed. "This is not about the right to die," Fieger said. "It is about the right not to suffer. The medical profession cannot be required by government to keep us alive against our will." To Fieger, the jury's decision demonstrated that "the people of America are not going to allow certain governmental officials to tell us at the end of our life how much we have to suffer."[12]

The legal and public opinion landscapes appeared to be changing in favor of assisted suicide. During Kevorkian's trial, the 9th U.S. Circuit Court of Appeals struck down Washington State's law against the practice, leading some to believe that Washington would become the second state after Oregon to legalize the right to die (it eventually did, as we saw in chapter 5, but not until 2008). In addition, a survey published in the February issue of the *New England Journal of Medicine* had found that two-thirds of Michigan residents and more than half of the state's doctors preferred legalizing assisted suicide to banning it. In light of the trends in public opinion and the law, some observers believed Kevorkian would never be convicted. One called any future attempt at prosecuting him "an exercise in futility."[13]

The doctor's second trial of the year and third overall, scheduled to begin in April, proved to be precisely that, but not before it became much more of a public spectacle than the previous attempt to convict Kevorkian. This time around, he was to be tried under the Michigan Supreme Court's 1994 ruling that assisted suicide is a common-law felony for his role in Marjorie Wantz's and Sherry Miller's 1991 deaths. Geoffrey Fieger began complaining to the media before the trial began. "Three years after the fact, my client is finally informed what he did was a crime, and I have to wait until five days before the trial before the judge makes up the elements of the law," he said. "That's reprehensible and, you should add, medieval." He was referring to Judge David Breck's announcement from a few days before that he would instruct the jury that the prosecution needed only to prove that Kevorkian knew the patient intended to commit suicide, that he provided the means by which it was accomplished, and that "he intended that they be used to commit the suicide." Breck had been petitioned by the prosecution to instruct the jury "on the difference between motive and intent." Given the judge's decision, Gregory Townsend was optimistic about the prosecution's chances. "I believe if the jury will merely follow the law, we will win a conviction," he said. "And it should be easier for them to follow the law." Townsend thought the fact that neither Wantz nor Miller was terminally ill would help his case. His colleague in the prosecutor's office, Lawrence Bunting, agreed, saying that he would argue that the two women had other options. "In this case," he said, "you have a lady who had multiple sclerosis—it was not terminal at the time—and you have a lady who the medical examiner testifies there was nothing physically wrong with her. She had a mental problem."[14]

Fieger shot back, clarifying that his client had never used a terminal illness as a criterion for deciding whether to help a patient. "The criteria is [sic] suffering," he explained, "and in many ways, Marjorie Wantz suffered more than any of his other patients. This is not about the right to die. This is about any competent individual's right to choose how much suffering she or he has to endure, and hers was horrific." He declared that Judge Breck's ruling "has absolutely no effect on us," and said he still planned to argue that Kevorkian's "sole intent was to relieve pain and suffering." Fieger, as much as anyone else, was aware that this trial had a political undercurrent. Republican Oakland County Prosecutor Richard Thompson was running for reelection in 1996, and his opponents had begun accusing him of wasting taxpayers' money on prosecuting Kevorkian. That three prosecutors in other Michigan counties had said they would not prosecute the doctor for the suicides he assisted in their jurisdictions did not help Thompson's chances of reelection. It was perhaps for these reasons that Thompson himself did not appear in court; instead, Skrzynski and Bunting led the prosecution.[15]

Kevorkian, for his part, took the opportunity to make a political statement. He showed up at the courthouse in a colonial-era costume, complete with a white wig, breeches, a vest, and buckle shoes. His intent to mock the proceedings was immediately clear. Once inside, he shouted, "If Thomas Jefferson justifies and endorses and advocates suicide for cancer, why am I in this courtroom?" He later gave reporters what he said was the text of an 1813 letter in which the third U.S. president discussed the advantages of using extracts from poisonous plants to painlessly end one's life. Kevorkian's dramatic arrival at the courthouse in full costume was a sign of things to come during the trial.[16]

Opening arguments proceeded as expected. Bunting, for the prosecution, appeared to be "almost pleading with jurors to heed the higher court ruling," according to a *New York Times* report. "We aren't creating law here; we aren't setting a pattern for the future," the prosecutor explained. "This is a very straightforward criminal case. He knew what he was doing. He intended to assist them in their suicides, and he did so." The defense countered by encouraging the jury to "strike a blow against tyranny." Fieger urged the jury to recognize that there was no written law against assisted suicide and to reach a verdict accordingly. With his flair for the dramatic, Fieger showed the jury a large blank sheet of paper. "Go to the law books and look up the law under which Dr. Kevorkian will be charged, and this is what you will see—nothing!" he exclaimed. "Five judges said there was a secret, unwritten law in force in 1991 that no one ever knew about. Does that make sense to you?" His conclusion was simple. "What we are talking about," he asserted, "is this relentless persecution of Dr. Kevorkian." He added, "No one could have the intent to violate a law that isn't written down and that no one knows about."[17]

Two days later, Kevorkian walked out of his own trial while Bunting was cross-examining Marjorie Wantz's husband. "To put me on trial without a written law is the definition of corruption," he asserted. Judge Breck informed the defendant, while the jury was out of the courtroom, that he would allow him to leave, with the understanding that he might have to return at a future date. The judge then explained to the jurors that Kevorkian had voluntarily exercised his right not to attend the trial. "I want to be convicted," Kevorkian told Fieger before the proceedings resumed. "Where there's no law, there's no crime . . . and let's see what history says in 10 years."[18]

When testimony resumed, the jurors once again saw dramatic video footage of the deceased. Sherry Miller practically forced her words out. "I have thought about this for a long time," she said quietly. "There's no turning back. I want to die. I waited too long, and I can't do anything myself." Marjorie Wantz, her eyes almost black from lack of sleep, added, "She got about my words exactly. I wish we could have done it a year ago—two years ago." She mentioned that she had twice tried to kill herself but failed. Some of the most damaging comments to the prosecution's case came from Wantz's husband, Bill, who testified over three days. The prosecution had tried to establish that Marjorie was clinically depressed. "I don't think Marg was depressed, and she was not nuts," her husband objected. "She was constantly in pain, and didn't like being in pain. She kept going to these doctors and every operation was supposed to finally solve the problem and every one just made it worse." The prosecutor asked whether she wanted to die. Wantz, carefully coached by Kevorkian's attorneys, said, "No. She knew that she would die, but she wanted to relieve her pain and suffering."[19]

Outside of court, Fieger continued to hammer home his themes, asking of reporters, "Do you for a moment think a jury in America will convict someone on an *ex post facto* law which isn't written down and which a court made up three years after the fact?"[20] Inside the courthouse, the trial grew increasingly tense, and even bitter. Prosecutors had spent much of the first month appealing a variety of matters to the state appellate court; there would be thirteen in all, virtually all of which were granted. When Kevorkian finally took the stand in early May, emotions were running high on both sides. Twice during Kevorkian's first day on the stand, Fieger asked Judge Breck to dismiss the case on the grounds that his client was being denied due process because of all of the prosecution's last-minute, successful appeals. "I am sympathetic and I am really surprised that the Court of Appeals would move ahead in this fashion," the judge admitted, but said that it was "out of my hands." That Kevorkian was being prosecuted for violating a common law was unusual enough; that so many of the prosecution's appeals were being granted during the trial led a professor of constitutional law to conclude that the authorities "clearly are determined to get Kevorkian."[21]

Kevorkian's testimony began quietly. "My motive," he explained, "was to do my duty as a physician. My intent was to relieve pain and suffering, not help them die. That was, unfortunately, necessary." But after appearing for the proceedings only sporadically during the first month of the trial, he quickly grew frustrated on the stand. "I never considered this a real trial based on real law," he replied when questioned by his attorney, "and I didn't want to give it any kind of validation. For anyone who would call this a real crime and this unwritten law real, I have nothing but contempt, though I do respect the judge and the family members." Turning to the jury at one point, he said, "This is an inquisition in which the only protection for a defendant is a jury. I don't fear conviction, especially when I am sure I was right. But I will not last long in jail, if my liberty is taken away, because nothing is more precious to me."[22]

The tension in the courtroom reached a peak during the second day of Bunting's cross-examination of Sharon Welsh, the lifelong best friend of Sherry Miller. The assistant prosecutor tried to get Welsh to state that she knew Kevorkian intended to illegally assist in a suicide. Welsh, who had helped the doctor place the mask over Miller's face, simply kept repeating that her best friend "wanted to end her pain and suffering." Bunting was aggressive in his persistence. The line of questioning ended with Welsh sobbing, and asking, "Why are you doing this to me? You can call it a physician-assisted suicide, you can call it murder, you can call it whatever you want, but Dr. Kevorkian ended Sherry's suffering." She pleaded with Bunting: "So stop this; please stop this."[23]

A few days later, Bunting began cross-examining Kevorkian. The following exchange was typical:

Kevorkian: This is not a trial! This is a lynching! There is no law! No law!

Bunting: Let's presume, just for the heck of it, that this is a courtroom and there is a judge and a jury and we are all really here.

Kevorkian: I won't presume it. You ain't got a case.

Judge Breck immediately called a recess at that point. It did not help. Kevorkian returned to the stand and repeated his belief that the concept of an unwritten law was nonsense. "We shouldn't even be here," he declared at one point. "Our Supreme Court is corrupt for having foisted this idiotic so-called law on Judge Breck." At another point, he declared that "The Supreme Court of this state is lying to the people of this state and this jury. You have a corrupt judicial system, a corrupt legislature, and you have a society that tolerates that." Kevorkian had no patience for Bunting's questions either, frequently turning to the judge and demanding, "Tell the prosecutor that's an improper question."[24]

Just hours after stepping down from the stand on Monday, May 6, Kevorkian demonstrated his defiance in a different way. He attended his twenty-eighth suicide. The next day, the Right-to-Die Society of Canada announced that right-to-die advocate Austin Bastable, fifty-three and suffering from multiple sclerosis, had simultaneously inhaled a fatal dose of carbon monoxide and activated a suicide machine as Kevorkian and several other doctors looked on. Kevorkian's assistant, Janet Good, at whose home in the Detroit suburb of Farmington Hills Bastable's suicide occurred, later clarified the circumstances of the death. In addition to Kevorkian, four other members of Physicians for Mercy were present; this would be the only assisted suicide they ever attended. Kevorkian repeatedly asked Bastable: "Are you sure you want

to do this?" Upon his death, one of the doctors signed a death certificate noting the cause as "patholysis." A Canadian funeral home picked
up the body from Good's home and drove the twenty-five miles back
across the border to Windsor, Ontario, where Bastable had been living.
For the first time in six years, neither Kevorkian nor Fieger acknowledged the suicide. Fieger only stated that he would have no comment.
When Kevorkian was asked about it as he walked into the courthouse
Tuesday morning, he answered vaguely, "As I have always said, the only
thing that counts for me is the suffering patient." He remained in the
courtroom for barely five minutes that day, leaving as soon as the prosecution called its final rebuttal witness. "I only came here out of respect
for the jury members," he said. [25]

Once the deliberations began, it did not take long for the six men
and six women to reach a verdict. After three days, they found Kevorkian not guilty of violating the state's common law. The news was delivered to Kevorkian while he was eating lunch in the courthouse cafe-
teria—and worrying that he might be convicted this time. "The jury
saved me," a visibly relieved Kevorkian said. His attorney agreed. "Despite a blatant attempt by the prosecution and certain judges to rig this
trial," Fieger told reporters, "the jury saw through it. Thank God for the
jury system." As in Kevorkian's previous trial, it had taken just three
votes for the jurors to reach unanimity. One of the jurors who originally
believed Kevorkian was guilty changed her mind while she was raking
leaves over the weekend. Referring to the common law under which
Kevorkian was being tried, she said, "I realized I didn't want someone
to come along three years from now and say that raking leaves back
then was illegal, you just didn't know it." All of the jurors reported being
deeply moved by the videotapes in which Wantz and Miller explained
their misery and begged to be allowed to end it. "What this proves is
that while this may be a sin to you," Kevorkian told reporters after the
verdict, "one thing is clear: For any enlightened human being, this can
never be a crime." The news that "the world's best known advocate of
doctor-assisted suicide" had been acquitted a third time quickly
traveled around the globe. [26]

✿ ✿ ✿

Austin Bastable's suicide was the first of eighteen that Kevorkian would attend in the five-month stretch between May and October 1996. To put that number in perspective, Kevorkian had attended twenty-seven in the previous *six years combined*. Clearly, his two recent acquittals emboldened him. He seemed untouchable, even to his opponents. "The safest place for Dr. Kevorkian is in a courtroom with a jury," said Arthur Caplan back in March. "They will never find Kevorkian guilty." The doctor's acquittal in the Wantz-Miller double suicide was just more evidence for Caplan's prediction. In fact, 1996 would prove to be Kevorkian's most active year yet, in terms of the number of suicides he attended.[27]

It was not just Kevorkian who was emboldened by the recent legal decisions in his favor; it was his potential patients as well. Of the doctor's twenty-six patients before 1996, seventeen were from Michigan. By contrast, only one of his eighteen patients during 1996 was from Kevorkian's home state; the other seventeen traveled from nearly a dozen different states, and as we saw in the case of Austin Bastable, a different country, in order to obtain the doctor's services. The sudden drop in the number of patients from Michigan fueled suspicions that Kevorkian had stopped reporting some of his local cases to the authorities. There was another important difference between the pre-1996 patients and those who died during that year: Where a patient's terminal status was an important aspect of the case before, it no longer seemed to matter—to Kevorkian and his lawyers, to the authorities, or to the public. The jury in the Wantz and Miller case had paved the way for this development when each of the members said that the fact that the two women had not been terminally ill was not an important issue. One final point should be made about the seventeen patients who committed suicide with Kevorkian's help between June 10 and October 22 of 1996: thirteen of them were women.[28]

After helping three patients end their lives in one ten-day period in the middle of June—Kevorkian's first assisted suicides since his most recent trial ended—a reporter with the *Chicago Sun-Times* pointed out that it was the doctor's "biggest burst of activity yet." With no outstanding charges against him, and with no charges brought against him in any of his last half-dozen assisted suicides, Kevorkian felt freer than ever before to continue doing what he had been doing since June 1990. The brazenness of assisting in a suicide during the Wantz-Miller trial had been a signal of things to come.[29]

Like Arthur Caplan, University of Michigan law professor Yale Kamisar was an opponent of Kevorkian. He also did not think the doctor would be stopped. "He seems to understand that he can become bolder because it's become increasingly clear that you can't get a conviction," said the professor. "Unless he trips up, unless someone testified she changed her mind . . . unless a spouse says, 'No, I told him not to do this,'" Kamisar predicted it would be next to impossible to successfully prosecute Kevorkian. "Otherwise, I think you have to resign yourself to the fact that he's just too good at what he does. He's too careful at what he does."[30]

The finger-pointing of state legislators and prosecutors in the wake of Kevorkian's latest acquittal certainly did not hurt the doctor's cause. State Representative Michael Nye admitted, "I don't see us doing anything in regard to assisted suicide." He tacitly blamed prosecutors: "We had the ban, he was found not guilty under the ban. We had the common law, he was found not guilty under that situation. What do we pass so he won't be found not guilty?" Carl Marlinga, Macomb County's prosecutor, accused legislators of "basically throwing in the towel and saying assisted suicide, for all intents and purposes, is legal in the state of Michigan." Marlinga continued, "The Legislature seems unable to engage in compromise. They have abdicated their responsibility and basically have let Dr. Kevorkian have his way."[31]

State and local politics also began to more obviously interfere in the investigation of Kevorkian's assisted suicides. The case of Bette Lou Hamilton was the first example. Geoffrey Fieger announced that the cause of the sixty-seven-year-old woman's death on June 20, 1996 was carbon monoxide poisoning, Kevorkian's method of choice since 1991. Dr. Dragovic refused to rule on the cause of death, however, because he judged the level of carbon monoxide to be "a toxic level, but not a lethal level." Dragovic casually alluded to a puncture mark on Hamilton's left arm, suggesting a lethal injection, but only to claim that the tests were unlikely to show whether she had been injected with a toxin such as potassium chloride. "It's like pouring a cup of water into a bucket of water and then trying to determine which part of the water came from the cup," Dragovic explained. "That's why they refer to potassium chloride as the perfect poison." The accusation being hinted

at by the medical examiner was clear: Hamilton was rendered unconscious by the carbon monoxide, and then killed by Kevorkian with a
lethal injection.[32]

The Hamilton case did not end there. According to Lieutenant Brian
Peters of the Pontiac Police Department, Hamilton's friend Jeanne
Bogen brought her body into Pontiac Osteopathic Hospital in a wheelchair on the evening of June 20, and left after informing the staff that an
attorney would arrive shortly. Geoffrey Fieger promptly showed up and
gave the hospital a Social Security number for the body. But Peters
went on to say that the police did not have the proper information to
identify the woman as Bette Lou Hamilton, and that she would remain
in the morgue until she could be identified. "Whether the Social Security number is wrong or the hospital copied it down wrong, I do not
know," the lieutenant stated. "I do know that the number we have for
the body was not issued by the United States government." Kevorkian's
lawyers could not believe it. "That's just baloney," exclaimed Michael
Schwartz. "This is outrageous. There is no question who this woman is.
They look at a picture, look at the body and identify her, simple as that.
Quite honestly," he added, "I don't know what they're trying to do."
Schwartz claimed that the police had been given Hamilton's driver's
license, so there should not have been a problem identifying her.
"They've done this before with a Virginia woman [whom Kevorkian had
helped to die]," he continued. "They've held the body in an attempt to
harass people in the past. The medical examiner can simply release the
body." Oddly, Bogen herself had not been contacted by the police.
When asked about that, Lieutenant Peters claimed he was not even
sure who Bogen was. The woman found that hard to believe. "If the
Detroit Free Press called me at 2:00 a.m. [the morning after Hamilton's
death], I'm sure the police know who I am by now." She added, "I think
this has something to do with the politics that are going on in Pontiac."[33]

By now, Kevorkian had stopped commenting on the suicides he
attended. A body would simply be dropped off at a hospital, and the
patient's name, home state, and illness would be provided to medical
staff. Kevorkian's attorneys had also begun withholding information,
including how long a patient had been in contact with their client and
the time, place, and means of each death. These tactics had become
routine for Kevorkian when, at the beginning of July, he applied for a

concealed-weapons permit out of fear of "right-wing nuts," as he called them, who opposed him and assisted suicide. Yet it was Kevorkian who brought Rebecca Badger to the hospital himself after she self-administered a lethal injection of potassium chloride on July 9. It was the first time Kevorkian himself had delivered a body in a long time. "There is some concern about putting the families out," Fieger explained, so Kevorkian thought it was better to do it himself.[34]

Soon after, in a July 29 luncheon speech before the National Press Club, Kevorkian openly chastised virtually every group that had tried to stand in his way. "Pass any law you want, I don't care," he chided the legislature. He called the U.S. Supreme Court justices "cowards." As a representative from the Christian Defense Coalition protested outside, Kevorkian also attacked organized religion: "Had Christ died in my van, with people around him who loved him, [it] would have been far more dignified." But the doctor reserved special criticism for the American Medical Association, which had denounced his brand of assisted suicide the previous month. Questioning the AMA's opposition to physician-assisted suicide, Kevorkian recalled past AMA positions that group medical practices, Blue Cross and Blue Shield insurance, and Medicare were unethical. "It turns out," he asserted, "that everything they oppose turns out to be ethical. The AMA is dishonest, disingenuous. In fact, they're criminally negligent." Fieger, who also spoke at the event, piled it on: "[The AMA has] never led on anything. Why would they lead on this?" The AMA declined to comment on Kevorkian's and Fieger's remarks.[35]

The same day as Kevorkian's speech, Dr. Dragovic publicly criticized Kevorkian. He began by pointing out that "a lot of [Kevorkian's patients were] physically incapacitated" rather than terminally ill. "They could have lived for many months, to many years," he claimed. In fact, of the roughly twenty cases he had been involved with, he believed only "four or five" people were "actually near death." He was frustrated by the case of Rebecca Badger, Kevorkian's most recent assisted suicide, because Fieger had claimed the woman had multiple sclerosis. "I can show you every slice from her brain and spinal cord," Dragovic had told the *Washington Post* after examining her, "and she doesn't have a bit of M.S. She looked robust, fairly healthy. Everything else is in order. Except she's dead."[36]

✿ ✿ ✿

Rebecca Badger was not the last patient whom Dr. Kevorkian wheeled into a hospital himself. He repeated it with Elizabeth Mertz on August 6. He did it again the following week with forty-two-year-old Judith Curren, accompanied this time by Dr. Georges Reding, a psychiatrist who had helped him with his previous few cases. By this point, according to one authoritative commentator, Kevorkian-assisted suicides were "barely newsworthy." Even Geoffrey Fieger said that assisted suicide "should not even be treated as news but as an everyday occurrence." The Curren case, however, would make a lot of news and prove to be anything but an everyday occurrence.[37]

Kevorkian had spent some of the day of Curren's death playing golf and making a public appearance to auction off his now-famous powder-blue cardigan for the Children's Leukemia Foundation. His attendance at the forty-two-year-old Massachusetts nurse's suicide that evening did not raise any more eyebrows than usual until newspapers across the country picked up the news that Curren's husband, a psychiatrist, had been arrested three weeks earlier on a charge of domestic violence. Kevorkian tried to explain that he had asked the couple about any domestic problems, as was his policy, and they had said that they had none. A couple of days later, he hinted that he might not have helped Curren end her life if he had known about the charge against her husband. "We try to guard against things like this with patient screening," he said.[38]

But the damage had been done. It was compounded by newspaper reports about Kevorkian's evolving methods. The *Tampa Tribune* was one of the first sources to report that Kevorkian had been resorting to lethal injections, rather than using his customary carbon monoxide, in his recent assisted suicides. Prosecutor Larry Bunting fueled the growing fire by saying "we don't know what's happening, and Kevorkian isn't telling anyone. Perhaps there's another physician involved. I just don't know." Kevorkian, for the first time in six years, was less than forthcoming. "I can't talk about that," he answered when asked about the means he provided to his most recent patients. All his attorney would say was, "Anything that was done, the patients did themselves," reiterating that some previous patients had stockpiled medication to use in their suicides.[39]

The pressure continued to mount when the *Boston Herald* published some troubling results from a report by the Suicide Research Center at Chicago's Columbia-Michael Reese Hospital. Nearly 70 percent of Kevorkian's patients—twenty-four of the thirty-five—had not been terminally ill, the study found. This finding had the potential to shift the public debate to the matter of whether a person who is not suffering from an incurable disease should have the right to assisted suicide. Additional findings were that more than two-thirds of Kevorkian's patients had been women, and that most of those had not been diagnosed as terminal (that is, having less than six months to live).[40]

In addition, the political maneuvering continued in Michigan. Bidding for reelection, Oakland County Prosecutor Richard Thompson had lost the Republican primary to David Gorcyca the week before Kevorkian helped Judith Curren die. Gorcyca was a relative newcomer who had campaigned on a promise not to waste taxpayers' money trying to convict Kevorkian "unless the Legislature gives me an enforceable law." State Senator Jim Berryman, a Democrat who planned to run for governor, had sought a statewide referendum on assisted suicide and blamed the religious right for acting as an obstacle to his plans. The bill he had tried to get passed that would have legalized the practice was "always blocked by Right to Life [of Michigan]," he claimed, "which controls a substantial number of legislators and doesn't want any legalization." He continued: "They won't allow a statewide vote and Jack Kevorkian won't stop, and no jury will convict him, so that is where we are, and it is embarrassing."[41]

The autopsy results on Judith Curren, released on August 19, showed no evidence of a physical disease, let alone a terminal illness. She suffered from chronic fatigue syndrome, was significantly overweight, and had a history of severe depression. Like other critics of Kevorkian, medical ethicist Arthur Caplan focused on the last of these: "You certainly don't want to be helping someone die because they can't deal with life's problems. And I think Kevorkian has gone out into a place where society just doesn't want to go." While the fact of the matter was that many of Kevorkian's patients, not just Curren, had not been terminally ill, Caplan and Richard Thompson, among others, believed that jurors might be less sympathetic toward Kevorkian for assisting in the suicide of someone with depression.[42]

In the week after Curren's death, Kevorkian attended three more suicides. Dr. Dragovic quickly ruled the first one, that of seventy-six-year-old Louise Siebens, who had been suffering from Lou Gehrig's disease, a homicide. "This one is self-explanatory," the medical examiner said. "There is no way this woman could have self-injected the poisons. She was poked all over." The autopsy report indicated that no fewer than six needle marks were present on her arms. Geoffrey Fieger, clearly frustrated by Dragovic's growing tendency to openly criticize Kevorkian in the press, sneered, "Yeah, Dr. Kevorkian has taken up Chinese needle torture. This is getting stupid. Let him say whatever he wants."[43]

Two days after Siebens's death, Kevorkian delivered two more bodies to Pontiac Osteopathic Hospital. He showed up in the emergency room with the first one early in the afternoon. "I have a patient in the car," he calmly told a staff member. "Can I borrow a wheelchair?" The patient was Patricia Smith, a forty-year-old nurse from Missouri. Shortly after 9:00 p.m., Kevorkian returned with the body of Pat DiGangi, a sixty-six-year-old former history professor at Brooklyn College. Both patients suffered from multiple sclerosis. Pontiac police officers attempted to question Kevorkian upon his return with DiGangi's body; Sergeant Ken Lewis claimed that Kevorkian then "became very loud and abusive toward the officers," and the doctor was arrested and charged with disorderly conduct. Geoffrey Fieger drove to the jail after the police informed him that Kevorkian was being held there. Dr. Dragovic, this time not bothering to wait for the autopsy results on either body, offered his assessment of what had happened. "This is a sad thing," he said. "Whenever they make some kind of mistake, as they did with Judith Curren, they try to dampen it by doing a couple of people who are dramatically incapacitated."[44]

David Gorcyca, fresh off of his successful primary campaign for county prosecutor, stated his belief that Kevorkian had "really pushed the envelope" in assisting Curren to die. Nevertheless, Gorcyca believed that attempting to prosecute him would "just waste a lot of time, prosecutorial resources and taxpayer money"—exactly what he had accused his opponent, Richard Thompson, of having done over the past six years. Like Thompson, however, he began referring to Oakland County as "the suicide mecca of the world," and challenged the state legislature to either legalize assisted suicide or pass a more stringent ban than the law that had lapsed nearly two years earlier. Less than a week later, Dr. Dragovic ruled Curren's death a homicide, as he had in twenty-seven of the thirty other Kevorkian cases he had been involved with. "Everything points to the fact that she was injected with the deadly substances," the medical examiner announced. "This is not physician-assisted suicide. It's physician-assisted death. When physicians act this way by inflicting this manner of death, it's in the category of homicide."[45]

The first week of September saw heightened drama. Kevorkian participated in his thirty-ninth suicide, delivering the body of seventy-three-year-old Jack Leatherman to a hospital in suburban Detroit on the evening of September 2. During an interview three days later, Kevorkian and Fieger claimed that the doctor had actually helped more patients to die than the thirty-nine he had reported, although they would not say exactly how many unreported assisted suicides there had been. "We aren't telling, now or ever," Fieger said, pointing out that because assisted suicide was not against the law, "we are under no obligation to say anything about it to anybody." Kevorkian tried to use the prospect of secret assisted suicides to attack his critics: "They always say I should provide death with dignity. Well, they should be satisfied now, because that is exactly what this is. This is the way it should be: at home, in private, with the family, peaceful, and without police or medical examiners or any other people who have no business there."[46]

The next day, in a bizarre episode, police officers and prosecutors broke in on a meeting in a room at the Bloomfield Township Quality Inn between Kevorkian, Janet Good, and a potential patient and her husband. Isabel Correa told reporters afterward, "I was very frightened. . . . My privacy has been violated. I was doing nothing wrong," adding, "I know what I'm doing. I want to die. I am not depressed." Good, Kevorkian's assistant, said that it "was just a meeting to see if she might be a candidate." The couple had traveled from Fresno, California, despite Isabel being in excruciating pain from a spinal cord condition that rendered her unable to walk or lie on either side of her body. "I think it is sad that I have to come across the United States to see a man like Kevorkian," she said. "There should be one in California so that I wouldn't have to come so far in such pain." The police confiscated a variety of the woman's personal belongings, including her pain medication and a rosary. They did not arrest Kevorkian, however, who described the scene as "proof we've got Nazi storm troopers and the Gestapo right here." He added: "But they aren't going to stop me."[47]

Proving his point, Kevorkian delivered Isabel Correa's body to William Beaumont Hospital the next day. Geoffrey Fieger triumphantly waved one of her sweaters during a press conference afterward. "This is a flag of freedom," he declared. "Despite the best efforts of the thugs who would take away her rights, she is free from her suffering." The dramatic attorney confirmed that his client had participated in undisclosed assisted suicides. He was asked how many. "More than one and less than 100," was the answer. Fieger also said that Kevorkian no longer believed it was necessary to report the suicides of seriously ill Michigan residents. "Why should we?" Fieger asked rhetorically. "This is no crime. We believe in death with dignity."[48]

The police quickly defended their decision to enter the hotel room during Kevorkian's meeting with Correa without a search warrant. Bloomfield Township Police Chief Jeffrey Werner said his officers had reason to believe that a suicide was about to occur, and denied that they had broken into the room. Someone had voluntarily allowed them to enter, he claimed. Fieger angrily disputed that story: "He's a liar. They said 'Jack, open the door or we'll kick it down.' I promise you we will be suing all those responsible for this outrage." Just a few days later, Fieger announced that Kevorkian filed a $25 million federal lawsuit against the Bloomfield Township Police Department and two prosecutors, including Lawrence Bunting, for violating his and Isabel Correa's civil rights when they "pushed in a door" in order to "save" Correa.[49]

Although the doctor was not arrested at the Quality Inn, some of his personal items were confiscated along with Isabel Correa's. Among them were a lethal injection machine, various toxic chemicals, and videotaping equipment. Authorities soon discovered that the videotape that contained Kevorkian's interrupted interview with Correa also included footage of Kevorkian and Janet Good meeting with a woman named Loretta Peabody and her husband at the couple's home in Ionia, Michigan. Peabody had died a week before Correa, on August 30. The cause was listed on the death certificate as multiple sclerosis. Kevorkian could be seen on the discovered tape discussing how to give the misleading impression that a death is due to natural causes.[50]

Fieger responded to the unexpected turn of events in predictable fashion. "I had no knowledge of Peabody," he claimed. "But if it were up to me, I'd tell all the families and friends of the patients to tell the police they went to Disneyland and fell off the mouse ride." Ionia County Prosecutor Raymond Voet was not as amused. "This is outrageous," he said. "Assisted suicide is against the law. The Michigan Supreme Court decided that in 1994." Despite knowing that Kevorkian had been acquitted of violating the common law, and that juries had failed to convict him twice before that, Voet insisted that he would enforce the law. He asked a circuit judge to convene a grand jury as a first step toward a possible indictment of Kevorkian for his role in Peabody's death. Less than a week later, Fieger acknowledged that Kevorkian attended her suicide, and proceeded to play two videotapes for reporters in which the woman begged for help in ending her life. By this point, her husband and daughter had both been subpoenaed by the grand jury. Sobbing after the tapes were shown, Peabody's daughter said, "We shouldn't have to be here. We should be left alone. The system needs to change so other people don't have to go through this anymore."[51]

On the same day that Fieger and Voet spoke to reporters about Peabody's appearance on the Correa videotape, police arrested a thirty-nine-year-old Ohio man who had showed up at Fieger's Southfield office. Larry Blakeman announced that he was there that morning to "stop Dr. Jack." When police arrived, they found an unloaded .22-caliber handgun and live ammunition in a suitcase in his car. "I came here for help," Blakeman explained during his arraignment, having changed his story. "It's not at all what it appears to look like. I came up here from Ohio for help from Dr. Kevorkian." He claimed to be suffering from severe neck and back pain. He also asked the judge if Fieger could represent him. Fieger announced plans to increase security at his office and for Kevorkian, stating that he was "absolutely convinced the man was there to assassinate Dr. Kevorkian or myself." The incident prompted authorities to grant Kevorkian an emergency thirty-day concealed weapon permit in response to the application he filed in July. Fieger was also granted a permit.[52]

At a speech at Northeastern University on September 29, Fieger announced that his client had "just moments ago" attended his forty-first suicide—that of Richard Faw, a North Carolina psychiatrist with colon cancer. The audience was shocked. Fieger's announcement represented a dramatic end to what had been a dramatic month.[53]

October began with more of the same, when Kevorkian helped paramedics treat a bicyclist who was hit by a car in West Bloomfield Township. A lieutenant with the fire department who responded to the scene told reporters that Kevorkian "came over and advised the paramedics that he had been observing the patient, and rendered an opinion. He said the patient didn't lose consciousness. This was very important information." Kevorkian, the very face of the national right-to-die movement for more than six years, seemed embarrassed by the unexpected publicity over the incident. "How did you find out?" he quietly asked a reporter. "It's not a story." Only half-kidding, he added, "I wish this wouldn't get out because you know the kind of jokes that will come. They'll say the guy looked up and thought it was worse than it was." Always sensitive to public relations, Fieger took the opportunity to soften Kevorkian's image. "He's a physician first and foremost," he said, adding that his client's actions did not surprise him. "He helps suffering human beings."[54]

Kevorkian would do so again, but under very different circumstances, three times in October. All three assisted suicides—Kevorkian's last in 1996—followed the same general pattern. After the procedure, Kevorkian dropped off the patient at a hospital, along with a card that contained the individual's name, illness, and other information. It was the specifics of each case that differed. The first, that of a Texas man who sought Kevorkian's help because he feared ending up in "one of those rat-infested nursing homes," was relatively uneventful.[55]

The second suicide, which occurred one week later, was anything but. It was reminiscent of the Correa case, in fact. On the evening of October 16, Kevorkian met Nancy DeSoto at a motel in Royal Oak. While he was leaving the parking lot, he was intercepted and detained by police, who claimed they stumbled upon the doctor during a routine patrol. Meanwhile, other officers had the motel's manager open the door to DeSoto's room. The fifty-five-year-old florist, who was confined to a wheelchair, insisted the police produce a warrant. When they could not, she ordered them out. Fieger accused the authorities of "Gestapo tactics," including illegal wiretaps and twenty-four-hour surveillance of his client. Lawrence Bunting called Fieger's accusations "so ridiculous, it's almost childish." Shortly after noon the next day, Kevorkian arrived at William Beaumont Hospital with a body, and handed a paper to emergency room staff. The name on the paper was Nancy DeSoto.[56]

Less than a week later, Kevorkian was present at the suicide of Barbara Collins, a retired microbiologist from Cape Cod with advanced ovarian cancer. Predictably, Dr. Dragovic ruled her death a homicide, claiming "it was obvious she was injected by someone else." He went on: "She couldn't have done it herself. For that, one has to have adequate professional skills and manual dexterity. Besides you have to use common sense. If she was going to do it herself, why didn't she do it back in Massachusetts?" Once again, Kevorkian left the body at the hospital, along with a card describing her illness. This time, according to Geoffrey Fieger, police stopped him as he drove away and confiscated his vehicle. "Police dragged Jack out of his car," he claimed, "beat him up and tried to steal his car, and then stole his car." He said Kevorkian was held for two hours on the side of the road before the police finally let him go. "This is plain and simple harassment . . . and thuggery," Fieger declared.[57]

Outgoing Oakland County Prosecutor Richard Thompson had had enough. At the end of October, he surprised observers by charging Kevorkian with nine felonies and ten misdemeanors in the deaths of ten people between June 20 and September 7. The indictment included three counts of assisting suicides—the most serious of the charges—as well as improperly removing bodies, possession of a controlled substance, and posing as a physician without a license. Because Thompson would be leaving office on December 31 after losing the Republican primary to David Gorcyca in August, his decision to indict Kevorkian was widely viewed as a last-ditch, very personal attempt to stop the doctor.[58]

Kevorkian was furious when he arrived at Michigan's 48th District Court for his arraignment on October 31. He demanded to be jailed. He referred to the lame-duck prosecutor as "a lying psychotic." He raised his right arm in the courtroom in a mock Nazi salute and said, "Heil." He also vowed to starve himself to death as soon as Judge Edward Avadenka set a $20,000 bond. "I prefer jail to bail," Kevorkian said. Fieger immediately filed an emergency motion to overrule the judge. "My client values his liberty more than he values his life," Fieger pleaded. "He will not take fluids or food [in jail]." The judge decided to waive the bond, stating, "I am not going to allow him to make himself a martyr."[59]

Kevorkian's associates Neal Nicol and Georges Reding were also indicted, although Janet Good, who was recently diagnosed with terminal pancreatic cancer, was not. "I am disappointed I wasn't charged," she said, "but I knew Thompson wouldn't have the nerve" because of her condition. Thompson himself did not bother to show up for the arraignment, instead declaring during a local radio interview that "these cases should go forward if we are to live under the rule of law." Outside the courthouse after the arraignment, Kevorkian was fatalistic. "This is the end of it," he announced. "Either Thompson dies or I die, by which I mean, either this dies as a legal issue or I do, and I don't care which, but this ends now."[60]

Thompson's decision to indict Kevorkian, two months to the day before he would leave office, put his successor in a difficult position. Both Gorcyca and Steven Kaplan, the Democratic candidate, had repeatedly stated during the campaign that they would not prosecute Kevorkian without an enforceable law in place. Of Thompson's unexpected decision, Gorcyca said, "I think the timing of these charges is very suspicious." He added that he resented what he viewed as an attempt by his predecessor to force him into action. Richard Thompson was looking more and more like he was pursuing a personal vendetta against Kevorkian.[61]

After a bizarre twist in the election process, it was Gorcyca who ended up inheriting the Kevorkian problem. Election Day results showed Kaplan to be the winner. But while he was doing a radio interview the next day, an election worker discovered an 18,000-vote error which, in a matter of minutes, handed thirty-four-year-old Gorcyca the position of prosecutor-elect. The young lawyer understood the gravity of the situation he would face. "Unfortunately," he said in an interview, "I know how I deal with that issue—assisted suicide—will define my career, and will do so very early on." He knew very well that the man he was succeeding had lost the position because of his relentless pursuit of Kevorkian. It was likely for that reason that Gorcyca delayed any immediate action of his own by blaming state legislators. "I'm looking for the legislature in Lansing to address [assisted suicide] once and for all," he said. He even appealed to Michigan's governor. "I told Governor Engler, 'Look, I need some help on this,'" he explained to reporters. "This issue is bigger than Oakland County." The governor responded by directing him to State Senator William Van Regenmorter, who was in the process of drafting legislation banning assisted suicide.[62]

The pursuit of Kevorkian was happening on another front as well. Two days after the election, he was indicted by a grand jury, and handcuffed and arrested coming out of a pawn shop he frequented in Waterford Township. Authorities drove him more than 100 miles to Ionia in an unmarked car, where he was charged with several crimes, including assisting in Loretta Peabody's suicide. "I'm afraid of these Nazi thugs," Kevorkian said when he was taken in shackles and an orange prison uniform to the Ionia courthouse. In the meantime, a pawnshop employee called Geoffrey Fieger, who drove to Ionia. The attorney was furious over what he called "these police state tactics of essentially kidnapping Dr. Kevorkian." And he questioned Ionian County prosecutor Raymond Voet's approach. "All he had to do is call me," he said, "and I would have brought [Kevorkian] to court. He always shows up in court when required to. Now which side is perpetuating the circus?" He added, "This is totalitarian. This is jack-booted thugs. They want to act like they see cops act on TV."[63]

Voet, who earned $59,000 a year as county prosecutor and had just convened the first grand jury in Ionia County's history, saw his job clearly. "My duty is to enforce the law," he said. "I have steeled myself to the fact that I may not have any political future, and if that is the case, so be it." Fieger, who had settled a case for $17.6 million earlier in the year—and received one-third of that amount for himself—saw things differently. "Mr. Voet is an amateur seeking publicity for his right-wing radical religious agenda," he asserted. "His legal acumen would be insufficient to get him a job in my law office as a courier. He's got a real surprise coming if this case even goes to trial. The judge should dismiss it immediately for lack of evidence, among other things." At various points, Fieger described Voet as "dumb," called him "a religious fanatic," and referred to him as "a spherical jackass."[64]

Fieger was equally upset with Voet for also indicting another of his firm's clients, Janet Good, calling the prosecutor's decision to charge a terminal cancer patient "the most vicious, foolhardy act a human being could undertake." Michael Schwartz, who accompanied Good to her arraignment, agreed. "No one with an ounce of humanity would have charged a seventy-three-year-old dying woman," he said with disgust. "How could he stoop so low? She'll never live through the trial." Voet took the criticism in stride, saying that it was "important to note that the grand jury decided on the indictments, not me." He added, "Everyone asks me why I don't drop the charges. Well, I don't have any proof that she is terminally ill, and I am not aware that sick people are exempt from the law." Good declared herself "so proud," and admitted that she "was almost offended when I wasn't charged last time," referring to Thompson's indictments of Kevorkian, Neal Nicol, and Georges Reding in October. Ultimately, the charges against Good were dropped.[65]

Kevorkian was released without bond after he promised not to attend any other suicides until his trial. But what that promise meant was not immediately clear. Fieger simply said, "I am not aware that he has ever been present at any suicide. He has sometimes been present when people have ended their horrific suffering," adding that "Dr. Kevorkian has been found not guilty in five cases where he essentially admitted what he did. Do you think the outcome will be any different?" Fieger had reason to be confident about an acquittal since Peabody's body had been cremated without an autopsy. "There is no body, there is no cause of death, there is no evidence of anything," he said. "They don't have a case," he insisted. "They don't have a body or a crime. This will be far easier than the other trials," he predicted. The question on many people's minds at the end of 1996 was whether it would get that far.[66]

7

"WELL, SIR, CONSIDER YOURSELF STOPPED"

A Leader's Fall and a Movement's Decline

Even before he took office on January 1, 1997, Oakland County Prosecutor David Gorcyca faced a dilemma. On one hand, his victorious primary campaign against his predecessor, Richard Thompson, essentially revolved around one accusation; namely, that Thompson had wasted taxpayers' money pursuing Jack Kevorkian for more than six years. On the other hand, the young attorney, who went on to narrowly defeat Democrat Steven Kaplan in the general election, did not want to appear to be soft on the man whom many believed was a serial killer. What was he going to do, many of the 1.2 million people in his district wondered, with the charges that Thompson had filed against Kevorkian the previous October?

The answer came less than two weeks into Gorcyca's term. He dismissed every single charge, saying they had been "written in haste" and proclaiming any new efforts to prosecute Kevorkian "an exercise in futility." Thompson's bitter reaction was that his successor had made "a political decision not to do his job." But Gorcyca did not believe the decision was his. "It is time for the Michigan Legislature to step up to the plate and pass a clearly enforceable law controlling assisted suicide," he stated. Still at odds about how to do that, with Democrats arguing for a statewide vote and Republicans desiring an outright ban, it would be almost another year before the state legislature took any action.[1]

Geoffrey Fieger welcomed the new prosecutor's decision to drop the charges against his client, even as Fieger knowingly attributed more to it than he should have. "We now have a unique opportunity in Michigan for doctors to work with patients to make end-of-life decisions without fear of prosecution or persecution," he said. "We are calling for physicians to come forward, now that it is clear that Mr. Gorcyca will not prosecute you." But Gorcyca had made it clear that he was not giving Kevorkian a free pass. "This does not mean that Dr. Kevorkian or anyone else now has a blank check to assist suicides," he warned. "At the right time and place, I will not hesitate to prosecute under the common law." It was an odd threat to make in light of his public declaration that "the common-law prohibition against assisted suicide is all but unenforceable." Perhaps that was why Kevorkian himself seemed only mildly interested in the new Oakland County prosecutor's course of action. "I have always felt free to help [a patient] when I can," he said. Kevorkian did not seem to care who held the office of Oakland County prosecutor.[2]

Still facing a trial in Ionia County in June for the assisted suicide of Loretta Peabody, Kevorkian attended his first two assisted suicides of 1997 on February 3. This year would prove to be the most active of his career, with a total of thirty people ending their lives in the doctor's presence. The body of the first, Elaine Day, was left in a van outside the medical examiner's office. Later in the day, Lisa Lansing's body was dropped off by a friend at the Pontiac Osteopathic Hospital. While neither Kevorkian nor Fieger explicitly stated that the doctor was involved, his attorney nevertheless made the circumstances of the deaths clear: "You have to have been born under a rock yesterday not to know who was involved in these cases."[3]

In the process of attending three more suicides in March, Kevorkian changed his tactics again. Rather than leaving a body in a vehicle at the medical examiner's office or wheeling a dead patient into the emergency room, he began leaving his patients' bodies where they died—in hotel rooms. Each time, a note was left with the body providing personal information about the deceased. The March 25 death of Janette Knowles was typical of the new pattern. A security officer at the Red Roof Inn in Warren, Michigan, received an anonymous call that evening. Upon entering the room, he found the seventy-five-year-old woman's body and a note listing Geoffrey Fieger as her representative.[4]

At the beginning of April, Kevorkian and Fieger received a cease-and-desist order from the state. The document warned Kevorkian that he faced up to four years in jail and a $2,000 fine for practicing medicine without a license if he participated in another assisted suicide. It was a desperate attempt to stop Kevorkian. Even the director of the Michigan Department of Consumer and Industry Services, the agency that was responsible for licensing physicians, admitted to "mak[ing] an assumption that Kevorkian will ignore the cease and desist as he has ignored the suspension [of his license]." At a press conference, Fieger described the order as "incomprehensible" and "tyrannical." Kevorkian, in what by now were considered typical theatrics, added "fascistic" before publicly burning the state document with a lighter.[5]

As if that public display of contempt for the cease-and-desist order were not enough, the body of a twenty-seven-year-old AIDS patient was found in a Romulus, Michigan, hotel just four days later, on April 8. Once again, Fieger declined to say whether his client had been present, although it was clear from the characteristics of the scene that he had been. The note that was left with the body again listed Fieger as the person to contact, but all that the attorney would say during a telephone interview from his vacation home in the Caribbean was that "she would have been the first AIDS patient" for Kevorkian.[6]

Kevorkian spent much of the rest of April and May in consultation with his attorneys, preparing for his upcoming fourth trial. He assisted in only one suicide during this time, that of Delouise Bacher at the beginning of May. At the end of the month, he scored a personal legal victory against the American Medical Association (AMA). After representatives of the group in October and November 1995 called him a "killer" and asserted that he engaged in "criminal conduct," Kevorkian filed a $10 million lawsuit in February 1996 for slander and defamation. Now, fifteen months later, a judge ruled that his lawsuit against the organization should go to trial. A Michigan appeals court would ultimately dismiss the suit in August 1999.[7]

❊ ❊ ❊

With about 55,000 residents, Ionia County was a significantly smaller venue for a Jack Kevorkian trial than Oakland County had been, with its population of 1.1 million. Apple orchards and water towers dotted the landscape, along with five state prisons. It was a rural community that had not elected a Democrat to a county job in sixty-five years. The courthouse, built in 1886, was too small for jury selection, so jurors were chosen in the Ionia Theatre across the red bricks of Main Street, and then escorted into the courthouse.[8]

The prosecutor, Ray Voet, felt confident on his home turf. Conceding that some county residents "are very anti-tax, very anti-big-government, very much protective of their own personal rights," he said that the people were "also very law-and-order, too. They expect their police and prosecutor to make sure the people who commit crimes are brought to justice." Many of them had probably also never seen an attorney like Geoffrey Fieger before, except on television. After arriving, the brash, sharply dressed lawyer said, "I like Ionia. I like the people. I like the judge. At the end of this, Ray Voet will have a nervous breakdown."[9]

Opening arguments took place on June 11. The prosecution urged jurors to put side "sympathy and prejudice"—those emotional aspects of assisted suicide that previous Kevorkian prosecutors had believed resulted in acquittals. "I'm not asking you to judge Loretta Peabody," Voet told the jurors. "I'm asking you to judge Jack Kevorkian." Geoffrey Fieger spent a good deal of his opening statement talking about Voet. He accused the prosecutor of engaging in a "witch hunt," harassing the Peabody family and other witnesses, and altering evidence. He shifted gears quickly, talking about Loretta Peabody's health, casually mentioning Kevorkian's three previous acquittals, and criticizing the state's common law against assisted suicide. It was a rare performance. And virtually none of it bore on the case at hand. Voet called it "the most outrageous, illegal opening statement I've seen in my life," and was practically forced to request a mistrial. Judge Charles Miel granted it the next day, ruling that the "number of problems are so great [sic], the court feels there's a high likelihood that the impartiality of one or two jurors" could be compromised. With that, the fourth trial of Jack Kevorkian was over.[10]

The doctor himself had not attended. According to Fieger, his client thought his presence might cause a disturbance. It seemed unlikely that Kevorkian would ever again stand trial for Loretta Peabody's death. The court would first have to determine who caused the mistrial, and if it found that the prosecutor was at all at fault, the case could not be brought again. Fieger was as bold as ever. "Both Judge Miel and the prosecutor know that Dr. Kevorkian is not coming back to court here," he told *Court TV*, adding his belief that Voet had "ended the case precipitously, because he knew what I was going to do to him." A bewildered Voet said afterward that it was "tough to come up empty-handed" and that he was unsure whether he would refile the charges against Kevorkian. "My theory is that Fieger's strategy was to blow up this case one way or another," he added. "It's as if he put gasoline in the jury box and lighted it."[11]

* * *

Two highly anticipated U.S. Supreme Court rulings on physician-assisted suicide were handed down at the end of June 1997. The decisions rejected challenges to two states' laws prohibiting the practice. In the first, *Washington v. Glucksberg*, the justices unanimously found that the right to assisted suicide was not protected under the Due Process Clause of the 14th Amendment. In a related unanimous decision, *Vacco v. Quill*, the high court ruled that New York State's ban on assisted suicide was constitutional. These proved to be landmark rulings in the right-to-die movement in the United States—rulings that effectively ended the debate over whether there was a constitutional right to die.[12]

State Senator William Van Regenmorter, whose own bill to ban assisted suicide was scheduled to be debated by the Michigan legislature later in the summer, believed the Supreme Court decisions would strengthen his case. "It is a powerful, powerful decision," he said, "with clear instructions that physician-assisted suicide is clearly dangerous." Other opponents of Kevorkian and of assisted suicide felt vindicated by the high court's rulings. Richard Thompson was one of them. But after having battled Kevorkian for so long, and ultimately losing his job for it, he was also wary. "The war is not over yet," he warned.[13]

Thompson was correct. As had been the case with judicial and legislative decisions in his home state of Michigan over the past seven years, Kevorkian did not seem to be affected by the U.S. Supreme Court decisions. When Fieger was asked if they made a difference to his client, he said, "Not to Dr. Kevorkian. Hell, no." In fact, in one of the doctor's boldest moves yet, he was present at a suicide just hours after the court issued its rulings. The body of a forty-year-old Nevada woman was found in a local motel with a note to call Geoffrey Fieger. Without discussing the possibility of his client's involvement, Fieger simply said that he represented the family of the deceased and read a statement from her father. Dr. Dragovic promptly ruled the death a homicide. Because of Dragovic's consistent refusal to classify Kevorkian's assisted deaths as suicides, those cases alone accounted for 10 percent of all homicides in Oakland County between 1990 and 1997.[14]

Less than a week later, on July 2, two more women's bodies were found. An anonymous tip led to the discovery of the first one in a motel in Roseville, northeast of Detroit. The other was found about an hour later by a maid in a Romulus motel. Geoffrey Fieger once again refused to state directly that Kevorkian was responsible. Instead, he said, "There's no question about what happened here. Everyone understands that Dr. Kevorkian provides assistance to end suffering." Fieger said both women were his clients. The attorney informed the press of their deaths after Kevorkian's own announcement about his next step. It involved his longtime associate, Janet Good, forming and leading a non-medical group to establish "reasonable and sensible" guidelines for practicing assisted suicide since the medical profession had refused to do so and Physicians for Mercy had disbanded sometime after Austin Bastable's May 1996 suicide.[15]

In the middle of August, Geoffrey Fieger announced that Kevorkian had actually been involved in "nearly 100 cases" of assisted suicide, which was more than double the number that was officially attributed to him. This surprising, if also exaggerated, news came as Fieger was providing the details of thirty-four-year-old Karen Shoffstall's suicide, which had occurred earlier that day. When asked by reporters to elaborate on his comment, Fieger said they had only made public the recent cases that involved people from other states; Michigan residents' assisted suicides had not been reported. "Dr. Kevorkian has continued to do exactly what he's been doing since day one," the attorney said. "Everybody knows it's Dr. Kevorkian." In fact, the typewritten note left with Shoffstall's body in a room at the Holiday Inn stated that both Kevorkian and his longtime associate, Janet Good, had been involved in the suicide.[16] It was the last time Good would assist Kevorkian in anything.

✿ ✿ ✿

Janet Good founded the Michigan chapter of the Hemlock Society in 1989, the year before Jack Kevorkian assisted in his first suicide. By that point, she had been a feminist and civil rights activist in Michigan for more than two decades. After working with the Archdiocese of Detroit in the mid-1960s to implement President Lyndon Johnson's "War on Poverty," Good served as director of Equal Employment Opportunity for the state's Employment Security Commission. Subsequently appointed to cochair a gubernatorial task force on sexual harassment, she played a key role in getting sexual harassment defined as an unlawful practice in Michigan's Elliott-Larsen Civil Rights Act of 1976. Good was also instrumental in establishing the state's Older Women's League, and became its first president. Her efforts on behalf of women got her elected to Michigan's Women's Hall of Fame in 1991.[17]

With so much rights-related activism behind her, she actively supported Kevorkian from the time she witnessed him help Janet Adkins with her suicide in June 1990. "I have worked for civil rights and women's rights and human rights for many years," she later said, "and [assisted suicide] seemed to me just another right we should have." In 1994, after the death of Kevorkian's sister, Good became the doctor's primary personal assistant, participating in everything from patient screening to attending assisted suicides. She had become indispensable to him. Good even allowed Kevorkian to use her home for an assisted death in May 1996. "When Austin Bastable died here," she later said, "I thought, 'How peaceful.' He was smiling. He wanted to make sure he was smiling when he died." By that point, Good's husband of more than fifty years, a retired Detroit police commander, had gone from opposing to supporting assisted suicide. Three months later, after pancreatic cancer had spread to her liver, she announced that she wanted a similar death. "I want to end my life gently, peacefully, painlessly—just like I've seen Dr. Kevorkian's patients die," she said.[18]

Less than one year later, on August 26, 1997, Janet Good did just that. Given how much she had devoted to women's rights, it was fitting that her death took place on the seventy-seventh anniversary of the enactment of the 19th Amendment, which gave women the right to vote. Geoffrey Fieger announced her death but, as usual, refused to say directly whether Kevorkian had been involved in it. "I can assure you," he simply said, "any help she asked for, she got." He publicly called on the medical examiner not to issue his usual ruling in Good's death. "I think it would be sacrilegious for Dr. Dragovic to put on her death certificate a homicide," Fieger asserted. The attorney also read a letter from Kevorkian, whom he described as "very, very upset" over his friend's death. "Janet's courage and strength of character," Kevorkian wrote, "far exceeded in quality and quantity that represented by the collective courts and legislatures of this morally benighted country. Janet exemplified the best in women: She fought for freedom, liberty, justice and compassion. I loved her. We will all miss her."[19]

☼ ☼ ☼

After assisting in Janet Good's suicide, Kevorkian's pace quickened. Between her death on August 26 and the end of the year, he would be present at eighteen suicides—an average of about one a week over that four-month period. By the middle of October 1997, a *New York Times* headline pointed out what had become obvious: "Kevorkian Encountering Fewer Hurdles in Suicides." Prosecutors in Michigan still had no state law against assisted suicide, and none were willing to try their luck prosecuting him a second time under the common law. Macomb County Prosecutor Carl Marlinga said, "I don't see any prosecutor going after him on the common law theory. It just won't hold up in court." Marlinga's belief even led him to meet with Kevorkian in October, at the doctor's request, to work out a more dignified way of handling the bodies of his patients. Kevorkian asked the prosecutor to allow patients' relatives to deliver their loved ones' bodies to funeral homes without being prosecuted. After telling Kevorkian that he would look into it, Marlinga wrote to the doctor three days later: "I regret to say that under Michigan law it is not possible to provide any assurance that such persons will not face possible criminal prosecution."[20]

As for the police, they had been content over the past year to speak to Fieger without even bringing in Kevorkian for questioning. A case against him could not be built solely on speculation about the circumstances of a suicide. And since Fieger and Kevorkian had stopped explicitly tying the doctor to deaths—indeed, had stopped providing virtually any details about the deaths he attended—speculation was precisely what prosecutors were left with. Even the Michigan Department of Consumer and Industry Services admitted that it did not have enough

evidence to charge Kevorkian with practicing medicine without a license. A law professor at the University of Detroit–Mercy summed up
the situation at the time by saying that it "appear[s] as if Jack Kevorkian
has been granted the implicit authority to be able to assist in suicides in
southeastern Michigan under the current state of the law."[21]

Kevorkian felt so free to continue aiding suicides that he announced
toward the end of October during a closed-circuit press conference
with reporters from across the country that he planned to begin offering
organs to patients in need of transplants. The organs would be harvested from his suicide patients. "Up to this point," he reasoned, "when
someone dies, it's negative. But then you give organs back. So here's a
case where we can end the suffering of a patient and get organs back to
save lives." Kevorkian intended the organs to be provided on a first-
come, first-served basis, with lungs and a heart likely being the first to
be harvested. The doctor's organ transplantation plan—which he had
been floating on and off for decades, as we saw in previous chapters—
was his latest challenge to organized medicine. "You'll notice that no
clinic comes forward and says we'll allow you to come in here and let
this patient end his suffering and give his organs to save three other
people's lives," he predicted. "You'll find out they won't do that."[22]

One week after the press conference, the body of an eighteen-year
veteran of the New York City Probation Department was discovered in
a Romulus, Michigan, hotel room. The note accompanying fifty-five-
year-old John O'Hara's body read: "Do Not Investigate: Contact Geoffrey Fieger." Kevorkian had by now attended more than a dozen suicides in Detroit-area hotels and motels. Some of the managers of those
establishments began to complain. "Our costs are significant, and Kevorkian isn't going to pay for this," explained the general manager of the
Comfort Inn in Romulus. "Never mind if the victim put the room on a
credit card. Try and get reimbursement for that," he said sarcastically.
The estimated cost to each business was a little under $1,000 per sui-
cide, according to hoteliers; that included nearly $600 to replace the
mattress and bed linens and to clean the carpets, as well as the loss of
the room for at least two days at a rate of $60 to $100 per night.
Kevorkian's activities were much more expensive than that, in fact.
Police costs of each investigation, plus anywhere between $4,000 and
$10,000 per autopsy, ran up taxpayers' bills. In addition, Kevorkian's
trials had cost hundreds of thousands of dollars, according to prosecu-

tors. Dr. Dragovic, the medical examiner, did not hesitate to point out that Kevorkian's clients "are imports into Michigan, and this is an excessive burden on the taxpayers."[23]

Kevorkian responded, if only indirectly, by staging his next assisted suicide—in a Roman Catholic church. Geoffrey Fieger claimed that Nadia Foldes, a seventy-four-year-old liver cancer patient from Queens, New York, had inhaled carbon monoxide on November 13 at a church that had "a sympathetic priest." Kevorkian then delivered the body to the emergency room of Pontiac Osteopathic Hospital. While Fieger declined to identify the church or the priest, he did offer the following observation: "Churches have traditionally been looked upon as places of sanctuary and refuge and to think that a church would not be an appropriate place to go into the next world is nonsense." He said that Foldes had chosen the church. "It was for the patient," he asserted, and was not in any way a political statement. He was responding to accusations that Kevorkian himself had chosen a church as the setting for Foldes's assisted suicide as retaliation against Cardinal Adam Maida of Detroit, who only days earlier had called on the roughly 1.5 million Catholics in southeastern Michigan to resume abstaining from meat on Fridays as penitence for assisted suicide, abortion, and the "culture of death" in the United States.[24]

Religious officials were outraged. Ned McGrath, a spokesperson for the Detroit Archdiocese, began by questioning the entire claim. "The only source of information we have on this is from Geoffrey Fieger," he correctly pointed out. "So, I guess unless and until credible information is brought forward for us to see, there's no need to investigate or even dignify such claims with comment." McGrath quickly reconsidered, however, and added, "No matter how or where this happened, what this tragic incident points to is the 'slippery slope' of assisted suicide. What's next? A supermarket, a schoolyard, a stadium? There appears to be no end to the publicity-driven attempts by these death brokers to manage and manipulate media coverage of this issue." The spokesperson for Cardinal O'Connor in New York was equally concerned about what Cardinal Maida called a "culture of death" in the United States, saying it "is not dignified, it is not appropriate for any individual to take his or her own life or to assist somebody else in taking his or her own life."[25]

With Foldes's death—and perhaps as a result of Detroit-area hotel managers' recent complaints—Kevorkian resumed his practice of personally delivering his patients' bodies to the hospital or to the medical examiner's office. By the beginning of December, he changed tactics again, shifting responsibility for a patient's suicide for the first time to someone else. That person was Georges Reding, a retired psychiatrist. Although Kevorkian was present at eighty-two-year-old Martha Wichorek's suicide on December 3, it was Reding who assisted in it. Fieger explained that Kevorkian had "decided that other doctors are going to be involved." Reding confirmed that he had begun what he called a "fellowship" in assisted suicide with Kevorkian, whom he referred to as his "medical hero." Fieger also issued a warning after Wichorek's death: "There'll be more."[26]

Fieger was correct. Before the year was out, Kevorkian and his new "apprentice" would be present at five more assisted suicides. Reding even accompanied Kevorkian in dropping off their patients' bodies at the hospital or the medical examiner's office. Once again, Kevorkian had forged into new territory by involving another doctor in assisted suicides. And, once again, authorities were unable to stop him. Captain Damon Shields of the Oakland County Sheriff's Office admitted as much after Kevorkian wheeled the body of Tampa resident Mary Langford into the medical examiner's office during the last weekend of December 1997. "Basically, the only crime that's been committed here is jaywalking," he said. "People here are of the opinion that, until the Legislature defines assisted suicide more clearly, it's almost a non-issue."[27]

In fact, the state legislature had been working on doing exactly that. On December 4, the Senate passed a new ban on assisted suicide by a vote of twenty-seven to eight. Like the temporary ban that expired in 1994, the new law would not apply to someone who prescribed drugs to relieve pain and suffering, even if the drugs increased the risk of death. At the same time, it closed the loophole in the previous law by stipulating that the drugs must be prescribed by a licensed physician who maintained a clinical practice in a fixed location within the state of Michigan. Once again, state legislators had crafted a law specifically to stop Jack Kevorkian. The doctor's opponents were hopeful. "It's really to the point where we need to get the attorney general or a prosecutor to say yes to prosecution of Kevorkian," said the deputy director for Michigan's medical licensing agency. "He's out of hand."[28]

While the bill was being debated in the House, Kevorkian called a press conference. He told reporters that he would starve himself to death in prison if he was ever convicted of assisting in a suicide. The primary purpose of the press conference, however, was to issue a challenge. Kevorkian plainly stated that he would not abide by any state law banning assisted suicide. It would be two and a half more months before the House voted on the ban that had passed the Senate in December. On March 12, 1998, the bill was approved by the House and sent back to the Senate for a vote on minor changes before it went to Governor Engler.[29]

By that point, Kevorkian had attended seven more suicides, including that of twenty-one-year-old Oakland University student Roosevelt Dawson. He was Kevorkian's youngest patient. Dawson had been paralyzed from the neck down and depended on a ventilator to breathe since a viral infection had attacked his spinal cord more than a year earlier. He had been hospitalized for the past five months. Not suffering from a terminal illness, Dawson had fought to be released from the hospital so he could seek Kevorkian's help in ending his life. He did just that, with his mother by his side, in their home on the evening of February 26, 1998.[30]

Criticism of Kevorkian quickly began to mount. He had aided in the suicides of nonterminal patients before, but the death of Roosevelt Dawson—a young college student who was severely incapacitated—seemed different. "He said he was only going to take terminally ill patients," said Ned McGrath. "Now, he makes the claim that he will decide who's terminally ill." Naturally, the spokesperson for the Detroit Archdiocese was still smarting from Fieger's claim that Kevorkian had assisted in a suicide in a Catholic church. But McGrath's criticisms of Kevorkian were becoming increasingly difficult to counter. "He said he would consult with patients' past records," he continued. "Then there was a man he assisted in December who had a history of mental illness, and they didn't catch it." Georges Reding, who also attended Dawson's death, retorted that anyone could choose assisted suicide because "we are all terminal." And Kevorkian simply said that a person's decision to live or die should be based on "quality of life."[31]

Kevorkian was less concerned about the growing criticism than he was about the behavior of the police officers who showed up at the Dawson home after Roosevelt's death. He complained that they had tried to interfere and mistreated the family, claiming they had confiscated Dawson's mother's glasses, which she had put on a pillow while she held her dying son. "I need my glasses for work," she explained. "They said, 'We can't release them.' What could you find on those glasses but a mother's tears?" The police also confiscated a "euthanasia device" and other medical equipment. Judge Breck gave them until noon on April 1 to bring a case against Kevorkian or return his equipment.[32]

Despite the growing concern that Kevorkian had become less strict about whom he would help die, he continued to deliver his patients' bodies to area hospitals with Georges Reding's help. He also continued to use lethal injection as the means of death. When Kevorkian helped sixty-six-year-old lung cancer patient Waldo Herman kill himself on Friday, March 13, Geoffrey Fieger announced that it was his client's 100th assisted suicide. It was the day after the Michigan House had approved a new ban on assisted suicide, which would make the practice a felony punishable by up to five years in prison and a $10,000 fine.[33]

After attending another suicide on March 26, the medical equipment that had been confiscated after Roosevelt Dawson's death in February—a "euthanasia device," syringes, chemicals, and an oxygen tank—was returned to Kevorkian. He promptly picked up his pace again, assisting in eight suicides between April 9 and June 7. The first five, all of which occurred during a sixteen-day stretch in April, proceeded smoothly. But upon delivering the sixth body to the hospital—that of twenty-six-year-old Matthew Johnson, who had been paralyzed from the neck down after a motorcycle accident—there was an altercation, and both Kevorkian and Reding were arrested. According to police reports, officers who were at William Beaumont Hospital on other business saw Kevorkian and told him they wanted to ask him some questions. Kevorkian took off his hat and glasses, saying "I'm going to get bloody," and grew agitated. Police tried to calm him down and held him by both arms. At that point, Reding came toward them with clenched fists. Kevorkian began yelling, "You'll have to kill me" and "Go to hell" at the officers. They knocked him down and handcuffed him. After spending the night in jail, Kevorkian remained defiant. He refused to enter the courtroom for his arraignment the next morning, and had to be brought in bound in handcuffs and sitting in a wheelchair.[34]

Things began to unravel quickly for Kevorkian around this time, primarily because his own behavior became increasingly erratic.[35] A crucial additional reason was that he suddenly lost Geoffrey Fieger as his legal counsel. The stated reason was that Fieger had decided to pursue a gubernatorial campaign, although people close to Kevorkian suggested that the two men had had a falling out and Kevorkian fired him.[36] Regardless of the reasons for Fieger's departure, Kevorkian was now being defended by Michael Schwartz and Michael Odette. Kevorkian said that if he went to trial on the charges of obstructing a police officer and resisting arrest for the tussle at the hospital, he wanted to act as co-counsel with Odette—which would entail cross-examining witnesses and calling his own experts to the stand. The attorney, who had worked almost exclusively on Kevorkian's civil cases to this point, saw no problem with that plan. "I think Jack deserves to have his day in court," he said. "If he wants to take part in it, I'm all for it." Odette saw it as an easy potential case. "The whole defense is you have a right to resist an unlawful arrest," he explained. He added that Kevorkian already had a list of almost ten witnesses he wanted to call should he go to trial for his and Reding's altercation with the police.[37]

On June 7, Kevorkian stunned observers—including many who supported him—by announcing that kidneys had been harvested from the body of a forty-five-year-old man whose suicide he assisted, and they were immediately available for a transplant. Having been removed at 11:00 a.m., Kevorkian claimed they would be healthy for transplantation until 11:00 p.m. the following day. The patient was John Tushkowski who, like two of Kevorkian's recent patients, was a quadriplegic. Kevorkian stated that Tushkowski's kidneys were removed according to protocols for organ transplantation, including sterile conditions and tests for various diseases. Since Tushkowski's family refused to cooperate with police, David Gorcyca immediately stated that charges were unlikely to be filed even though Michigan law required organ harvesting to be done in a licensed medical facility with two doctors present— one to pronounce the patient dead and the other to harvest any organs from the body. The medical examiner spared few details in discussing the corpse. "They didn't remove his sweater. They just pulled it up, then cut the belly," Dr. Dragovic explained. "This is not a situation to be compared with the highly skilled act of organ procurement surgery. . . . We're talking about a chopped-up body." He ruled Tushkow-ski's death a homicide.[38]

Critics of Kevorkian's latest "stunt," as they called it, wasted no time making their voices heard. The director of the University of Michigan Transplant Center was one of the first to offer an opinion. Dr. Robert Merion put the matter succinctly: "Dr. Kevorkian is persisting in confusing the public and making a mockery of the important and delicate issue of organ donation." Kevorkian was adamant, however, that his organ transplant idea was "totally moral in every aspect compared to what we do today." He claimed during a press conference that about 250 people—none of whom were doctors—had called to inquire about Tushkowski's kidneys. He also pointed out that six to ten people die every day because of a lack of donor organs.[39]

Even some of Kevorkian's allies thought his harvesting of Tushkow-ski's kidneys—which ultimately went unclaimed—crossed a line. Michael Odette abruptly withdrew from the doctor's legal defense team over it at the end of June. "Jack's been good to me, and good for business," he said. "Most criminal defense attorneys would love to represent Jack Kevorkian. I believe in assisted suicide, but he went too far this time, and I want no part of it anymore." It was a severe blow, both to the doctor's public image and, on the heels of Geoffrey Fieger's departure to focus on his gubernatorial campaign, to his legal defense. Michael Schwartz, who had assisted Fieger on Kevorkian's previous criminal cases, would now be in charge.[40]

Kevorkian found himself in increasingly difficult circumstances after Fieger's and Odette's departures. On July 16, he received a subpoena from Michigan's Department of Consumer and Industry Services. The agency that was responsible for medical licensing wanted the records of forty-two people it alleged Kevorkian had helped to die since it had issued the cease-and-desist order that Kevorkian publicly burned in April 1997. In addition, a new state law banning assisted suicide was due to go into effect on September 1, 1998. Two months later, Michigan residents would vote on a ballot measure to legalize physician-assisted suicide and Kevorkian would go on trial for his May 7 scuffle with police at William Beaumont Hospital. In light of these upcoming events, it is perhaps not surprising, in retrospect, that Kevorkian would take a break after assisting in John Tushkowski's suicide at the beginning of June. He would not attend another death for more than three months—his longest stretch between patients in a year and a half. The summer of 1998 was the calm before the storm.[41]

❋ ❋ ❋

On September 15, 1998, exactly two weeks after Michigan's new ban on assisted suicide took effect, Jack Kevorkian sat with Thomas and Melody Youk in the couple's Waterford, Michigan, home. Thomas, a fifty-two-year-old accountant, was in the advanced stages of Lou Gehrig's disease. He could not move his arms or legs, and his speech was barely intelligible. Once an amateur race car driver who restored old Porsches, he was now confined to a wheelchair. As had more than 100 people before him, he had decided to end his life with Kevorkian's help.[42]

Kevorkian, as was his custom, videotaped the preliminaries. He presented Thomas with a consent form and asked whether he needed more time to think about his decision. The doctor said, "Let's not hurry into this." Thomas signed the form, which stated that he would die by "direct injection." Two days later, on September 17, Kevorkian returned to the Youks' home to assist in Thomas's death. Again, he turned on the video camera. After struggling to find a suitable vein, the doctor said, "We're ready to inject your right arm. OK? Okey-dokey?" and injected Thomas with secobarbital sodium, a barbiturate, to put him to sleep. His chin fell onto his chest; he did not respond when Kevorkian asked him if he was awake. The doctor administered two more injections: a muscle relaxant to stop his breathing followed by potassium chloride to stop his heart. Kevorkian later told reporters that it was the first time he had recorded the "actual event" of death.[43]

After Youk's death, Kevorkian quietly sent the unedited videotape to CBS for its top-rated and long-running national news show *60 Minutes*. David Gorosh, who had recently replaced Michael Schwartz as Kevorkian's legal counsel, claimed he had no idea that his new client had done so. "I certainly didn't advise him to send the tape to *60 Minutes*," he said. "As a legal adviser, I certainly wouldn't advise him to do that." Gorosh speculated that Kevorkian was "simply indicating, 'Either prosecute me and leave it there, or don't prosecute me and let's leave it once and for all.'" The attorney was correct. "I want a showdown," Kevorkian told a reporter for the *Oakland Press*. "I want to be prosecuted for euthanasia. I am going to prove that this is not a crime, ever, regardless of what words are written on paper." He continued, "I am tired of all the hypocrisy and we're going to end this, one way or another."[44]

❀ ❀ ❀

When Michigan voters went to the polls in November 1998, Oregon was the only state in which physician-assisted suicide was legal. Across the country, people waited to find out whether the home state of Dr. Death himself would become the second. Proposal B was a ballot measure that would allow doctors to prescribe a lethal dose of medication for terminally ill patients who wished to kill themselves. The language that appeared on the ballot was as follows:

The proposal would:

1. allow a Michigan resident or certain out-of-state relatives of Michigan residents confirmed by 1 psychiatrist to be mentally competent and 2 physicians to be terminally ill with 6 months or less to live to obtain a lethal dose of medication to end his/her life;
2. allow physicians, after following required procedures, to prescribe a lethal dose of medication to enable a terminally ill adult to end his/her life;
3. establish a gubernatorially appointed, publicly-funded oversight committee, exempt from Open Meetings Act and whose records, including confidential medical records, and minutes are exempt from Freedom of Information Act;
4. create penalties for violating the law.

Kevorkian himself opposed the measure, saying it was too restrictive. Ultimately, Michigan voters did too: 71 percent voted against it.[45]

Just two days later, Kevorkian was found guilty of misdemeanor assault and resisting arrest for the May 7 fracas at William Beaumont Hospital. It was the first time he was convicted of anything in more than eight years of wrangling with authorities. Defiant as ever, Kevorkian challenged prosecutors to send him to jail, where he would go on a hunger strike as a form of protest. Kevorkian also asked Judge Sawicki to give him the maximum sentence of ninety days. The judge imposed fines instead, and sentenced Kevorkian to two years' probation.[46]

✿ ✿ ✿

The first dramatic step in the showdown that Kevorkian so desperately wanted took place more than two months after Thomas Youk's death, when Kevorkian appeared on the opening segment of *60 Minutes* on the evening of Sunday, November 22, 1998. During the interview, Mike Wallace played an edited version of the video of Thomas Youk's death. Kevorkian provided "macabre play-by-play," as one news account called it, to the fifteen million households that tuned in. During the interview, Kevorkian explained that Youk "felt very afraid of choking to death . . . and I couldn't have him suffer in that kind of frame of mind." Wallace asked Kevorkian whether he had killed Youk. "I did," Kevorkian responded. As for administering the lethal injection, Kevorkian explained that "actually, this is better than assisted suicide. I explained that to [Thomas]. Better control. And then he did agree, which I think, I didn't force him to agree, he did agree." He viewed a physician administering a lethal injection as "faster, cleaner and easier" than a patient using his homemade suicide machine, and called Youk's death his "first euthanasia." Kevorkian added that if he was convicted, he would starve himself to death in prison. Melody Youk defended the doctor during the interview, telling Wallace that she was "so grateful to know that someone would relieve [Thomas] of his suffering." She made her position clear. "I don't consider it murder," she stated. "I consider it the way things should be done."[47]

Kevorkian, his lawyer David Gorosh, Neal Nicol, and a few others watched the broadcast over dinner. According to his lawyer, Kevorkian had been "hoping it would be a piece that was sensitive to the family. He was pleased." The next day, Kevorkian issued an ultimatum to authorities through his lawyer. Gorosh told reporters that Kevorkian had "indicated if he's not charged in a week, he's made the assumption that the prosecution isn't going to move against him and he'll go about assisting people in need." Gorosh expressed his own hope that prosecutors "will come to the opinion this isn't something that should be taken to a courtroom. The issue of euthanasia should be debated. I think it would be unfortunate if [they] went ahead and charged Dr. Kevorkian with a crime." The attorney's comments were at odds with those of his client. Kevorkian had told the *Oakland Press*, "I want to be prosecuted for euthanasia" for his role in Youk's death. And he had told Mike

Wallace that he had deliberately crossed the line from assisted suicide to euthanasia so that he would be arrested. Kevorkian insisted that he either wanted to be charged and acquitted or, if convicted, to starve himself to death in prison.[48]

By the second day after the broadcast, the backlash against Kevorkian was unlike anything he had experienced in his more than eight-year assisted-suicide campaign. The American Medical Association issued a statement condemning Kevorkian as "a self-admitted zealot killing another human being to advance his own interests and ego-driven urge to martyrdom." One prominent media critic called Youk's euthanasia a "stunt death." Ned McGrath of the Detroit Archdiocese said, "What I saw on my TV screen was a publicity-hungry, unlicensed pathologist killing a visibly troubled, vulnerable man." More than a few observers pointed out that the airing of the videotape on *60 Minutes* occurred during the last weekend of "sweeps month," when audience sizes are measured to establish advertising rates. The episode had yielded the show its highest ratings of the season. Dr. Timothy Quill, a longtime critic of Kevorkian whom we met in chapter 3, offered his opinion of Youk's death. "This killing was not patient driven," he argued. "It was all about Kevorkian trying to advance Kevorkian, to flout the laws. It had nothing to do with the core issues involved here." Even Geoffrey Fieger briefly resurfaced for an interview on CNN. He told the host of *Talk Back Live* that while he admired Kevorkian's bravery, he would not participate in his former client's "martyrdom." Proponents of assisted suicide remained quiet.[49]

David Gorosh seemed to change his own story when he explained that he had advised Kevorkian against submitting the video to CBS. But, he said, Kevorkian is "a hard man to predict." He also offered a somewhat feeble defense of his client's actions. "The issue comes down to whether the citizens of this community feel what he did is a crime," he said. "There is no criminal intent here. There is no malice. How could mercy be considered murder?" Prosecutor David Gorcyca took a very different view: "What was most disturbing . . . was the total lack of compassion exhibited for Mr. Youk in the last few moments of his life." He also questioned Kevorkian's character and his stated motives. "I saw a nonchalant, callous, businesslike approach involving the death of a person for the purpose of satisfying an attention-starved ego. It would have been more appropriate to submit the tapes to local law-enforce-

ment agencies than a national TV show, if Kevorkian wanted to legiti-
mately challenge the statute in a course of law."[50]

Gorcyca took action the day after the broadcast by issuing a subpoena to *60 Minutes*—but not to Kevorkian—for the unedited version of
the videotape. He explained that he did not want to make a decision
about whether to prosecute the doctor until he had seen the video in its
entirety. However, in an effort to set the tone for the debate that had
already begun, he referred to Kevorkian's action not as assisted suicide
or as euthanasia but as something fundamentally different under the
law. "After viewing the edited portions of the video last night," he said,
"it appeared a homicide was committed in violation of the laws of the
state of Michigan."[51]

Two days later, armed with the state law that had gone into effect on
September 1, Gorcyca charged Kevorkian with first-degree murder,
among other crimes. "In this case, there is an obvious violation of the
law," the prosecutor said, "which I will not turn my back to." He asserted that Kevorkian's actions fit the definition of premeditated murder and that Thomas Youk's consent was not a legal defense. Seeking to
defend himself against the charge of wasting taxpayers' money prosecuting Kevorkian—the charge he had leveled against his predecessor,
Richard Thompson, during their primary contest—Gorcyca made it
clear that he had no choice. "I did not bring this upon Dr. Kevorkian,"
he said. "He did it to himself." Kevorkian immediately surrendered and
appeared for arraignment, smiling. In an attempt to show how serious
they were, the prosecution argued during the twenty-minute arraignment that Kevorkian should be locked up immediately. "He will kill
again," warned assistant prosecutor Jennifer Stout. "He has demonstrated complete and utter disregard for orders such as this." The judge,
however, released Kevorkian on a $750,000 personal bond, on the con-
dition that he not participate in a "mercy killing . . . or any other thing
you wish to call it." The doctor replied, "Your honor, there won't [even]
be a parking ticket."[52]

Kevorkian's critics welcomed not only the murder charge, but the
charges for assistance to a suicide and delivery of a controlled substance
as well. A lawyer for the International Anti-Euthanasia Task Force said,
"It's about time. Unless the rule of law means nothing in this country,
Jack Kevorkian belongs in jail." Even pro–assisted-suicide groups questioned Kevorkian's motives. The executive director of the Hemlock So-

ciety, Faye Girsh, believed Gorcyca's decision to file a murder charge was legally appropriate. "This was what Jack Kevorkian wanted," she said. "He chose to do this to make a point to the American public." Girsh added, "You can't pick your martyrs in a struggle like this. Sure, you'd like to pick Marcus Welby [instead of Kevorkian]," referencing the family physician with the wonderful bedside manner on the 1970s television show. Barbara Coombs Lee, executive director of Compassion in Dying, said the doctor's actions "bear no relationship to our cause or what we stand for." Interestingly, it was one of Kevorkian's former lawyers, Michael Schwartz, who came to the doctor's defense, if only to point out that the charges were contradictory. "You can't say that there was a suicide and at the same time say there was a homicide," he said. "Homicide is not a suicide—that's impossible."[53]

To everyone's surprise, David Gorosh announced at the arraignment that Kevorkian would represent himself at trial, with help from two legal advisers: Gorosh himself and Wayne State University law professor Robert Sedler, who had not defended a criminal case in three decades. Perhaps no one was more surprised than Kevorkian's former attorney, Geoffrey Fieger, who by now had lost the gubernatorial election with less than 38 percent of the vote. He believed Kevorkian's decision to act as his own lawyer was a mistake. "I can tell you what the results will be if he represents himself," he said. "He will go to jail and starve." He suggested that Kevorkian wanted to represent himself because "either consciously or unconsciously, he wants to hurt himself. He has a self-destructive impulse that comes out regularly." Fieger told *Newsweek* magazine that he would not help Kevorkian this time. "I don't assist my clients in their own suicides," he quipped.[54]

At the beginning of December, Judge Phyllis McMillen ordered Kevorkian to stand trial on all three charges against him. "The intent to kill was premeditated," the judge found, "and thought out beforehand." The following week, Kevorkian pleaded not guilty to first-degree murder and vowed, once again, to go on a hunger strike if he was sent to prison. His trial was scheduled for March 1999. If convicted of the murder charge, he faced mandatory life in prison.[55]

✿ ✿ ✿

Oakland County prosecutors and Jack Kevorkian spent a long Michigan winter preparing for the doctor's fifth trial. At the beginning of March, just weeks before the trial, prosecutors made an important tactical decision. Judge Jessica Cooper had ruled that if prosecutors pursued the assisted suicide charge against Kevorkian, the defense could present testimony about the doctor's role in relieving patients' pain and suffering; if they only pursued the murder charge instead, any testimony about relieving pain and suffering would be inadmissible. Such testimony was exactly what prosecutors thought had earned Kevorkian his two prior acquittals. Dropping the assisted suicide charge would be "a calculated risk," Gorcyca conceded. "But," he continued, "that kind of testimony has proved lethal to our case in the past. . . . What you had is jurors, even male jurors, crying. To overcome that kind of emotional testimony at trial is almost impossible." It was a risk, maybe, but one that Gorcyca did not hesitate to take. He dropped the assisted suicide charge. The jury would not hear testimony about Thomas Youk's pain and suffering.[56]

While the prosecution was deciding which charges to pursue, the members of the defense team were figuring out their respective roles. Kevorkian wanted to defend himself. Gorosh disagreed with that approach. "We've tried to persuade him that the lawyers should try the case," Gorosh told reporters. "He's an incredibly charming man, he's as honest as the day is long, and I think jurors would appreciate that. That said, a criminal trial is a complicated thing. . . . Although Dr. Kevorkian is quite brilliant, he isn't schooled in the law." Kevorkian did not think he needed to be, and insisted that he at least wanted to cross-examine Dr. Dragovic himself and deliver the closing argument. "There are certain points I can bring out better than any attorney," Kevorkian contended. "There are certain questions I can ask." Observers noted that such a disagreement would never have happened, let alone become public, with Geoffrey Fieger on the defense team. They also noted the thirty-year-old Gorosh's "softer style" and comparative lack of trial experience.[57]

Kevorkian prevailed. Despite Judge Cooper's misgivings and her extensive questioning of Kevorkian, she allowed him to defend himself. "Do you understand you could spend the rest of your life in prison?" she asked. "There's not much of it left," Kevorkian replied. Judge Cooper was patient with Kevorkian, as she proved to be throughout the trial, also asking him whether he knew what the inside of a state prison looked like. Kevorkian told her that he had seen the movie *The Shawshank Redemption* twice. She also informed the doctor that anything he said in court could be used against him in future proceedings. Kevorkian answered, "I plan to say nothing but the truth."[58]

Upon hearing the news that his former client would be defending himself, Geoffrey Fieger expressed his opinion from the sidelines. "Kevorkian may be the most brilliant man I've ever met," Fieger said. "But the country is going to get a look at a side of this man they will not like. This is going to be ugly. This is going to be embarrassing. He wants to be a martyr. This is about focusing attention on himself." Public opinion of Kevorkian had withered since he had tried to harvest John Tushkowski's kidneys, and Fieger's comments did not help his former client's cause. In fact, he stated his belief that Kevorkian "didn't have to push the envelope this far. [Thomas Youk's death] fits the legal definition of murder." To make matters even worse, the day before the trial began, one of Kevorkian's legal advisers admitted not knowing what the defendant's strategy was going to be.[59]

During opening statements, Kevorkian himself did not seem to know either. The prosecutor, John Skrzynski, was clear with the jurors. "Begin to focus on what Jack Kevorkian does," he told them, "and what Jack Kevorkian says, and what you will see is a man breaking the law. Jack Kevorkian killed Tom Youk, and Jack Kevorkian does not have the right to kill." When it was his turn, Kevorkian claimed that he had acted solely out of compassion for Youk and suggested that he had not committed a crime. "To have a crime," he reasoned, "you need a vicious will and a vicious act." Skrzynski objected on the grounds that Kevorkian was arguing law rather than summarizing his case. The judge agreed and dismissed the jury so Kevorkian could explain to her what he was trying to say. "What I was trying to prove here is that I didn't have the intent to kill, just as the executioner doesn't," Kevorkian explained. "His intent is to do his duty, because he may despise what he is doing. But he's forced to do it by his position." This was the second trial in which Kevorkian had likened himself to an executioner. The first time, he had the savvy Geoffrey Fieger to rein him in and ultimately win over the jury. This time, he did not. "I despise a human being dying in my hands," he pleaded. "But my intent wasn't to kill the person. I thought it was my duty as a physician to do this."[60]

Procedurally, the first day of testimony did not go any better for Kevorkian. The prosecution opened and closed its case in the morning, presenting the videotape and excerpts from the *60 Minutes* episode, and calling three witnesses. Kevorkian cross-examined two of them, including Dr. Dragovic. When he asked the medical examiner whether he was personally opposed to euthanasia, Judge Cooper quickly struck the question as legally impermissible. By dropping the assisted suicide charge, the prosecution had severely hampered the defense. That fact became even more evident as soon as Kevorkian tried to call Melody Youk as the first witness for the defense. Judge Cooper was forced to dismiss the jury for the second time. "Sir, what you seek to introduce is not cognizable under the laws of the State of Michigan," she tried to explain. Neither Melody nor Thomas Youk's brother Terry could testify that Thomas had given consent because consent was not a legal defense for murder. "And I know that you disagree with that," she told Kevorkian, "and I know that that's what you want to talk to the jury about. But you can't. The jury doesn't decide whether the law is correct." Once again, she stated her belief that Kevorkian should not be representing himself. "You need to have counsel here," she told him, "and in the waiver of counsel you put yourself in a difficult position." She ordered the defense to submit a brief by the next morning, laying out its arguments for calling Melody Youk and Terry Youk.[61]

Kevorkian and his advisers did so, asking that Melody and Terry be allowed to testify that this had been a mercy killing, not a murder, and that Thomas had consented, thus supporting Kevorkian's claims. The prosecution responded by asserting that the statements by family members on the day of Thomas's death were made under the assumption that they would be used as part of a criminal defense. "This was an event orchestrated by defendant to push his own public agenda," the brief read. "Here the statements made by defendant to Tom Youk's family members were the epitome of self-serving declarations, which defendant prepared and intended to be used at his future trial, and are not admissible." Judge Cooper ruled in favor of the prosecution, and Kevorkian informed her that he had no witnesses to call. The defense rested without calling any witnesses or presenting any evidence.[62]

All Kevorkian had left was his closing argument. Before he delivered it, Judge Cooper reminded the seven women and five men of the jury that their job was to follow the state statute, not try to change it. She added that euthanasia was not at issue and that even if Thomas Youk had given his consent, that was not a legally acceptable defense. She instructed the jurors to evaluate whether Kevorkian's actions met the standards of first-degree murder, second-degree murder, or involuntary manslaughter. It was at the request of the prosecution that the judge added involuntary manslaughter as a possible finding, since second-degree murder was automatically added any time a person was charged with first-degree murder in Michigan. Kevorkian thought the suggestion of manslaughter was outrageous. "The prosecution has charged me with first-degree murder," he told the judge. "I don't think they should back down. That's cowardice."[63]

Nevertheless, Kevorkian proceeded to raise all of these points in his closing anyway. "He calls it a murder, a crime, a killing," began Kevorkian, gesturing toward Skrzynski. "I call it medical science. Tom Youk didn't come to me saying, 'I want to die, kill me.' He said, 'Please help me.' There was medical affliction. Medical service is exempt from certain laws." Kevorkian insisted, as he chopped one hand into the palm of the other, that his intent was "to end [Youk's] torture finally and definitively." He appealed to the jury: "You don't want to put him to sleep and have him reawake in the same condition he was before. That wasn't the aim. The aim was a final solution to incurable agony." Kevorkian continued to paint the picture of a requested mercy killing rather than a premeditated murder. He also appealed to jurors' reason. "There are certain things that words on paper can never make a crime," he argued. "There are certain acts that by sheer common sense are not crimes." He ended on a more personal note and, ultimately, with a warning. "Just look at me. Honestly now, honestly. Do you see a criminal? Do you see a murderer? Do you see what's called a killer? If you do then you must convict. And then take the harsh judgment of history or the harsher judgment of your children and grandchildren if they ever come to need that precious choice."[64]

To counter Kevorkian's invocation of the civil rights struggles of Rosa Parks and Dr. Martin Luther King Jr. during his closing statement, Skrzynski alluded during his to the Nazis' explanation of its mass killings as a form of euthanasia. "There are 11 million souls buried in Europe who could tell you that there are some catastrophic effects when you make euthanasia law," he asserted. "Some awful things can come from that." He replayed a portion of the video during which Youk moaned just before he was injected, and wondered aloud whether he had asked Kevorkian to stop at the last minute. "This is a methodical killing of a human being," he suggested. "You cannot get around that." Skrzynski also questioned Kevorkian's motives. "He's making a political statement," he argued to the jury. "He kills a man to further his political agenda. . . . He's willing to sacrifice this man for his cause [and] he wants you to make a new exception to the murder statute." He continued: "There's nobody watching [Kevorkian] do this. He chooses whose suffering is worth it. He's not accountable to anyone. And when he asks you to give him that power, because he is surely asking you to forget the law and give him that power, it will be an unaccountable power." The prosecutor presented Kevorkian as a less than compassionate doctor, stating that he "came like a medical hit man in the night with his bag of poison." Echoing the judge, Skrzynski told the jurors that the trial was not about assisted suicide or the right to die. "It's about Jack Kevorkian's right to kill. Jack Kevorkian murdered Thomas Youk. He killed Thomas Youk and he does not have the right to kill."[65]

The jury deliberated for five hours on Thursday night before asking Judge Cooper to resume the next morning. During its deliberations on Friday, Kevorkian, finally realizing the folly of his decision to represent himself, asked the judge whether lawyers could immediately begin representing him. Astonished, Judge Cooper asked, "Now?" before granting his request. But it did not matter. Just before 5:00 p.m., the jury announced its decision: Jack Kevorkian was guilty of second-degree murder. The defendant merely blinked as the verdict was read. The judge released him on bond until his sentencing in mid-April. "No assisted suicide" in the meantime, she warned him. "No injection. No anything." The fifth and final trial of Jack Kevorkian was over after less than six hours in the courtroom.[66]

❉ ❉ ❉

On April 13, 1999, Judge Jessica Cooper sentenced Jack Kevorkian to ten to twenty-five years in prison for second-degree murder. She added three to seven years for delivering a controlled substance without a license. "This trial was not about the political or moral correctness of euthanasia," she explained to the defendant during sentencing. "It was about you, sir. It was about lawlessness." She went on to reprimand

Kevorkian. "You had the audacity to go on national television, show the world what you did and dare the legal system to stop you. Well, sir, consider yourself stopped."[67]

Through five criminal trials, nearly nine years of constant media coverage, and more than 100 assisted deaths, Jack Kevorkian had single-handedly kept the debate over assisted suicide in the public spotlight. When his sentence was announced in the Pontiac, Michigan, courthouse that day, it all but disappeared.

CONCLUSION
Death with Dignity—After Kevorkian

Most of the reactions to Jack Kevorkian's lengthy sentence were predictable. His critics applauded the fact that a "medical hitman" was finally going to prison, while his supporters asserted that ten to twenty-five years was unduly harsh. Judge Jessica Cooper even had to be placed under police protection after receiving death threats from some in the latter camp.[1]

The most interesting reactions came from assisted-suicide advocates who implicitly acknowledged Kevorkian's importance to their cause while simultaneously distancing themselves from him and predicting that the right-to-die movement would continue in his absence. "The way he carried out this last case shows how far outside the mainstream he really was," said one activist in Oregon. "His conviction clears the air and allows us to discuss this subject in a rational way." Faye Girsh, president of the Hemlock Society, had a bit more praise for Kevorkian, but also did not lament his exit from the public stage. "He's focused this debate. He's raised the issue around the world," she asserted. "If he is out of the picture, the debate will go on. This is not a matter that is going to rise and fall on the basis of one person." The Reverend Russell Burck of Rush-Presbyterian St. Luke's Medical Center in Chicago said, "The debate will continue but will be somewhat relieved by Kevorkian's absence because he throws an element of hysteria into it."[2]

One of the points I have tried to make throughout this book is that the visibility of the assisted-suicide debate and the right-to-die movement *did* rise on the basis of one person between 1990 and 1999. It also fell on the basis of that same person's disappearance from the public spotlight. When Jack Kevorkian was sent to prison in the spring of 1999, the right-to-die movement lost its most visible and important leader, and with him, its ability to attract sustained media attention.[3]

☼ ☼ ☼

"His self-destruction was as precise and predictable as a class in anatomy." That is how Jack Kevorkian's longtime friends and associates Neal Nicol and Harry Wylie summed it up in their 2006 book *Between the Dying and the Dead*.[4] After an eight-year crusade, after aiding in more than 100 people's suicides, after three acquittals and a mistrial, how did Kevorkian's career as a right-to-die activist come to such an end? How was he finally stopped after being unstoppable for so many years?[5]

Several developments by the end of 1997 and beginning of 1998, in retrospect, seemed to spell Kevorkian's doom. First, he lost Geoffrey Fieger. The ostensible reason was Fieger's decision to run for governor of Michigan. The real reason was the rift that had grown between two stubborn, driven men who found themselves increasingly disagreeing about tactics and strategy. Calling the rift between Kevorkian and Fieger "predictable," Nicol and Wylie described their intense relationship as follows: "They were best of friends, yet they were always at odds. They dined out together almost weekly and Jack was frequently invited to Geoffrey's home for dinner. They often went to movies together. Yet Jack's neighbour Harry Wylie recalls whenever he heard, from a considerable distance, Jack screaming on the phone, he knew he was probably talking with Fieger." Nicol and Wylie also suggested that the "chief wedge" driven between Fieger and Kevorkian was the latter's insistence on representing himself if he went to trial for obstructing a police officer and resisting arrest over the May 1998 altercation at the hospital.[6]

Whatever the reasons for the split—neither man, to my knowledge, ever discussed its causes—it was a deadly blow to Kevorkian, both legally and in terms of public relations. Fieger, by all accounts, was (and still is) a formidable trial attorney.[7] His knowledge of the law and its loopholes, as well as his brilliance in the courtroom, were on full display during Kevorkian's three acquittals and the mistrial. Prosecutors, disarmed by both the lack of a clear state statute and jurors' emotional identification with Kevorkian's patients, were no match for Fieger. Outside the courtroom, he was just as effective on behalf of his most famous client. Fieger carefully managed Kevorkian's public image whether he was addressing the media, insulting judges and prosecutors, or delivering a speech. He was, in today's terminology, Kevorkian's "handler." Few attorneys could have successfully stepped into his shoes, especially as Kevorkian's behavior became more confrontational and he began to lose public support as a result.[8]

One might trace the beginnings of what one author called Kevorkian's "radicalized" practices to late August 1997, immediately after his assistance in his friend Janet Good's suicide.[9] As we have seen, he went on to assist in eighteen more deaths during the last four months of 1997, a pace unparalleled in the previous seven years. It was not just Kevorkian's pace that changed but his tactics. Instead of dropping off his patients at local hospitals, he began leaving their bodies in hotel rooms, which caused an outcry from local hotel managers. Kevorkian's October 1997 announcement that he would begin harvesting organs from his patients surprised everyone, including some of his supporters. In November, he carried out an assisted suicide in a Roman Catholic church. At the beginning of December, another doctor, Georges Reding, assisted in the suicide of one of Kevorkian's patients for the first time. When Kevorkian assisted in the suicide of a severely incapacitated twenty-one-year-old Oakland University student at the end of February 1998, concerns emerged about the rigor of his patient selection process.[10] Just a few months later, Kevorkian and Reding were arrested after the fight with police officers at William Beaumont Hospital. Geoffrey Fieger, no doubt sensing that things were falling apart, parted ways with Kevorkian around this time. A significant public relations misstep followed soon after, when Kevorkian harvested John Tushkowski's kidneys on June 7, 1998. It resulted in the loss of another of his lawyers, as we saw in chapter 7, and a great deal of negative publicity.

On top of that, Michigan's new law banning assisted suicide was due to go into effect on September 1, 1998, which meant that prosecutors would have a legal weapon to use against Kevorkian for the first time since 1994. Kevorkian immediately gave them a chance to do so when he assisted in Thomas Youk's death. The method Kevorkian used all but guaranteed a criminal trial. For the first time in over 100 cases, Kevorkian administered the lethal injection himself—and purposely videotaped it to prove it to the world. The brazenness of showing himself killing another person on national television could not be abided by prosecutors. They had to charge Kevorkian. And he gave them all the evidence against him that they needed. Yet he helped them even further by choosing to represent himself at what was subsequently judged to be one of the trials of the century.[11]

As Jack Kevorkian had been threatening for several years, he had wanted to provoke a showdown.[12] He finally did so with the Thomas Youk case. Kevorkian's personal fall brought an end to the most active decade that this country's right-to-die movement had ever seen. With Kevorkian's incarceration, the movement once again declined into abeyance, losing all of the sustained visibility that it had enjoyed during the 1990s. To be sure, the debate over death with dignity would briefly flare up in 2005, as we will see below, and again in 2014 over the case of Brittany Maynard (see the introduction). But in the fifteen years since Kevorkian's imprisonment, the movement has not managed to generate the kind of sustained media or public attention that "Dr. Death" did during the 1990s. That Brittany Maynard so quickly came to be called the "face" of dying with dignity underscores the fact that no one was able to take center stage after Kevorkian's exit.

✺ ✺ ✺

In April 2000, after spending almost exactly a year in various Michigan correctional facilities, Prisoner #284797 made national and international headlines when he was given the Gleitsman Foundation's Citizen Activist Award for Humanitarianism. It came with an $85,000 prize. Thomas Youk's wife and brother accepted the award on Jack Kevorkian's behalf. "He risked his personal freedom and today he is in a very small cell," Melody Youk said, "alone but not forgotten."[13] Indeed, Kevorkian had spent a good deal of his first year in prison answering fan mail, much of which came from outside the United States.[14]

In the spring of 2000, Hemlock's Faye Girsh admitted that losing Kevorkian was proving to be a blow to the right-to-die movement. "It's both a relief to not have him on the scene and unfortunate because attention to the problem has dwindled," she said. With the ambivalence that had long characterized the sentiments of the movement's organizational leaders about Kevorkian, she added, "I think what he did was heroic, but it was misguided."[15] Many other observers offered the same opinion. "Obviously, he's not the spokesperson most movements would want," said Alan Meisel, the director of the University of Pittsburgh's Center for Bioethics and Health Law. "He was clearly a loose cannon and not a responsible person. However, I suppose he did bring this issue into public view far better than anyone else did."[16] In the years immediately following Kevorkian's imprisonment, the consensus among right-to-die advocates quickly became that while they did not want to live with him, they were having a difficult time living without him. Their movement had lost its public face—and, as a result, its audience.

Kevorkian was in the news, but only briefly, two more times during the summer of 2000. Barbara Walters had wanted to conduct an interview with him, inside prison, for the news program *20/20*. It would require Walters and ten other people to be admitted to the prison for nine hours. After a county judge ordered the Michigan Department of Corrections to allow the interview, a state appellate court blocked the ruling at the end of July.[17] The following month, Kevorkian's legal team asked Judge Jessica Cooper to free him on bail while they appealed his murder conviction. Kevorkian was suffering from high blood pressure and other health problems, they said. The judge denied the request.[18]

By the end of 2001, Kevorkian exhausted his appeals at the state level. The U.S. Supreme Court, after refusing to hear his case in October 2002, subsequently rejected his appeal in November 2004. In between, the 6th U.S. Circuit Court of Appeals had dismissed his petition for bail and a U.S. district judge had denied his petition for a writ of habeas corpus. "There's no doubt I expect to die in prison," Kevorkian told a reporter during his first telephone interview from Thumb Correctional Facility in April 2004. Reflecting on his recently rejected appeals and his five years in prison, he resorted to his old accusation that the state was crushing individual liberty and rights. "All the big powers, they've silenced me," he said. "So much for free speech and choice on this fundamental human right." He also, however, continued to promise not to assist in any more suicides if he were released.[19]

By the end of 2004, with his federal appeals exhausted and his health deteriorating, Kevorkian and his attorney, Mayer Morganroth, needed a different approach. They asked the Michigan Parole Board early in

2005 to recommend to Governor Jennifer Granholm that the seventy-six-year-old Kevorkian be released on the grounds that he suffered from hepatitis C, high blood pressure, and arthritis. Morganroth, an old friend of Geoffrey Fieger's, asked for a recommendation to pardon Kevorkian or to commute his sentence. "I'm really concerned," Morganroth said when Kevorkian had to undergo bilateral hernia surgery in February 2005. "His health is quite poor."[20] Still, the governor said she would not consider pardoning Kevorkian.[21]

✿ ✿ ✿

As Mayer Morganroth petitioned the parole board for his client's release from prison, a different story returned the debate over the right to die to the national headlines early in the spring of 2005. On March 31, less than two weeks after her feeding tube had been removed, a forty-one-year-old Florida woman died. The acrimonious fifteen-year saga of Theresa "Terri" Schiavo had finally come to an end.

By stirring up memories of the Karen Ann Quinlan and Nancy Cruzan cases of the 1970s and 1980s, the Schiavo case reignited the debate over passive euthanasia, or the withdrawal of life-sustaining treatment from a significantly debilitated or terminally ill patient. Schiavo had collapsed in her St. Petersburg home in February 1990. After eight years of watching her persist in a vegetative state, unresponsive to various forms of speech and physical therapies, Michael Schiavo petitioned a circuit court in 1998 to remove his wife's feeding tube. Terri's parents opposed it. The legal and political battles that ensued were unprecedented for a right-to-die case. Not even in the Quinlan and Cruzan cases had there been so many suits, appeals, motions, petitions, and hearings, at both the federal and state levels. By court order, Schiavo's feeding tube was removed for the first time on April 24, 2001; it would be reinserted several days later after an appeal. Even President George W. Bush got involved, flying to Washington, D.C. from a vacation in Texas in order to sign legislation to keep her alive. By early 2005, all federal appeals were exhausted, and the hospice facility's staff removed Schiavo's feeding tube on March 18.[22]

Terri Schiavo's death at the end of March 2005 brought an end to the most controversial passive euthanasia case since that of Nancy Cruzan. And it focused the public's attention, if only briefly, on a larger debate that had not been heard since Jack Kevorkian was sent to prison six years earlier—that of the right to die. The public debate promptly disappeared again, even as assisted suicide became legal in four states between 2008 and 2014—disappeared, that is, until the Brittany Maynard case toward the end of 2014.

◦ ◦ ◦

It would take several more appeals to the Michigan parole board, over a period of two years, before Mayer Morganroth and Jack Kevorkian finally got their wish. On December 13, 2006, two members of the board approved Kevorkian's release on June 1, 2007, which was the date on which he had always been eligible for parole. Kevorkian had promised the board that he would not participate in any more assisted suicides or counsel potential patients; rather, he would work toward legalizing the practice. "You can put any conditions you want on me," he had said. "I'm not going to do it again. Anything that will bring me back to prison, I will avoid. Prison is not a place to live." David Gorcyca, the Oakland County prosecutor who had put Kevorkian behind bars, said that he would not appeal the board's decision to release Kevorkian. Fearing that his client would not live to see June 1, Morganroth again petitioned Governor Granholm to commute the sentence. Again, she refused, but did order an independent medical evaluation of the increasingly frail Prisoner #284797.[23]

On June 1, 2007, Jack Kevorkian slowly walked out of Lakeland Correctional Facility, wearing his trademark light-blue cardigan. The reactions to his reappearance were virtually indistinguishable from those he had consistently elicited during the previous decade. Opponents like Paul Long, vice president of public policy for the Michigan Catholic Conference, were outraged that he had been paroled. "This is a man who is known to have killed more people than any other person in Michigan's history, and he's being set free two years early," he exclaimed.[24] Ed Rivet of Michigan Right to Life used more colorful language to describe Kevorkian. "It's important to remember that this man was on a ghoulish death crusade," he said. "He was dumping bodies all over the place. This guy is a twisted individual."[25]

Leaders of right-to-die organizations were only slightly more welcoming. "[Kevorkian] was a profound symbol of the covert and clandestine process of dying," said Barbara Lee, the president of Compassion & Choices, the largest death with dignity group in the country. "But we don't really need that kind of championship these days. What we need are sane, rational laws."[26] A former president of the Hemlock Society of Michigan was a bit more direct. "To some, Dr. Kevorkian was a hero," he said. "To others, he is one of the reasons we didn't succeed. Rather than waiting for it to be legal, he went and did it, and that seemed to energize the opponents." Geoffrey Fieger, who had mended fences with his former client after his release from prison, denounced those who tried to distance themselves from Kevorkian. "These people have done nothing regarding the issue, and Jack has," he said in a telephone interview. "If we depended on them to get anything done, nothing would get done."[27]

Fieger appeared to be correct. On the legal front, nothing had changed during Kevorkian's eight years in prison. Oregon was still the only state in which assisted suicide was permissible. Coincidentally, at the time of Kevorkian's release, the California Legislature was about to vote on the Compassionate Choices Act, a bill similar to the one approved by Oregon voters thirteen years earlier. Democrat Lloyd Levins, who cosponsored the bill, was nervous about the timing and began framing the bill as a way to prevent any would-be Kevorkians from taking matters into their own hands. "[Kevorkian] did a lot for the national dialogue way back when, but he also got carried away," he said. "Actually, he is the perfect reason we need this law in California. We don't want there to be more Dr. Kevorkians."[28] The bill failed, as had recent bills and ballot measures in a half-dozen other states.[29]

¤ ¤ ¤

True to his word, Jack Kevorkian sought to effect legal change by running for a seat in the U.S. House of Representatives in 2008. Campaigning on the importance of the 9th Amendment, which says that rights that are not specifically addressed by the Constitution are reserved for the people—including, in Kevorkian's interpretation of it, the right to die—he garnered less than 3 percent of the vote.[30]

While Kevorkian lost in his bid for a seat in Congress, the right-to-die movement won on that election day. Voters in Washington State approved Initiative 1000, establishing the Death With Dignity Act and joining Oregon as the only two states in which assisted suicide was legal.[31] The following year, 2009, the Montana Supreme Court effectively legalized assisted suicide in Big Sky Country when it upheld a lower court's ruling that a physician could use a patient's consent as a defense against the charge of assisting in a suicide.[32] Suddenly, after quiet legal and judicial losses in a number of states between 1994 and 2008, the right-to-die movement had achieved two loud victories in the two and a half years since Jack Kevorkian had been paroled.

Kevorkian himself scored a public-relations victory in 2010 when *You Don't Know Jack*, a movie about his life starring Al Pacino, premiered on HBO in April.[33] The film was well received by critics and won Pacino several accolades, including a Golden Globe, an Emmy, and a Screen Actors Guild award for his portrayal of Kevorkian. "Dr. Death," it seemed, had been vindicated and his reputation rehabilitated. Photographed on the red carpet with Pacino and other members of the cast and crew, a beaming Kevorkian, now an octogenarian, clearly enjoyed his continuing cultural resonance. The movie "brings tears to my eyes," he said, "and I lived through it."[34]

* * *

Vermont and New Mexico became the fourth and fifth states to legalize assisted suicide in 2013 and 2014, respectively. These most recent victories for the right-to-die movement, coupled with Brittany Maynard's very public decision to end her life in the fall of 2014, signal that assisted suicide will remain a debatable practice, both in the United States and around the world, in the years ahead. Indeed, medical ethicist Arthur Caplan, one of Jack Kevorkian's old opponents, offered the following prediction in the days leading up to Maynard's planned suicide: "My forecast is that we are going to see more push to put these [assisted suicide] laws in front of state legislatures and to get them on state ballots. We are going to see more states move in this direction." The reasons Caplan offered have as much to do with societal trends as they do with Brittany Maynard herself: "Now we have a young woman getting people in her generation interested in the issue. Critics are worried about her partly because she's speaking to that new audience, and they know that the younger generation of America has shifted attitudes about gay marriage and the use of marijuana, and maybe they are going to have that same impact in pushing physician-assisted suicide forward."[35] Whether the changing culture will produce another Kevorkian-type public figure remains to be seen.

✿ ✿ ✿

Janet Adkins, Janet Good, Thomas Youk, and all of Jack Kevorkian's other patients were laid to rest long ago. On June 3, 2011, just over a year after the premier of *You Don't Know Jack*, the eighty-three-year-old Kevorkian joined them. The tombstone of Jack Kevorkian, M.D., in White Chapel Memorial Park Cemetery in Troy, Michigan, reads simply: "He sacrificed himself for everyone's rights."

NOTES

INTRODUCTION

1. Griffin 2014.
2. Compassion & Choices 2014; Shoichet 2014.
3. See, by way of comparison, Cha 2014; DuBois 2014; Durando 2014; "Right-to-Die Advocate Brittany Maynard Ends Life" 2014.
4. "News Q&A" 2005.
5. Humphry and Clement 1998:5.
6. Filene 1998:190.
7. Hillyard and Dombrink 2001:244.
8. Dowbiggin 2003:100.
9. See, by way of comparison, Fox et al. 1999; Gailey 2003.
10. Eckholm 2014a.
11. Death With Dignity National Center 2014.
12. Wilson 2014.

1. "A SELF-IMPOSED MISSION"

1. Belkin 1990; Irwin 1990b; "Suicide Doctor Warned on Use of Device" 1989.
2. Belkin 1990; Moss 1990.
3. Belkin 1990; Wilkerson 1990b.
4. Kevorkian 1991:222.
5. Belkin 1990; Mansnerus 1990; "The Tape: 'I Want to Get Out'" 1990.

6. Belkin 1990; Kevorkian 1991:222; Reid 1990; Risen 1990; Wilkerson 1990a; "Woman 'Aching to Die' Puts Suicide Machine to Test" 1990.

7. Belkin 1990; Kevorkian 1991:223; Wilkerson 1990b.

8. Kevorkian 1991:223.

9. "The Tape: 'I Want to Get Out'" 1990.

10. Beck et al. 1990; Belkin 1990; Jenish 1990.

11. "Dying, Dr. Kevorkian's Way" 1990; Irwin 1990b; "Woman 'Aching to Die' Puts Suicide Machine to Test" 1990.

12. Belkin 1990; Borger 1990a.

13. See Kevorkian 1991:229 for the note.

14. Kevorkian 1991:28.

15. Kevorkian 1991:29.

16. See, by way of comparison, Taylor 1989.

17. Dowbiggin 2003:7.

18. Dowbiggin 2003:82.

19. Dowbiggin 2003:94.

20. See, by way of comparison, Kevorkian 1957a, 1958.

21. See, by way of comparison, Kevorkian and Wessel 1959.

22. Kevorkian and Groner 1965.

23. Kevorkian 1991:30.

24. Kevorkian 1991:40.

25. Kevorkian 1991:40.

26. Borger 1990a.

27. Kevorkian and Bylsma 1961:413.

28. Kevorkian and Bylsma 1961:416.

29. Kevorkian and Bylsma 1961:417.

30. Kevorkian and Bylsma 1961:417.

31. Kevorkian and Bylsma 1961:418.

32. Kevorkian et al. 1964:24.

33. Kevorkian et al. 1964:25.

34. Kevorkian et al. 1964:25.

35. Kevorkian et al. 1964:25–26.

36. Kevorkian et al. 1964:26.

37. Nicol and Wylie 2006:63–65.

38. Kevorkian et al. 1964:26.

39. Kevorkian et al. 1964:27.

40. Kevorkian et al. 1964:27.

41. Kevorkian and Marra 1964:112.

42. Kevorkian and Marra 1964:117.

43. Kevorkian and Groner 1965:925.

44. Kevorkian and Marra 1964:117.

45. Borger 1990a.
46. Filene 1998.
47. Borger 1990a.
48. Kevorkian 2001.
49. Dowbiggin 2003:134.
50. Dowbiggin 2003:135.
51. See, by way of comparison, McCarthy and Zald 1977; Everett 1992.
52. Risen 1990.
53. Borger 1990a.
54. Risen 1990.
55. Kevorkian 1956:1264, emphasis added.
56. Kevorkian 1957b:1660.
57. Kevorkian 1957b:1663.
58. Kevorkian 1961a.
59. Kevorkian 1961a:54.
60. Kevorkian 1961a:62.
61. Kevorkian 1961b.
62. Kevorkian 1961b:261.
63. Kevorkian 1961b:257.
64. Kevorkian 1961b:266.
65. Kevorkian 1961b:271.
66. Risen 1990.
67. Risen 1990; Wilkerson 1990b.
68. Dowbiggin 2003:149.
69. Kevorkian 2001:15.
70. Kevorkian 1985a.
71. Kevorkian 1991:137.
72. Kevorkian 1985a:225.
73. Kevorkian 1985a:215.
74. Kevorkian 1985a:216.
75. Kevorkian 1985a:216.
76. Kevorkian 1985a:225.
77. Kevorkian 1985a:225.
78. See, by way of comparison, Kevorkian 1991:138–58.
79. Kevorkian 1991:138.
80. Kevorkian 1985a:225.
81. Kevorkian 1991:45.
82. Kevorkian 1986a, 1985b, 1985c.
83. Kevorkian 1985b:313.
84. Kevorkian 1985c:532.
85. Kevorkian 1986a; see, by way of comparison, Kevorkian 1991:253–56.

86. Kevorkian 1986b:1057.
87. Kevorkian 1986b:1059.
88. Kevorkian 1986b:1059.
89. Kevorkian 1987:1240.
90. Kevorkian 1987:1240, emphasis added.
91. Kevorkian 1989, 1988a.
92. Kevorkian 1988b:3.
93. Kevorkian 1988b:2.
94. Kevorkian 1988b:1.
95. Kevorkian 1988b:9.
96. Kevorkian 1989:562.
97. Kevorkian 1989:564.
98. Kevorkian 1989:564–65.
99. Braunstein and Wang 1988.
100. Kevorkian 1988a:94.
101. Belkin 1990; "Death-Row Murderers" 1989; Risen 1990; Wilkerson 1990b.

2. "THEY'LL BE AFTER ME FOR THIS"

1. Belkin 1990.
2. Anderson 1991; Belkin 1990; Reid 1990; Wilkerson 1990a.
3. Wilkerson 1990a.
4. Reid 1990.
5. Irwin 1990b.
6. Altman 1990; Belkin 1990; "Dying, Dr. Kevorkian's Way" 1990.
7. Belkin 1990; Irwin 1990b; Kevorkian 1991:228.
8. "Judge Sets Hearing on Suicide Machine" 1990; Wilkerson 1990a.
9. "Suicide Doctor Warned on Use of Device" 1989.
10. McAdam 1982.
11. Belkin 1990; Mansnerus 1990; Reid 1990; Wilkerson 1990b.
12. "'Everybody Plays God,' Doctor Says" 1990; Moss 1990.
13. "Doctor Helps Woman Suicide" 1990; "Final Solution of 'Dr. Death'" 1990; Reid 1990; Risen 1990; "Woman 'Aching to Die' Puts Suicide Machine to Test" 1990; Yeaman 1990.
14. "Final Solution of 'Dr. Death'" 1990; Yeaman 1990.
15. "Final Solution of 'Dr. Death'" 1990.
16. "'Everybody Plays God,' Doctor Says" 1990.
17. Borger 1990b.
18. Jenish 1990; Mauro 1990.

19. Beck et al. 1990.
20. Beck et al. 1990.
21. Jenish 1990.
22. Beck et al. 1990.
23. Jenish 1990.
24. Wilkerson 1990a.
25. Seven 1990.
26. Belkin 1990.
27. Belkin 1990.
28. Duffy et al. 1990.
29. Altman 1990.
30. Altman 1990.
31. "Quotations of the Day" 1990.
32. Belkin 1990.
33. Wilkerson 1990a.
34. Mauro 1990.
35. Belkin 1990.
36. Belkin 1990.
37. Belkin 1990.
38. Belkin 1990.
39. "'Everybody Plays God,' Doctor Says" 1990.
40. Mauro 1990.
41. Duffy et al. 1990.
42. Seven 1990.
43. Risen 1990.
44. Risen 1990.
45. Beck et al. 1990.
46. Jenish 1990.
47. Beck et al. 1990.
48. Irwin 1990a; Schmidt 1990.
49. Seven 1990.
50. Cameron 1990; Seven 1990.
51. Cameron 1990.
52. Cameron 1990.
53. "Euthanasia Equals Murder" 1990:28.
54. Mansnerus 1990.
55. Risen 1990.
56. "No Use of Suicide Device" 1990.
57. "Inventor of Suicide Machine Finally Hires Lawyer" 1990.
58. "Inventor of Suicide Machine Finally Hires Lawyer" 1990; "Suicide Device on Trial" 1990.

59. Fieger Law 2014.
60. Irwin 1990a.
61. Leavitt and Marsh 1990a.
62. Schmidt 1990.
63. Wilkerson 1990a.
64. Irwin 1990b; Wilkerson 1990a.
65. Wilkerson 1990a.
66. Leavitt and Marsh 1990b.
67. Borger 1990b.
68. Wilkerson 1990a.
69. Irwin 1990b; Meehan 1990.
70. Meehan 1990.
71. Wilkerson 1990a.
72. See, by way of comparison, Risen 1990.
73. Irwin 1990b.
74. "Euthanasia Equals Murder" 1990; Wilkerson 1990a.
75. Wilkerson 1990a.
76. Meehan 1990.
77. Meehan 1990.
78. "The Tape: 'I Want to Get Out'" 1990.
79. Rucci 1991.
80. Anderson 1991; Schmidt 1990; "Suicide Doctor Goes Free" 1990.
81. Anderson 1991; Irwin 1990a; "Kevorkian Prosecutor Won't Try To Appeal" 1990; Schmidt 1990.
82. "Kevorkian Prosecutor Won't Try To Appeal" 1990.
83. Anderson 1991.
84. Meehan 1990.
85. Anderson 1991.
86. Malone 2011.
87. Irwin 1990b.
88. Schmidt 1990.
89. Wilkerson 1990b.
90. Borger 1990a.
91. Wilkerson 1991b.
92. Schmidt 1990.
93. Anderson 1991.
94. Risen 1990.

3. "A SERIAL MERCY KILLER ON OUR HANDS"

1. Goodman 1991.
2. Wilkerson 1991b.
3. Wilkerson 1991b.
4. Wilkerson 1991b.
5. Goodman 1991.
6. Rucci 1991.
7. Goodman 1991.
8. Goodman 1991.
9. "Doctor to Test Ruling on Suicide" 1991.
10. Lee 1991a.
11. Bullard and Marshall 1991.
12. Bullard and Marshall 1991.
13. Lee 1991a.
14. "Kevorkian's Silence about Deaths Postpones Decision on Charges" 1991.
15. Castaneda 1991a; Lee 1991a.
16. "Kevorkian's Silence about Deaths Postpones Decision on Charges" 1991.
17. Lee 1991a.
18. Lee 1991a.
19. Wilkerson 1991a.
20. Wilkerson 1991a.
21. Edmonds and Castaneda 1991; "Judge Says Suicide Doctor Does a 'Service'" 1991; "Kevorkian's Silence about Deaths Postpones Decision on Charges" 1991; "'No Qualms,' Says Women in Video before Suicide" 1991; Wilkerson 1991a.
22. Lee 1991a.
23. Wilkerson 1991a.
24. Lee 1991a.
25. Wilkerson 1991a.
26. Lee 1991a; Wilkerson 1991a.
27. Edmonds and Castaneda 1991; Wilkerson 1991a.
28. Lee 1991a.
29. "'No Qualms,' Says Women in Video before Suicide" 1991.
30. Castaneda 1991a; Lee 1991a.
31. Lee 1991a; "'No Qualms,' Says Women in Video before Suicide" 1991.
32. "'No Qualms,' Says Women in Video before Suicide" 1991.

33. Edmonds and Castaneda 1991; "Kevorkian's Silence about Deaths Postpones Decision on Charges" 1991.

34. Wilkerson 1991a.

35. "Kevorkian's Silence about Deaths Postpones Decision on Charges" 1991.

36. Wilkerson 1991b.

37. Wilkerson 1991a.

38. Bullard and Marshall 1991; Wilkerson 1991a.

39. Wilkerson 1991a.

40. Wilkerson 1991a.

41. Edmonds and Castaneda 1991.

42. Rucci 1991.

43. Lee 1991b; "Michigan Board Suspends License of Doctor Who Aided in Suicides" 1991.

44. "Doctor in Suicides Assails U.S. Ethics" 1991.

45. Rucci 1991.

46. Rucci 1991.

47. Wilkerson 1991a.

48. Humphry 1992; see, by way of comparison, Dowbiggin 2003:169.

49. Humphry 1992.

50. Bernstein 1991.

51. Altman 1991.

52. "Calif. Doc-Assisted Suicide Movement Is Dead Set against Dr. Kevorkian's Stance" 1991.

53. "Calif. Doc-Assisted Suicide Movement Is Dead Set against Dr. Kevorkian's Stance" 1991.

54. "2 Doctor-Assisted Suicides Ruled Homicides" 1991; Castaneda 1991b.

55. "2 Doctor-Assisted Suicides Ruled Homicides 1991"; Lee 1991c.

56. Castaneda 1991b; "Prosecutor Seeks Murder Charges against Doctor" 1991.

57. "Prosecutor Seeks Murder Charges against Doctor" 1991.

58. Castaneda 1992b.

59. "Suicide Device Inventor Charged with Murder" 1992.

60. "Inventor of Suicide Machine Tied to Death of Dentist in California" 1992.

61. "Inventor of Suicide Machine Tied to Death of Dentist in California" 1992.

62. "Kevorkian's Preliminary Hearing Ends" 1992.

63. "Judge Delays Hearing in 'Dr. Death' Case" 1992; "Kevorkian's Trial Ordered" 1992.

64. Olszewski 1992.

65. Olszewski 1992.
66. Olszewski 1992.
67. "Dr. Death Strikes" 1992; "Kevorkian Provided the Gas for Woman's Suicide" 1992.
68. Castaneda 1992a; Lee 1992.
69. Castaneda 1992a.
70. "Kevorkian Provided the Gas for Woman's Suicide" 1992.
71. Castaneda 1992a.
72. "Kevorkian Provided the Gas for Woman's Suicide" 1992.
73. Castaneda 1992a.
74. Lee 1992.
75. Lee 1992.
76. "Death at Kevorkian's Side Is Ruled Homicide" 1992.
77. Rucci 1992.
78. "Death No. 5 for Doctor" 1992; "Doctor Assists in Another Suicide" 1992; Rucci 1992.
79. Ulrich 1992.
80. "Doctor Bid for Auction of Organs" 1992; "Kevorkian Counseling Five People" 1992; "'Sell Off' Organs 1992.
81. "Doctor Bid for Auction of Organs" 1992.
82. "Doctor Bid for Auction of Organs" 1992.
83. "Suicides in Michigan" 1992.
84. "2 Commit Suicide, Aided by Michigan Doctor" 1992; "Critics Question New Ban on Aided Suicide" 1992; "Kevorkian Helps Two More Take Their Own Lives" 1992; Moss 1992b.
85. "Kevorkian Helps Two More Take Their Own Lives" 1992.
86. "2 Commit Suicide, Aided by Michigan Doctor" 1992; Moss 1992a; "Kevorkian Helps Two More Take Their Own Lives" 1992; Smith 1993.
87. See, by way of comparison, Seelye 1992.
88. "'Dr. Death' Thrilled by Battle after Suicide Help Outlawed" 1992; "Suicides in Michigan" 1992.
89. Moss 1992a.
90. Moss 1992a; "'Dr. Death' Thrilled by Battle after Suicide Help Outlawed" 1992; Seelye 1992; "Suicides in Michigan" 1992.

4. "WE'RE SOME FRIENDS OF DR. KEVORKIAN'S"

1. Hobbs 1993b.
2. Suddes 1993.

3. Suddes 1993.

4. Hobbs 1993b.

5. Suddes 1993.

6. Hobbs 1993b.

7. Suddes 1993.

8. Hobbs 1993a.

9. Suddes 1993.

10. Hobbs 1993a.

11. "Dr. Death's Toll 11" 1993.

12. "Call for Instant Ban on Assisted Suicide" 1993; Castaneda and Hall 1993; Stone 1993.

13. "Call for Instant Ban on Assisted Suicide" 1993.

14. Castaneda and Hall 1993; Stone 1993.

15. Castaneda 1993e; "Doctor May Face Murder Charge" 1993.

16. Castaneda 1993l.

17. Castaneda and Davis 1993b.

18. Castaneda and Davis 1993a.

19. Castaneda 1993l.

20. Castaneda and Davis 1993a.

21. "Doctor May Face Murder Charge" 1993; "Prosecutors Search Kevorkian's Home" 1993; Walsh 1993b.

22. "Doctor May Face Murder Charge" 1993; Theimer 1993.

23. Castaneda 1993a; "Kevorkian-Aided Suicide Investigated as Homicide" 1993; Walsh 1993a.

24. "Doctor May Face Murder Charge" 1993; Theimer 1993.

25. "Wife Denies Man Asked Kevorkian to Stop" 1993.

26. "Doctor May Face Murder Charge" 1993; "Prosecutors Search Kevorkian's Home" 1993.

27. "Kevorkian-Aided Suicide Investigated as Homicide" 1993; Smith 1993.

28. "Kevorkian's Backers Outnumber His Foes at Michigan Protest" 1993.

29. Castaneda 1993a; "Kevorkian to Await Ruling on Suicide Law" 1993; Smith 1993.

30. "Prosecutor Says He Won't Charge Kevorkian Now but Seeks Inquest" 1993.

31. Smith 1993.

32. "Right-to-Die Group Stages a Rally for Kevorkian" 1993.

33. "Kevorkian to Defy Ban" 1993; Talbot 1993.

34. "A Conversation with 'Dr. Death'" 1993.

35. "A Conversation with 'Dr. Death'" 1993.

36. "A Conversation with 'Dr. Death'" 1993.

37. "A Conversation with 'Dr. Death'" 1993.

38. "Kevorkian Inquest" 1993.

39. "Judge Bans 'Dr. Death'" 1993.

40. Marshall 1993a.

41. Lee 1993.

42. Marshall 1993c.

43. "A Helping Hand?" 1993.

44. "A Helping Hand?" 1993; Castaneda 1993d, 1993h; Lee 1993.

45. "Suicide Help Ban Lifted" 1993.

46. "Judge Voids Michigan Law on Assisted Suicide" 1993.

47. Marshall 1993c.

48. "Suicide Ban Back" 1993.

49. See, by way of comparison, Wilkerson 1993.

50. Humphry 1993.

51. Morganthau et al. 1993.

52. Atkinson 1993a; "'Dr. Death' Charged on Suicide" 1993; "Kevorkian Witness Again" 1993; Terry 1993a.

53. Atkinson 1993a; Castaneda 1993f; "Kevorkian's Prosecutor Could Almost Defend Him" 1993; Terry 1993a.

54. Atkinson 1993a; Castaneda 1993f; "Kevorkian's Prosecutor Could Almost Defend Him" 1993; Terry 1993a.

55. Walsh 1993b.

56. Castaneda 1993f, 1993j.

57. Castaneda 1993f.

58. "Kevorkian Asks Judge to Dismiss a Charge of Assisting in a Suicide" 1993; "Kevorkian Decision Postponed" 1993.

59. "Kevorkian Asks Judge to Dismiss a Charge of Assisting in a Suicide" 1993; "Kevorkian Decision Postponed" 1993; "Man Tells Kevorkian on Video: 'I Want to Die'" 1993.

60. "Kevorkian Decision Postponed" 1993.

61. "Kevorkian Asks Judge to Dismiss a Charge of Assisting in a Suicide" 1993.

62. Prodis 1993a; "Officials Debate How to Handle Kevorkian Case" 1993; "Suicide Doctor Gets a Trial Date, and a Warning" 1993.

63. "Right-to-Die Group Stages a Rally for Kevorkian" 1993.

64. "Kevorkian Charged a 2d Time Under Suicide Law" 1993; Marshall 1993b.

65. "'Dr. Death' Faces New Trial" 1993; "Kevorkian Is Facing 2d Trial" 1993; "Suicide Doctor Gets a Trial Date, and a Warning" 1993.

66. "Death's Dissident" 1993; "Kevorkian, Pushing for Jail, Aids in Suicide in His Home" 1993; Terry 1993b.

67. Castaneda 1993k; "Kevorkian, Pushing for Jail, Aids in Suicide in His Home" 1993.

68. "Kevorkian, Pushing for Jail, Aids in Suicide in His Home" 1993.

69. "200 Supporters Seek Release of Doctor Aiding in Suicides" 1993; Castaneda 1993g; "Dr. Death on Hunger Strike in Custody" 1993; "Kevorkian Leaves Jail After 3 Days" 1993.

70. "He's No Kevorkian Supporter, But Man Frees Suicide Doctor" 1993; "Kevorkian Leaves Jail After 3 Days" 1993.

71. Atkinson 1993b; Castaneda 1993c; Terry 1993b.

72. "Kevorkian Is Charged Again with Aiding a Suicide" 1993; "More Charges for 'Dr. Death'" 1993; "Police Search Kevorkian's Apartment" 1993.

73. "Kevorkian Is Charged Again with Aiding a Suicide" 1993; "Kevorkian Returns to Jail, Threatens to Starve to Death" 1993; "More Charges for 'Dr. Death'" 1993.

74. Atkinson 1993a; "Kevorkian Returns to Jail, Refusing to Pay His Bond" 1993; "Kevorkian Returns to Jail, Threatens to Starve to Death" 1993.

75. Prodis 1993b.

76. "3rd Trial for Doctor" 1993; "Dr. Death Heart Fear" 1993; "Kevorkian Back in Cell Despite Ruling" 1993; "Kevorkian Is Taken to Emergency Room with Pains in Chest" 1993; "Weak but Defiant, Kevorkian Continues Jailhouse Hunger Strike" 1993.

77. Prodis 1993c.

78. "Clarifying Decision, Judge Voids All of Suicide Law" 1993; Johnson 1993; "Kevorkian Back in Cell Despite Ruling" 1993; "Kevorkian Is Freed After Pledging to Refrain from Aiding Suicides" 1993; Robinson 1993.

79. "Kevorkian Leaves Hospital After Recuperating" 1993; "Kevorkian Is Freed After Pledging to Refrain from Aiding Suicides" 1993; "Tethered to Home" 1993; "Weak but Defiant, Kevorkian Continues Jailhouse Hunger Strike" 1993.

80. "Kevorkian Won't Aid More Suicides" 1993.

81. Bertelson 1993.

82. "Death's Dissident" 1993.

83. Bertelson 1993.

84. "Kevorkian Begins Ballot Drive for Suicide Measure" 1994.

85. "Kevorkian Is Freed After Pledging to Refrain from Aiding Suicides" 1993.

86. "Kevorkian Is Charged in Doctor's Suicide" 1994.

87. "Court Hears Arguments on Assisted Suicide Ban" 1994.

88. "Kevorkian Begins Ballot Drive for Suicide Measure" 1994.

89. Schmucker 1994.

90. "Kevorkian Begins Ballot Drive for Suicide Measure" 1994.

91. "Kevorkian Begins Ballot Drive for Suicide Measure" 1994; "Kevorkian Pleads for Legalization of Assisted Suicide" 1994.

92. "Kevorkian Pleads for Legalization of Assisted Suicide" 1994.

93. "Kevorkian Begins Ballot Drive for Suicide Measure" 1994; "Kevorkian Pleads for Legalization of Assisted Suicide" 1994.

94. "Kevorkian Begins Ballot Drive for Suicide Measure" 1994; "Kevorkian Pleads for Legalization of Assisted Suicide" 1994.

95. Castaneda 1994.

96. "Suicide Law Still in the Dock as Kevorkian's Trial Nears" 1994.

97. Castaneda 1994.

5. "A GAME OF CAT AND MOUSE"

1. "Kevorkian Trial Opens with a Surprise" 1994; "Using Surprise Strategy, Kevorkian's Lawyers Seek Acquittal" 1994; Waugh 1994.

2. "Kevorkian Trial Opens with a Surprise" 1994; "Using Surprise Strategy, Kevorkian's Lawyers Seek Acquittal" 1994; Waugh 1994.

3. "Judge Won't Drop Charge against Kevorkian" 1994; Lewin 1994a.

4. "Kevorkian Takes Stand in Own Defense" 1994; "Kevorkian Testifies Intent Was to End Victim's Suffering" 1994.

5. "Kevorkian Takes Stand in Own Defense" 1994.

6. "Kevorkian Takes Stand in Own Defense" 1994; "Kevorkian Testifies Intent Was to End Victim's Suffering" 1994.

7. "Kevorkian Takes Stand in Own Defense" 1994; "Kevorkian Testifies Intent Was to End Victim's Suffering" 1994; Lewin 1994b.

8. "Kevorkian Attorney Defends 'Kindness'" 1994; Lewin 1994b.

9. Lewin 1994a, 1994b.

10. Lewin 1994a, 1994b.

11. "Suicide-Assist Ban in Legal Limbo after Kevorkian Acquittal" 1994.

12. Goodman 1994; "Murder Charges against Kevorkian" 1994; "Suicide Aid Ban Ruled Invalid by Mich. Court" 1994.

13. See, by way of comparison, Eastland 1994; Goodman 1994; Krauthammer 1994.

14. "Suicide Rights" 1994.

15. Dewar 1994.

16. "Kevorkian and Hitler Art" 1994; "Kevorkian Explains Idea for Hitler Art Show" 1994.

17. "Top Michigan Court Reinstates Assisted-Suicide Ban, for Now" 1994.

18. "Kevorkian's Ballot Drive on Suicide Aid Stumbles" 1994.

19. Stephens 1994.

20. "Kevorkian's Ballot Drive on Suicide Aid Stumbles" 1994.
21. "Kevorkian's Sister, 68, Dies" 1994.
22. Holyfield 1994.
23. Eckholm 2014b; Oregon Health Authority 2014.
24. Davis 1994; "Kevorkian Assists Michigan Suicide" 1994.
25. Davis 1994; "Kevorkian Assists Michigan Suicide" 1994.
26. "Kevorkian: Doctors' Aid Not Needed" 1994.
27. "Court Ruling Could Mean 17 More Kevorkian Trials" 1994; "Kevorkian Vows to Keep Fighting Laws Barring Assisted Suicide" 1994; "Michigan Court Upholds Ban on Assisted Suicide" 1994.
28. "Court Ruling Could Mean 17 More Kevorkian Trials" 1994; "Kevorkian Vows to Keep Fighting Laws Barring Assisted Suicide" 1994; "Michigan Court Upholds Ban on Assisted Suicide" 1994.
29. "Court Ruling Could Mean 17 More Kevorkian Trials" 1994; "Kevorkian Vows to Keep Fighting Laws Barring Assisted Suicide" 1994; "Michigan Court Upholds Ban on Assisted Suicide" 1994.
30. "Court Ruling Could Mean 17 More Kevorkian Trials" 1994; "Kevorkian Vows to Keep Fighting Laws Barring Assisted Suicide" 1994; "Michigan Court Upholds Ban on Assisted Suicide" 1994.
31. "Court Ruling Could Mean 17 More Kevorkian Trials" 1994; "Kevorkian Vows to Keep Fighting Laws Barring Assisted Suicide" 1994; "Michigan Court Upholds Ban on Assisted Suicide" 1994.
32. "Kevorkian Cases Dropped" 1995; Leavitt 1995.
33. "Ban on Assisted Suicide Upheld" 1995.
34. "High Court Nixes Kevorkian Plea" 1995.
35. Bennet 1995.
36. Atkinson 1995; Bennet 1995.
37. Atkinson 1995; Bennet 1995.
38. Castaneda 1995a.
39. Bennet 1995.
40. Castaneda 1995a.
41. Castaneda 1995a.
42. Castaneda 1995b; "Kevorkian Once Again Aids Suicide" 1995.
43. "Angry Michigan Court Upholds Injunction against Kevorkian" 1995.
44. Castaneda 1995b, 1995c; "Kevorkian Once Again Aids Suicide" 1995; Peterson 1995.
45. Castaneda 1995b; "Kevorkian Once Again Aids Suicide" 1995.
46. Castaneda 1995b.
47. "Kevorkian at 24th Death" 1995; "Kevorkian Ousted from 'Obitorium' to Assist Suicides" 1995.
48. Cook 1995.

49. Cook 1995.

50. Curriden 1996.

51. "Kevorkian Attends 25th Assisted Suicide" 1995; "Kevorkian There at Death of Skokie Woman" 1995.

52. "Kevorkian Attends 25th Assisted Suicide" 1995; "Kevorkian There at Death of Skokie Woman" 1995.

53. "Kevorkian Attends 25th Assisted Suicide" 1995; "Kevorkian There at Death of Skokie Woman" 1995.

54. "Doctor Seeks to Quash Case of Murder in Suicide Deaths" 1995.

55. "Doctor Seeks to Quash Case of Murder in Suicide Deaths" 1995; "Dr. Death to Go on Trial" 1995; "New Charges on Deaths" 1995.

56. "Cancer Finding in Suicide Case of Kevorkian" 1995; "Dr. Death Helps 'Cancer' Patient" 1995.

57. "Doctors Offer Some Support to Kevorkian" 1995; "Kevorkian Forms Right-to-Die Group" 1995.

58. "Doctors Offer Some Support to Kevorkian" 1995; "Kevorkian Forms Right-to-Die Group" 1995.

59. "Doctors Offer Some Support to Kevorkian" 1995; "Kevorkian Forms Right-to-Die Group" 1995.

60. "Doctors Offer Some Support to Kevorkian" 1995.

6. "I PREFER JAIL TO BAIL"

1. "Kevorkian Attends Another Death; Woman's Body Is Left in Van" 1996.

2. "Kevorkian Attends Another Death; Woman's Body Is Left in Van" 1996; Marchione 1997.

3. "Kevorkian and the Issue of Assisted Suicide Will Go on Trial for Second Time" 1996.

4. "2 Views of Kevorkian: Killer or Comforter" 1996; "Doctor Death's 'Hidden Motive'" 1996.

5. "Court Ruling Aids Case against Kevorkian" 1996.

6. "Kevorkian Jury Watches Tape of Patient Who Chose Suicide" 1996.

7. Lawder 1996.

8. "Kevorkian Says He Aims to Ease Suffering, Not to Hasten Death" 1996.

9. "Dr. Kevorkian's Intent" 1996.

10. "Kevorkian Case Now in Jury's Hands after Defense Uses 'Kindness' Plea" 1996; "Released Kevorkian Jurors Favor Acquittal" 1996.

11. Anderson 1996; Helmore 1996; "Kevorkian Acquitted" 1996.

12. Anderson 1996; Helmore 1996; "Kevorkian Acquitted" 1996.

13. Anderson 1996; Castaneda 1996b; Helmore 1996; "Kevorkian and the Issue of Assisted Suicide Will Go on Trial for Second Time" 1996.

14. "Kevorkian Going on Trial for 4th Time in Suicides" 1996; "Prosecutors Are Ordered to Show Kevorkian's Intent Was to Kill" 1996.

15. "Kevorkian Dresses as Jefferson at New Trial" 1996; "Kevorkian Going on Trial for 4th Time in Suicides" 1996.

16. "Kevorkian Dresses as Jefferson at New Trial" 1996.

17. "Kevorkian Faces Suicide Prosecution without a Law Being Cited" 1996.

18. "Trial Turns to Statements about Death on Videotape" 1996; "U.S. Suicides Doctor Quits 'Corrupt' Trial'" 1996.

19. "Trial Turns to Statements about Death on Videotape" 1996.

20. "Trial Turns to Statements about Death on Videotape" 1996.

21. Lessenberry 1996b, 1996c.

22. Lessenberry 1996b.

23. Lessenberry 1996b.

24. "Kevorkian Attacks State Powers for Anti-Suicide Acts" 1996; Lessenberry 1996a.

25. "Despite Trial, Kevorkian Is at a Suicide" 1996; "Kevorkian Back at Trial as Talk of Detroit Is of Another Suicide" 1996; Nichols 1996; Nicol and Wylie 2006.

26. "Jury Acquits 'Dr. Death'" 1996; Lessenberry 1996c; Walsh 1996a.

27. Castaneda 1996b.

28. Lessenberry 1996c, 1996i.

29. Yuhn 1996.

30. Yuhn 1996.

31. Yuhn 1996.

32. "Coroner Questions Death Cause" 1996.

33. Hebert 1996.

34. Charen 1996; Irwin 1996; "Kevorkian Applies for Concealed Weapon" 1996.

35. Castaneda 1996c; "Kevorkian Has a Lively Time Slamming the AMA" 1996.

36. Castaneda 1996c; Charen 1996.

37. Beveridge 1996; Lessenberry 1996e.

38. Beveridge 1996; Lessenberry 1996e.

39. "Kevorkian-Related Deaths Use Various Drugs" 1996; Lessenberry 1996e.

40. Castaneda 1996a; Falcone 1996.

41. Lessenberry 1996e.

42. "Dr. Death Stands Accused" 1996; Mulvihill 1996; Zernike 1996.

43. Martin 1996.

44. Clark 1996; "Kevorkian Held Briefly After 2d Suicide in Day" 1996; Mueller 1996.

45. "Drugs Didn't Affect Decision in Woman's Suicide, Sources Say" 1996; Hayward 1996; Walsh 1996b.

46. "Lawyer: Kevorkian Got Involved Because Man's Doctor Wouldn't" 1996; Lessenberry 1996i.

47. "Lawyer: Kevorkian Got Involved Because Man's Doctor Wouldn't" 1996; Lessenberry 1996i, 1996f.

48. Lessenberry 1996f.

49. "Kevorkian Is Suing Police, Prosecutors" 1996; Lessenberry 1996f.

50. Lessenberry 1996f, 1996k.

51. Lessenberry 1996f, 1996k; "New Admission Puts Kevorkian Suicide List at 46" 1996.

52. "Arrested Man Says He Wanted to Commit Suicide" 1996; "Kevorkian to Carry Gun" 1996; Lessenberry 1996k.

53. "Kevorkian Aids 41st Death" 1996; Taylor 1996.

54. "Kevorkian Aids Rescue of Bicyclist" 1996.

55. "Another Body Left at Hospital by Kevorkian" 1996; Castaneda 1996d; Lasalandra and Weber 1996; "Kevorkian Assists Texas Man's Suicide" 1996.

56. "Another Body Left at Hospital by Kevorkian" 1996; Castaneda 1996d; Lasalandra and Weber 1996.

57. Lasalandra and Weber 1996.

58. Lessenberry 1996h; "Old Foe Takes Parting Shot at Kevorkian" 1996; Varner 1996.

59. Lessenberry 1996h; "Old Foe Takes Parting Shot at Kevorkian" 1996; Varner 1996.

60. Lessenberry 1996h; "Old Foe Takes Parting Shot at Kevorkian" 1996; Varner 1996.

61. Lessenberry 1996g, 1996h.

62. "Kevorkian Likely to Get a Break" 1996; Lessenberry 1996h.

63. Lessenberry 1996g, 1996j; White 1996.

64. "Hemlock Society Founder Indicted With Kevorkian" 1996; Lessenberry 1996j; Walsh 1996c.

65. "Hemlock Society Founder Indicted With Kevorkian" 1996; Lessenberry 1996d; Walsh 1996c.

66. Lessenberry 1996g, 1996h; White 1996.

7. "WELL, SIR, CONSIDER YOURSELF STOPPED"

1. "A Prosecutor Drops Kevorkian Charges" 1997.

2. "A Prosecutor Drops Kevorkian Charges" 1997.

3. "Kevorkian's Attorney Hints at Doctor's Involvement in Deaths" 1997.

4. "Body Linked to Kevorkian Again" 1997.

5. "Stop Aid, State Tells Kevorkian" 1997.

6. "AIDS Patient's Note Names Kevorkian Lawyer" 1997.

7. "Kevorkian Libel Suit" 1999; "Kevorkian's Suit" 1997.

8. White 1997.

9. White 1997.

10. "Mistrial Declared in Kevorkian Case after Lawyer's Statement" 1997; Tangonan 1997.

11. "Kevorkian's Trial Ends in Disarray Yet Again" 1997; "Mistrial Declared in Kevorkian Case after Lawyer's Statement" 1997.

12. Dowbiggin 2003; Katz 1997.

13. "Dr. Kevorkian Unaffected by Ruling, Says His Attorney" 1997.

14. Brown 1997; "Doctored Stats" 1999; "Dr. Kevorkian Unaffected by Ruling, Says His Attorney" 1997; "Kevorkian Said to Aid Suicide as High Court Rules" 1997.

15. Hughes 1997.

16. Gearty and Saltonstall 1997; Hanlon 1997; "Lawyer Puts Kevorkian Cases at 'Nearly 100'" 1997.

17. Michigan Women's Historical Center & Hall of Fame 2014.

18. "Kevorkian Aide Plans Her Own Death" 1996; Stout 1997.

19. "Janet Good" 1997; Nicol and Wylie 2006.

20. "Kevorkian Encountering Fewer Hurdles in Suicides" 1997; Mishra 1997.

21. "Kevorkian Encountering Fewer Hurdles in Suicides" 1997; Mishra 1997.

22. "Kevorkian to Harvest Organs from Suicides for Transplanting" 1997.

23. Breen 1997; Lopez 1997.

24. "Church Dismisses Kevorkian's Claim" 1997; Laurence 1997; Shin 1997; Smith 1993.

25. "Church Dismisses Kevorkian's Claim" 1997; Laurence 1997; Shin 1997.

26. "2 Assisted Suicides" 1997; Edozien 1997; "Kevorkian Associate Helps Woman in Suicide" 1997; "Kevorkian Questioned in Death" 1997; Saltonstall 1997.

27. Edozien 1997; "Kevorkian Friend Aided Suicide, Lawyer Says" 1997; "Kevorkian Questioned in Death" 1997; "Officials: Ill Woman Died With Kevorkian" 1997.

28. Mishra 1997; "New Assisted Suicide Ban" 1997.

29. "Kevorkian Deaths Total 100" 1998; "Kevorkian Promises Starvation If Convicted" 1998.

30. "Kevorkian Accuses Police of Interfering" 1998; "Student, 21, Ends Life With Kevorkian Help" 1998; "Tragic Loss" 1998; "'We Are All Terminal': Kevorkian Program Helps More People Die on Their Own Terms" 1998.

31. "Kevorkian Accuses Police of Interfering" 1998; "Kevorkian Gets Back Euthanasia Gear" 1998; "'We Are All Terminal': Kevorkian Program Helps More People Die on Their Own Terms" 1998.

32. "Kevorkian Accuses Police of Interfering" 1998; "Kevorkian Gets Back Euthanasia Gear" 1998; "'We Are All Terminal': Kevorkian Program Helps More People Die on Their Own Terms" 1998.

33. Cornell 1998; "Kevorkian Deaths Total 100" 1998; "Kevorkian's Latest" 1998.

34. "Kevorkian Arrested After Dropping Off Body" 1998; "Kevorkian Delivers 2" 1998; "Kevorkian Delivers Another Body to Hospital" 1998; "Kevorkian Gets Back Euthanasia Gear" 1998; "Kevorkian Intends to Be His Own Co-Counsel If He Is Tried Again" 1998; Reel 1998.

35. Lessenberry 1999.

36. Nicol and Wylie 2006.

37. "Kevorkian Intends to Be His Own Co-Counsel If He Is Tried Again" 1998.

38. "Kevorkian Has Kidneys to Give" 1998; "Mutilation Alleged in Kevorkian Case" 1998.

39. "Kevorkian Rips Critics of Organ Donor Offer" 1998.

40. "Kevorkian Lawyer Says Client 'Went Too Far'" 1998.

41. Hunter 1998; "Medical License at Issue for Kevorkian in Deaths" 1998.

42. Belluck 1998; Morello 1998a.

43. Belluck 1998; Haberman and Gregorian 1998a, 1998b.

44. Belluck 1998.

45. Johnson 1998; Leo 1999; "Michigan Assisted Suicide Measure Rejected" 1998.

46. "Right To Die Doctor Fined" 1998.

47. Belluck 1998; "'Dr. Death' Raises the Stakes—On TV" 1998; Haberman and Gregorian 1998a, 1998b; Huff and Siemaszko 1998; Johnson 1998; Morello 1998a; "Prosecutor Seeking Tape of Lethal Injection" 1998.

48. Belluck 1998; Dedman 1998; Haberman and Gregorian 1998a, 1998b; Huff and Siemaszko 1998; Morello 1998a.

49. Dedman 1998; Foer and Hammel 1998; Huff and Siemaszko 1998; Johnson 1998; Morello 1998a; Stead 1998a.

50. Dedman 1998.

51. Huff and Siemaszko 1998; Morello 1998a; "Prosecutor Seeking Tape of Lethal Injection" 1998.

52. Glaberson 1998; Haberman and Connor 1998; Johnson 1998; "Murder or Mercy?" 1998; Puente 1998; Rovner 1998; Stead 1998b.

53. Haberman and Connor 1998; Johnson 1998; Shapiro 1998; Stead 1998a.

54. Haberman and Connor 1998; Johnson 1998; Kennedy 1998; "Kevorkian Legal Plan Faulted" 1998; "Lawyer: Kevorkian 'Wants to Hurt Himself'" 1998; Morello 1998b.

55. "Dr. Death to Stand Trial" 1998; "Euthanasia Crusader on New Charge" 1998; "Kevorkian Not Guilty" 1998; Lusetich 1998; Morello 1998b.

56. Belluck 1999b, 1999d; Claiborne 1999; "Death Charge Cut" 1999.

57. Belluck 1999b; Bluth 1999; Hyde 1999e.

58. Bluth 1999; Hyde 1999b, 1999e; Johnson 1999.

59. Johnson 1999.

60. Bluth 1999; Hyde 1999e.

61. Belluck 1999d.

62. Belluck 1999c; Claiborne 1999; Hyde 1999f.

63. Belluck 1999a, 1999c; Claiborne 1999; Hyde 1999d.

64. Belluck 1999c; Hyde 1999d.

65. Belluck 1999c; Claiborne 1999.

66. Belluck 1999a; Claiborne 1999; "Guilty of Murder" 1999; Hyde 1999a; Lessenberry 1999; McGinn et al. 1999; Rovner 1999; Tait 1999; "The Suicide Doctor Is Convicted of Murder" 1999.

67. Hyde 1999c; Johnson 1999; "Kevorkian Trial Update" 1999; "Kevorkian Will Be Sentenced Today on Murder Conviction" 1999; Murphy 1999; Shapiro 1999c; Willing 1999a, 1999b.

CONCLUSION

1. "Judge Gets Death Threats" 1999.

2. Drell 1999; "Kevorkian Will Be Sentenced Today on Murder Conviction" 1999; Parker 1999.

3. See, by way of comparison, DeCesare 2013.

4. Nicol and Wylie 2006: 214.

5. See, by way of comparison, O'Shaughnessy 1998.

6. Nicol and Wylie 2006:215; see, by way of comparison, Shapiro 1999b.

7. "Primetime Lawyer" 1999.

8. Lessenberry 1999.
9. See, by way of comparison, Rodick 2007.
10. O'Shaughnessy 1998.
11. Rodick 2007.
12. Morello 1998b.
13. "Dr. Death Wins Humanity Prize" 2000.
14. Murphy 2000.
15. Murphy 2000.
16. Taylor 2001.
17. "ABC Interview with Kevorkian Barred" 2000.
18. "Free Ailing Kevorkian, Lawyers Ask" 2000; "Suicide Advocate Denied Bail" 2000.
19. "Appeals Court Hears Kevorkian Arguments" 2001; Hall 1999; "I Will Die in Jail, Says Kevorkian" 2004; "Kevorkian Loses" 2003; "Kevorkian's Conviction for Murder to Stand" 2001; "McVeigh Conspirator, Kevorkian Among Rejected Top Court Cases" 2002; "No Freedom for Dr. Death" 2004; Sloat 2002.
20. "Kevorkian Leaves Prison for Hernia Surgery" 2005.
21. "Kevorkian's Release Sought by Attorney" 2005; "Lawyer Asks Parole Board to Release Kevorkian" 2004; "Lawyer: Kevorkian's Life at Risk" 2006; "Primetime Lawyer" 1999.
22. Frey 2005; Levesque 2003; "Schiavo's Parents Turn to Court of Public Opinion" 2005.
23. "Dr. Death Parole" 2006; Gray 2006; "Lawyer: Kevorkian's Life at Risk" 2006.
24. Huffstutter 2007.
25. Davey 2007a.
26. Huffstutter 2007.
27. Davey 2007a.
28. Davey 2007a.
29. Huffstutter 2007; "Kevorkian Plans Post-Prison Role" 2007; Vogel 2007.
30. Davey 2007b; Michigan Department of State 2014.
31. Washington State Department of Health 2014.
32. "Mont. Court: State Law Doesn't Prevent Assisted Suicide" 2009.
33. Strauss 2010.
34. Krieger 2010.
35. Caplan 2014.

REFERENCES

"1 Trial Ordered for Kevorkian." 1993. *Pittsburgh Post-Gazette*, December 15, p. A8.

"2 Assisted Suicides." 1997. *Pittsburgh Post-Gazette*, November 23, p. A15.

"2 Commit Suicide, Aided by Michigan Doctor." 1992. *New York Times*, December 16, p. A21.

"2 Doctor-Assisted Suicides Ruled Homicides." 1991. *New York Times*, December 19, p. A29.

"2 Views of Kevorkian: Killer or Comforter." 1996. *New York Times*, February 21, p. A16.

"200 Supporters Seek Release of Doctor Aiding in Suicides." 1993. *New York Times*, November 6, p. 22.

"3rd Trial for Doctor." 1993. *Herald Sun* (Melbourne, Australia), December 15.

"ABC Interview with Kevorkian Barred." 2000. *San Diego Union-Tribune*, July 30, p. A20.

"AIDS Patient's Note Names Kevorkian Lawyer." 1997. *Milwaukee Journal Sentinel*, April 10, p. 5.

Altman, Lawrence K. 1990. "Use of Suicide Device Sets in Motion Debate on a Disturbing Issue." *New York Times*, June 12, p. C3.

———. 1991. "Doctor Says He Gave Patient Drug to Help Her Commit Suicide." *New York Times*, March 7.

Anderson, Charles-Edward. 1991. "Suicide Doctor Wins Dismissal: Citing Murky Michigan Law, Judge Says No Crime Committed." *ABA Journal* 77 (February): 22–23.

Anderson, Kelly L. 1996. "Kevorkian Acquitted a 2nd Time." *Chicago Sun-Times*, March 9, p. 3.

"Angry Michigan Court Upholds Injunction against Kevorkian." 1995. *New York Times*, May 15, p. 14.

"Another Body Left at Hospital by Kevorkian." 1996. *New York Times*, October 18, p. A22.

"Appeals Court Hears Kevorkian Arguments." 2001. *Houston Chronicle*, September 12, p. A8.

"Arrested Man Says He Wanted to Commit Suicide." 1996. *Columbus Dispatch*, September 22, p. 7F.

Atkinson, P. 1993a. "Dr. Death's Vow to Die for His Rights." *Herald Sun* (Melbourne, Australia), December 2.

———. 1993b. "No. 20 for Dr. Death." *Herald Sun* (Melbourne, Australia), November 24.

———. 1995. "Dr. Death Snubs the Judiciary." *Herald Sun* (Melbourne, Australia), May 10.

Bai, Matt. 1998a. "A Loose Cannon's Campaign." *Newsweek*, July 13, p. 27.

———. 1998b. "Death Wish." *Newsweek*, December 7, p. 31.

"Ban on Assisted Suicide Upheld." 1995. *New York Times*, March 10, p. A2.

Beck, Melinda, Karen Springen, Andrew Murr, Lucille Beachy, Mary Hager, Frank Washington, and Suzie Boss. 1990. "The Doctor's Suicide Van." *Newsweek*, June 18, p. 46.
Belkin, Lisa. 1990. "Doctor Tells of First Death Using His Suicide Device." *New York Times*, June 6, p. A1.
Belluck, Pam. 1998. "Prosecutor to Weigh Possibility of Charging Kevorkian." *New York Times*, November 23, p. A12.
———. 1999a. "Dr. Kevorkian Is a Murderer, the Jury Finds." *New York Times*, March 27, p. A1.
———. 1999b. "For Kevorkian, a Fifth, but Very Different, Trial." *New York Times*, March 20, p. A1.
———. 1999c. "Kevorkian Appeals to Emotions of Jurors as They Begin Weighing Murder Charges." *New York Times*, March 26, p. A14.
———. 1999d. "Kevorkian Stumbles in His Self-Defense." *New York Times*, March 24, p. A20.
Bennet, James. 1995. "Dr. Kevorkian Assists at His 22d Suicide." *New York Times*, May 9, p. A20.
Bernstein, Amy. 1991. "Mercy Mission?" *U.S. News & World Report*, March 18, p. 22.
Bertelson, Christine. 1993. "Dr. Kevorkian Enjoys His Work Too Much." *St. Louis Post-Dispatch*, December 30, p. 1B.
Betzold, Michael. 1993. *Appointment with Doctor Death*. Troy, MI: Momentum.
———. 1997. "The Selling of Doctor Death." *New Republic*, May 26, p. 22.
Bever, Lindsey. 2014. "How Brittany Maynard May Change the Right-to-Die Debate." *Washington Post*, November 3, http://www.washingtonpost.com/news/morning-mix/wp/2014/11/03/how-brittany-maynard-may-change-the-right-to-die-debate-after-death/.
Beveridge, John. 1996. "Dr. Death's 35th Suicide Client 'Not Terminally Ill.'" *Daily Telegraph* (Sydney, Australia), August 19, p. 19.
Bluth, Andrew. 1999. "Kevorkian Says His Role in Death Was 'Duty.'" *New York Times*, March 23, p. A18.
"Body Found with Note to Call Attorney." 1997. *Milwaukee Journal Sentinel*, October 15, p. 11.
"Body Linked to Kevorkian Again." 1997. *Washington Post*, March 26, p. A7.
Borger, Gloria. 1990a. "The Odd Odyssey of 'Dr. Death.'" *U.S. News & World Report*, August 27, p. 27.
———. 1990b. "The Shadows Lurking Behind Dr. Death." *U.S. News & World Report*, December 17, p. 30.
Braunstein, Philip, and Felix Wang. 1988. "A Simple Bedside Method for the Prompt Diagnosis of Brain Death." *Western Journal of Medicine* 148(4): 453–54.
Breen, Virginia. 1997. "City Man Calls on Dr. Death." *Daily News* (New York), October 31, p. 4.
Brovins, Joan, and Thomas Oehmke. 1993. *Dr. Death: Dr. Jack Kevorkian's Rx: Death*. Hollywood, FL: Frederick Fell.
Brown, Laura. 1997. "Kin: Pain Drove Woman to Suicide." *Boston Herald*, June 28, p. 5.
Bullard, Janice, and Steve Marshall. 1991. "Doctor Assists 2 Other Suicides." *USA Today*, October 24, p. 3A.
"Calif. Doc-Assisted Suicide Movement Is Dead Set against Dr. Kevorkian's Stance." 1991. *Modern Healthcare*, December 16, p. 48.
"Call for Instant Ban on Assisted Suicide." 1993. *Courier-Mail* (Brisbane, Australia), February 10.
Cameron, Mindy. 1990. "Death with Dignity: A Salute to Janet." *Seattle Times*, December 16, p. A22.
"Cancer Finding in Suicide Case of Kevorkian." 1995. *New York Times*, November 19, p. 35.
Caplan, Arthur. 2014. "Terminally Ill Woman Chooses Suicide, May Influence a New Generation." *Medscape*, October 28, http://www.medscape.com/viewarticle/833603.
Castaneda, Carol J. 1991a. "Pre-Suicide Video: 'I Want to Die.'" *USA Today*, October 29, p. 3A.

————. 1991b. "'Suicide Doctor's' Lawyer Denies Pair Was Murdered." *USA Today*, December 20, p. 2A.

————. 1992a. "Defiant 'Dr. Death' Present at Another Suicide." *USA Today*, May 18, p. 3A.

————. 1992b. "'Dr. Death' Calls for Specialists." *USA Today*, January 24, p. 2A.

————. 1993a. "Aided-Suicide Ban Faces Challenge." *USA Today*, March 1, p. 6A.

————. 1993b. "Flouting of Suicide Ban Overshadows Debate." *USA Today*, December 2, p. 8A.

————. 1993c. "Kevorkian Attends 20th Suicide." *USA Today*, November 23, p. 3A.

————. 1993d. "Kevorkian Defies Law, Aids Suicide." *USA Today*, May 17, p. 1A.

————. 1993e. "Kevorkian Extends Suicide String." *USA Today*, February 16, p. 3A.

————. 1993f. "Kevorkian Prosecutor Under Fire." *USA Today*, September 9, p. 3A.

————. 1993g. "Kevorkian Refuses Food, Offers of Bail." *USA Today*, November 8, p. 2A.

————. 1993h. "Kevorkian Tests Michigan Law." *USA Today*, May 17, p. 3A.

————. 1993i. "Lively Lawyer Behind 'Dr. Death.'" *USA Today*, August 18, p. 3A.

————. 1993j. "Michigan Charges 'Dr. Death.'" *USA Today*, August 18, p. 3A.

————. 1993k. "Prosecutors Get Tough So Kevorkian Will 'Get Message.'" *USA Today*, October 26, p. 2A.

————. 1993l. "Two States Target Kevorkian." *USA Today*, February 24, p. 3A.

————. 1994. "Kevorkian Sets Off New Furor, Vows to Aid Another Suicide." *USA Today*, March 30, p. 9A.

————. 1995a. "22nd Suicide for 'Dr. Death'/Kevorkian Attends Death in Mich. of Retired Clergyman." *USA Today*, May 9, p. 2A.

————. 1995b. "Kevorkian Turns to 'the Macabre'/Body Is Found in a Van Owned by 'Dr. Death.'" *USA Today*, May 15, p. 3A.

————. 1995c. "Law Can't Pin Down Elusive 'Dr. Death.'" *USA Today*, August 22, p. 2A.

————. 1996a. "A New Question Amid Suicide Debate: What If Patient Isn't Fatally Ill?" *USA Today*, August 23, p. 3A.

————. 1996b. "Assisted Suicide Becoming the Law That Jack Built." *USA Today*, March 11, p. 3A.

————. 1996c. "'Dr. Death' Denounces His Detractors." *USA Today*, July 30, p. 8A.

————. 1996d. "Police Try, Fail to Stop Kevorkian." *USA Today*, October 18, p. 3A.

Castaneda, Carol J., and Robert Davis. 1993a. "As Ban Looms, Kevorkian Helps 2 More Die." *USA Today*, February 19, p. 3A.

————. 1993b. "House at the End of Life's Road." *USA Today*, February 22, p. 1A.

Castaneda, Carol J., and Mimi Hall. 1993. "'Dr. Death' Assists Again." *USA Today*, February 9, p. 3A.

"CBS Will Give Kevorkian Tape to Prosecutor." 1998. *Chicago Sun-Times*, November 25, p. 34.

Cha, Ariana. 2014. "Brittany Maynard: Why She Was Unusual But Not Unique." *Washington Post*, November 3, http://www.washingtonpost.com/news/to-your-health/wp/2014/11/03/brittany-maynard-why-she-was-unusual-but-not-unique/.

Charen, Mona. 1996. "Pain, Suicide and Dr. Kevorkian." *Tampa Tribune*, August 5, p. 7.

Cheyfitz, Kirk. 1997. "Suicide Doctor May Go on Trial." *Daily Telegraph* (Sydney, Australia), January 6, p. 22.

"Church Dismisses Kevorkian's Claim." 1997. *St. Petersburg Times*, November 15, p. 7A.

Claiborne, William. 1999. "Kevorkian, Arguing Own Defense, Asks Jury to Disregard Law." *Washington Post*, March 26, p. A2.

"Clarifying Decision, Judge Voids All of Suicide Law." 1993. *New York Times*, December 15, p. A24.

Clark, Greg. 1996. "Nurse Said Goodbyes Early, Then Ended Life with Kevorkian Assist." *Rocky Mountain News* (Denver), September 1, p. 30A.

Compassion & Choices. 2014. "The Brittany Maynard Fund." http://www.thebrittanyfund.org/.

Condren, David. 1997. "Police in Michigan Say Kevorkian was Present for Death of Dunkirk Native." *Buffalo News*, September 2, p. 2D.

"A Conversation with 'Dr. Death.'" 1993. *Newsweek*, March 8, p. 48.

Cook, Rhonda. 1995. "Condemned Inmate Wants to Donate Organs." *Atlanta Journal-Constitution*, June 16, p. 1D.

Cornell, Tim. 1998. "Kevorkian IDs West Roxbury Man He Helped to Die." *Boston Herald*, March 9, p. 6.

"Coroner Questions Death Cause." 1996. *Columbus Dispatch*, June 23, p. 2B.

"Court Hears Arguments on Assisted Suicide Ban." 1994. *New York Times*, January 7, p. A16.

"Court Ruling Aids Case against Kevorkian." 1996, *Plain Dealer* (Cleveland), February 24, p. 9A.

"Court Ruling Could Mean 17 More Kevorkian Trials." 1994. *Houston Chronicle*, December 15, p. A4.

"Critics Question New Ban on Aided Suicide." 1992. *Plain Dealer* (Cleveland), December 17, p. 5A.

Curriden, Mark. 1996. "Inmate's Last Wish Is to Donate Kidney." *ABA Journal* 82 (June): 26.

Davey, Monica. 2007a. "Kevorkian Freed After Years in Prison for Aiding Suicide." *New York Times*, June 2, p. A8.

———. 2007b. "Still a Gruff, Passionate Advocate for Assisted Suicide." *New York Times*, June 4, p. A12.

Davis, Robert. 1994. "Kevorkian Assists in 21st Death." *USA Today*, November 28, p. 3A.

"Death at Kevorkian's Side Is Ruled Homicide." 1992. *New York Times*, June 6, p. A10.

"Death Charge Cut." 1999. *Weekend Australian*, March 13, p. 14.

"Death No. 5 for Doctor." 1992. *Herald Sun* (Melbourne, Australia), September 28.

"Death-Row Donation." 1993. *Pittsburgh Post-Gazette*, October 17, p. A7.

"Death-Row Murderers Could Be Lifesavers." 1989. *Newsweek*, January 9, p. 49.

Death With Dignity National Center. 2014. "Death with Dignity Around the U.S." http://www.deathwithdignity.org/advocates/national.

"Death's Dissident." 1993. *Economist*, November 13, p. 34.

DeCesare, Michael. 2013. "Toward an Interpretive Approach to Social Movement Leadership." *International Review of Modern Sociology* 39(2): 239–57.

Dedman, Bill. 1998. "Death 'Appeared a Homicide,' State Says." *New York Times*, November 24, p. A16.

"Despite Trial, Kevorkian Is at a Suicide." 1996. *New York Times*, May 8, p. A20.

Dewar, Helen. 1994. "Kevorkian for Governor?" *Washington Post*, May 28, p. A12.

"Doctor Assists in Another Suicide." 1992. *New York Times*, September 27, p. 32.

"Doctor Bid for Auction of Organs." 1992. *Herald Sun* (Melbourne, Australia), October 29.

"Doctor Death's 'Hidden Motive.'" 1996. *Daily Telegraph* (Sydney, Australia), February 22, p. A16.

"Doctored Stats." 1999. *Newsweek*, April 19, p. 8.

"Doctor Helps Woman Suicide." 1990. *Courier-Mail* (Brisbane, Australia), June 7.

"Doctor in Suicides Assails U.S. Ethics." 1991. *New York Times*, November 3, p. A30.

"Doctor May Face Murder Charge." 1993. *Advertiser* (Adelaide, Australia), February 27.

"Doctor Seeks to Quash Case of Murder in Suicide Deaths." 1995. *New York Times*, August 30, p. A12.

"Doctors Offer Some Support to Kevorkian." 1995. *New York Times*, December 5, p. A21.

"Doctor to Test Ruling on Suicide." 1991. *New York Times*, February 8, p. A18.

Dowbiggin, Ian. 2003. *A Merciful End: The Euthanasia Movement in Modern America*. New York: Oxford University.

"'Dr. Death' Charged on Suicide." 1993. *Courier-Mail* (Brisbane, Australia), August 19.

"'Dr. Death' Faces New Trial." 1993. *Herald Sun* (Melbourne, Australia), October 13.

"Dr. Death Finds Suicide 'Tough.'" 1993. *Hobart Mercury* (Tasmania, Australia), March 2.

"Dr. Death for Trial." 1997. *Sunday Mail* (Brisbane, Australia), May 18, p. 65.

"Dr. Death Heart Fear." 1993. *Herald Sun* (Melbourne, Australia), December 14.

"Dr. Death Helps 'Cancer' Patient." 1995. *Courier-Mail* (Brisbane, Australia), November 10.

"Dr. Death Link to Fourth Suicide." 1997. *Hobart Mercury* (Tasmania, Australia), September 22.

"Dr. Death on Hunger Strike in Custody." 1993. *Herald Sun* (Melbourne, Australia), November 8.

"Dr. Death Parole." 2006. *Advertiser* (Adelaide, Australia), December 15, p. 35.

"'Dr. Death' Raises the Stakes—On TV." 1998. *Newsweek*, November 30, p. 33.

"'Dr. Death' Says He'll Kill Himself If Jailed." 1999. *Gazette* (Montreal), March 21, p. A7.

"Dr. Death Stands Accused." 1996. *Daily Telegraph* (Sydney, Australia), August 21, p. 29.

"Dr. Death Strikes." 1992. *Sunday Mail* (Brisbane, Australia), May 17.

"'Dr. Death' Thrilled by Battle after Suicide Help Outlawed." 1992. *Los Angeles Times*, December 20.

"Dr. Death to Go on Trial." 1995. *Daily Telegraph Mirror* (Sydney, Australia), December 29.

"Dr. Death to Stand Trial." 1998. *Daily Telegraph* (Sydney, Australia), December 11, p. 41.

"Dr. Death Wins Humanity Prize." 2000. *Herald Sun* (Melbourne, Australia), April 12, p. 39.

"Dr. Death's Second Thoughts." 2006. *Los Angeles Times*, June 25, p. M6.

"Dr. Death's Toll 11." 1993. *Courier-Mail* (Brisbane, Australia), February 6.

"Dr. Kevorkian Unaffected by Ruling, Says His Attorney." 1997. *St. Louis Post-Dispatch*, June 27, p. 16A.

"Dr. Kevorkian's Intent." 1996. *Pittsburgh Post-Gazette*, March 5, p. A5.

Drell, Adrienne. 1999. "Dr. Death's Crusade Lives On." *Chicago Sun-Times*, May 13, p. 6.

"Drugs Didn't Affect Decision in Woman's Suicide, Sources Say." 1996. *Tampa Tribune*, August 30, p. 15.

DuBois, Steven. 2014. "Brittany Maynard Galvanizes Right-to-Die Efforts." AP, November 4, http://abcnews.go.com/Health/wireStory/brittany-maynard-galvanizes-die-efforts-26675770.

Duffy, Brian, David Makovsky, Marjory Roberts, Kenneth Sheets, Gerson Yalowitz, Nick Cumming-Bruce, Jeffery L. Sheler, and Don L. Boroughs. 1990. "A Very Chilling Bedside Manner." *U.S. News & World Report*, June 18, p. 10.

Durando, Jessica. 2014. "Brittany Maynard, Right to Die Advocate, Ends Her Life." *USA Today*, November 3, http://www.usatoday.com/story/news/nation-now/2014/11/02/brittany-maynard-/18390069/.

"Dying, Dr. Kevorkian's Way." 1990. *New York Times*, June 7, p. A22.

Eastland, Terry. 1994. "Shameless in Seattle." *American Spectator*, July, pp. 57–58.

Eckholm, Erik. 2014a. "Aid in Dying Movement Takes Hold in Some States." *New York Times*, February 7, p. A16.

———. 2014b. "Judge Affirms a Right to 'Aid in Dying.'" *New York Times*, January 14, p. A16.

Edmonds, Patricia, and Carol J. Castaneda. 1991. "Tale of 2 Suicides." *USA Today*, October 25, p. 1A.

Edozien, Frankie. 1997. "Kevorkian & Partner Assist in 2 Suicides." *New York Post*, December 28, p. 31.

"Euthanasia Crusader on New Charge." 1998. *Advertiser* (Adelaide, Australia), December 25.

"Euthanasia Equals Murder." 1990. *Economist*, December 15, p. 28.

Everett, Kevin D. 1992. "Professionalization and Protest: Changes in the Social Movement Sector, 1961–1983." *Social Forces* 70:957–75.

"'Everybody Plays God,' Doctor Says." 1990. *USA Today*, June 8, p. 6A.

"Evidence Is Reported On Suicide Assistance." 1993. *New York Times*, November 26, p. A31.

Falcone, David. 1996. "Many Patients Not Diagnosed as Having a Terminal Illness." *Boston Herald*, August 18, p. 16.

Fieger, Geoffrey. 1993. "Don't Blame Kevorkian." *USA Today*, March 4, p. 12A.

Fieger Law. 2014. "Geoffrey Fieger." http://www.fiegerlaw.com/about-us/geoffrey-fieger/.

Filene, Peter G. 1998. *In the Arms of Others: A Cultural History of the Right-to-Die in America*. Chicago: Ivan R. Dee.

"Final Solution of 'Dr. Death.'" 1990. *Advertiser* (Adelaide, Australia), July 4.

Foer, Franklin, and Sara Hammel. 1998. "Death in Prime Time." *U.S. News & World Report*, December 7, p. 55.

Fox, Elaine, Jeffrey J. Kamakahi, and Stella M. Capek. 1999. *Come Lovely and Soothing Death: The Right to Die Movement in the United States*. New York: Twayne.

Franchine, Philip. 1997. "Berwyn Father Mourned." *Chicago Sun-Times*, October 5, p. 7.

"Free Ailing Kevorkian, Lawyers Ask." 2000. *St. Petersburg Times*, August 24, p. 9A.

Frey, Jennifer. 2005. "Terri Schiavo's Unstudied Life." *Washington Post*, March 25, p. C1.

Gailey, Elizabeth A. 2003. *Write to Death: New Framing of the Right to Die Conflict, from Quinlan's Coma to Kevorkian's Conviction*. Westport, CT: Praeger.

Gearty, Robert, and Dave Saltonstall. 1997. "From Surfboard to Cane MS Drove Woman to Kevorkian." *Daily News* (New York), August 15, p. 8.

Gilmore, Janet. 1995. "Kevorkian Gets Millionaire's Award." *Times-Picayune* (New Orleans), December 4, p. A3.

Glaberson, William. 1998. "Kevorkian Case Difficult to Prosecute, Experts Say." *New York Times*, November 26, p. A18.

Goodman, David. 1991. "Michigan Decision Bars Use of Suicide Machine." *Oregonian*, February 6, p. A1.

Goodman, Ellen. 1994. "Assisted Suicide Winds Way Toward High Court." *Oregonian*, May 17, p. B9.

Gray, Kathleen. 2006. "Dr. Death Set to Taste Freedom." *Ottawa Citizen*, December 14, p. A12.

Griffin, Alaine. 2014. "Video Inspires Right-To-Die Supporters." *Hartford Courant*, October 12, p. A5.

"Guilty of Murder." 1999. *Economist*, April 3.

Haberman, Maggie, and Tracy Connor. 1998. "Dr. Death Takes a 'Holiday' After Arrest." *New York Post*, November 26, p. 6.

Haberman, Maggie, and Dareh Gregorian. 1998a. "Dr. Death: I Talked Him Into It— Helped Man on Videotape Get Over His 'Reluctance.'" *New York Post*, November 23, p. 4.

———. 1998b. "Dr. K: Arrest Me or I'll (Help) Kill Again." *New York Post*, November 23, p. 4.

Hall, Jon. 1999. "Friends Say Kevorkian Ceases Role in Suicides, Including His Own." *Boston Globe*, September 19, p. A3.

Hanlon, Michael. 1997. "Parents Want Murder Charge for Kevorkian." *Toronto Star*, August 21, p. A17.

Hayward, Ed. 1996. "Kevorkian Patient was Killed, ME Rules." *Boston Herald*, August 29, p. 1.

Hebert, Emily. 1996. "Police Refuse to Release Body of Kevorkian's Latest Patient." *Columbus Dispatch*, June 25, p. 3C.

Helmore, Edward. 1996. "Suicide Doctor Faces Third Trial." *Observer* (London), March 10, p. 21.

"A Helping Hand?" 1993. *Economist*, May 22.

"Hemlock Society Founder Indicted With Kevorkian." 1996. *Atlanta Journal-Constitution*, November 10, p. 9A.

"He's No Kevorkian Supporter, But Man Frees Suicide Doctor." 1993. *Atlanta Journal-Constitution*, November 9, p. A7.

"High Court Nixes Kevorkian Plea." 1995. *Boston Herald*, April 25, p. 16.

Hillyard, Daniel, and John Dombrink. 2001. *Dying Right: The Death with Dignity Movement*. New York: Routledge.

Hobbs, Michael A. 1993a. "Kevorkian Says Legislative 'Hysteria' Deterred Him from Coming to Ohio." *Plain Dealer* (Cleveland), January 16, p. 5B.

———. 1993b. "Move Begun to Outlaw Assisted Suicides; Kevorkian Says He May Help Ohioans End Lives." *Plain Dealer* (Cleveland), January 8, p. 3B.

Holyfield, Jeff. 1994. "Assisted Suicide Ban Before Court." *Chicago Sun-Times*, October 5, p. 30.

Hosenball, Mark. 1993. "The Real Jack Kevorkian." *Newsweek*, December 6, p. 28.

Huff, Richard, and Corky Siemaszko. 1998. "Homicide, Prosecutor Sez But Won't Charge Kevorkian Until He Sees Full Tape." *Daily News* (New York), November 24, p. 7.

Huffstutter, P. J. 2007. "Suicide Doctor Paroled After 8 Years." *Los Angeles Times*, June 2, p. A10.

Hughes, John. 1997. "Kevorkian Role Suspected in Two Apparent Suicides." *Chicago Sun-Times*, July 3, p. 3.

Humphry, Derek. 1991. *Final Exit: The Practicalities of Self-Deliverance and Assisted Suicide for the Dying*. Eugene, OR: Hemlock Society.

———. 1992. "Dr. Kevorkian's Assisted Suicide Tactics Could Derail Law Reform." *Hemlock Quarterly* 47:4–5.

———. 1993. "Time to Reform Law on Assisted Suicide." *New York Times*, June 2, p. A18.

Humphry, Derek, and Mary Clement. 1998. *Freedom To Die: People, Politics and the Right-To-Die Movement*. New York: St. Martin's.

Hunter, Janet. 1998. "Kevorkian Ignores File Order." *Ottawa Citizen*, July 26, p. A10.

Hyde, Justin. 1999a. "Dr. Death Pays the Price." *Courier-Mail* (Brisbane, Australia), March 29, p. 14.

———. 1999b. "Euthanasia Trial." *Advertiser* (Adelaide, Australia), March 24.

———. 1999c. "Jailed Doctor's Protest." *Advertiser* (Adelaide, Australia), April 16, 1999.

———. 1999d. "Kevorkian Case Goes To Jury." *Chicago Sun-Times*, March 26, p. 26.

———. 1999e. "Kevorkian Defends Self in Murder Trial." *Chicago Sun-Times*, March 23, p. 21.

———. 1999f. "Kevorkian Rests Case With No Witnesses." *Atlanta Journal-Constitution*, March 25, p. 3A.

"Inventor of Suicide Machine Finally Hires Lawyer." 1990. *Oregonian*, August 23, p. D4.

"Inventor of Suicide Machine Tied to Death of Dentist in California." 1992. *New York Times*, February 13, p. B14.

Irwin, Jim. 1990a. "Michigan Legislature Challenged to Resolve Assisted Suicide Issue." *Oregonian*, December 16, p. D3.

———. 1990b. "Testimony Begins in Kevorkian Case." *Oregonian*, December 13, p. C4.

———. 1996. "Kevorkian Takes Body to Hospital After Aiding Suicide." *Chicago Sun-Times*, July 11, p. 3.

"I Will Die in Jail, Says Kevorkian." 2004. *Herald Sun* (Melbourne, Australia), April 13, p. 29.

"Janet Good." 1997. *Chicago Sun-Times*, August 27, p. 79.

Jenish, D'Arcy. 1990. "The Right to Die." *Maclean's*, June 25, p. 24.

Johnson, Dirk. 1998. "Kevorkian Faces a Murder Charge in Death on Video." *New York Times*, November 26, p. A1.

———. 1999. "Kevorkian Sentenced to 10 to 25 Years in Prison." *New York Times*, April 14, p. A1.

Johnson, Doug. 1993. "Michigan Ruling May Not Affect Charges Against Kevorkian." *Christian Science Monitor*, December 15, p. 7.

Johnson, Kevin. 1999. "New Trial, Greater Risks for Kevorkian." *USA Today*, March 22, p. 3A.

"Judge Bans 'Dr. Death.'" 1993. *Herald Sun* (Melbourne, Australia), April 28.

"Judge Delays Hearing in 'Dr. Death' Case." 1992. *USA Today*, March 13, p. 3A.

"Judge Gets Death Threats." 1999. *Weekend Australian*, April 17, p. 16.

"Judge Says Suicide Doctor Does a 'Service.'" 1991. *New York Times*, October 27, p. A21.

"Judge Sets Hearing on Suicide Machine." 1990. *Oregonian*, October 4, p. D5.

"Judge Voids Michigan Law on Assisted Suicide." 1993. *Jet*, June 7, p. 4.

"Judge Won't Drop Charge Against Kevorkian." 1994. *Houston Chronicle*, April 26, p. A2.

"Jury Acquits 'Dr. Death.'" 1996. *Daily Telegraph* (Sydney, Australia), May 15.

Katz, Ian. 1997. "US Supreme Court to Rule on 'Right to Die.'" *Guardian* (London), January 8, p. 13.

Kennedy, Helen. 1998. "Kevorkian Has a Death Wish: Lawyer." *Daily News* (New York), November 30, p. 12.

Kestin, Sally. 1998. "Suicide Raises New Questions." *Tampa Tribune*, January 1, p. 7.

Kevorkian, Jack. 1956. "The Fundus Oculi and the Determination of Death." *American Journal of Pathology* 32(6): 1253–69.

———. 1957a. "Incidence of Carcinoid Tumors: Review of Necropsy and Surgical Specimens at the University of Michigan." *Medical Bulletin* 23(8): 276–81.

———. 1957b. "Rapid and Accurate Ophthalmoscopic Determination of Circulatory Arrest." *Journal of the American Medical Association* 164(15): 1660–64.

———. 1958. "Staining Reactions of Basigranular and Carcinoid Tumor Cells, With Special Reference to a Modified Giemsa Method." *American Journal of Clinical Pathology* 30(1): 37–44.

———. 1961a. "The Eye in Death." *Clinical Symposia* 13:51–62.

———. 1961b. "The Fundus Oculi as a 'Post-mortem Clock.'" *Journal of Forensic Sciences* 6(2): 261–72.

———. 1966. "Our Unforgivable Trespass." *Clinical Pediatrics* 5(12): 40–41.

———. 1984. "A Coherent Grid System of Coordinates for Precise Anatomical Localization." *Anatomia Clinica* 6(3): 183–93.

———. 1985a. "A Brief History of Experimentation on Condemned and Executed Humans." *Journal of the National Medical Association* 77(3): 215–26.

———. 1985b. "Medicine, Ethics, and Execution by Lethal Injection." *Medicine and Law* 4:307–13.

———. 1985c. "Opinions on Capital Punishment, Executions and Medical Science." *Medicine and Law* 4:515–33.

———. 1986a. "A Comprehensive Bioethical Code for Medical Exploitation of Humans Facing Imminent and Unavoidable Death." *Medicine and Law* 5:181–97.

———. 1986b. "The Long Overdue Medical Specialty: Bioethiatrics." *Journal of the National Medical Association* 78(11): 1057–60.

———. 1987. "Capital Punishment and Organ Retrieval." *Canadian Medical Association Journal* 136:1240.

———. 1988a. "Cerebral Blood Circulation and Brain Death." *Western Journal of Medicine* 149(1): 94.

———. 1988b. "The Last Fearsome Taboo: Medical Aspects of Planned Death." *Medicine and Law* 7:1–14.

———. 1989. "Marketing of Human Organs and Tissues Is Justified and Necessary." *Medicine and Law* 7:557–65.

———. 1991. *Prescription—Medicide: The Goodness of Planned Death.* Buffalo, NY: Prometheus.

———. 2001. "Solve the Organ Shortage: Let the Bidding Begin!" *American Journal of Forensic Psychiatry* 22(2): 7–15.

Kevorkian, Jack, and Glenn W. Bylsma. 1961. "Transfusion of Postmortem Human Blood." *American Journal of Clinical Pathology* 35(5): 413–19.

Kevorkian, Jack, and Donald P. Cento. 1973. "Leiomyosarcoma of Large Arteries and Veins." *Surgery* 73(3): 390–400.

Kevorkian, Jack, Donald P. Cento, J. R. Hyland, W. M. Bagozzi, and E. Van Hollebeke. 1972. "Mercury Content of Human Tissues During the Twentieth Century." *American Journal of Public Health* 62(4): 504–13.

Kevorkian, Jack, and Clarence Groner Jr. 1965. "Survival of Cadaver Red Cells in Healthy Human Recipients." *Military Medicine* 130:922–26.

Kevorkian, Jack, and John J. Marra. 1964. "Transfusion of Human Corpse Blood Without Additives." *Transfusion* 6:112–17.

Kevorkian, Jack, Neal Nicol, and Edwin Rea. 1964. "Direct Body-Body Human Cadaver Blood Transfusion." *Military Medicine* 129:24–27.

Kevorkian, Jack, and Wolfgang Wessel. 1959. "So-Called 'Nuclear Pellets' ('*Kernkugeln*') of Pineocytes." *American Medical Association Archives of Pathology* 68:513–24.

"Kevorkian Accuses Police of Interfering." 1998. *Milwaukee Journal Sentinel*, March 1, p. 8.

"Kevorkian Acquitted." 1996. *Maclean's*, March 18, p. 33.

"Kevorkian Aide Plans Her Own Death." 1996. *Chicago Sun-Times*, September 16, p. 52.

"Kevorkian Aids 41st Death." 1996. *New York Times*, September 30.

"Kevorkian Aids Rescue of Bicyclist." 1996. *Chicago Sun-Times*, October 5, p. 8.
"Kevorkian Ally." 1997. *Pittsburgh Post-Gazette*, May 8, p. A10.
"Kevorkian and Hitler Art." 1994. *New York Times*, May 19, p. B7.
"Kevorkian and the Issue of Assisted Suicide Will Go on Trial for Second Time." 1996. *New York Times*, February 12, p. A10.
"Kevorkian Appeal Cites Ineffective Counsel." 1999. *New York Times*, May 23, p. 18.
"Kevorkian Applies for Concealed Weapon." 1996. *Milwaukee Journal Sentinel*, July 7, p. 8.
"Kevorkian Arrested After Dropping Off Body." 1998. *Milwaukee Journal Sentinel*, May 8, p. 11.
"Kevorkian Asks Judge to Dismiss a Charge of Assisting in a Suicide." 1993. *New York Times*, August 27, p. 7.
"Kevorkian Assists in Suicide." 1996. *Atlanta Journal-Constitution*, August 7, p. 7A.
"Kevorkian Assists Michigan Suicide." 1994. *Christian Science Monitor*, November 28, p. 8.
"Kevorkian Assists Texas Man's Suicide." 1996. *Chicago Sun-Times*, October 11, p. 21.
"Kevorkian Associate Helps Woman in Suicide." 1997. *Milwaukee Journal Sentinel*, December 4, p. 4.
"Kevorkian at 24th Death." 1995. *Herald Sun* (Melbourne, Australia), June 28.
"Kevorkian Attacks State Powers for Anti-Suicide Acts." 1996. *Washington Post*, May 7, p. A8.
"Kevorkian Attends 25th Assisted Suicide." 1995. *Globe and Mail* (Toronto), August 23.
"Kevorkian Attends Another Death; Woman's Body Is Left in Van." 1996. *New York Times*, January 30, p. A11.
"Kevorkian Attorney Defends 'Kindness.'" 1994. *Times-Picayune* (New Orleans), April 29, p. A12.
"Kevorkian Back at Trial as Talk of Detroit Is of Another Suicide." 1996. *New York Times*, May 10, p. A16.
"Kevorkian Back in Cell Despite Ruling." 1993. *Houston Chronicle*, December 14, p. A8.
"Kevorkian Begins Ballot Drive for Suicide Measure." 1994. *New York Times*, January 31, p. A13.
"Kevorkian Case Now in Jury's Hands after Defense Uses 'Kindness' Plea." 1996. *Rocky Mountain News* (Denver), March 8, p. 53A.
"Kevorkian Cases Dropped." 1995. *New York Times*, January 15, p. 17.
"Kevorkian Charged a 2d Time Under Suicide Law." 1993. *New York Times*, September 15, p. A20.
"Kevorkian Counseling Five People." 1992. *St. Petersburg Times*, October 29, p. 6A.
"Kevorkian Deaths Total 100." 1998. *New York Times*, March 15, p. 18.
"Kevorkian Decision Postponed; Look at Law's Constitutionality to Precede any Focus on Doctor." 1993. *St. Louis Post-Dispatch*, August 28, p. 4B.
"Kevorkian Delivers Another Body to Hospital." 1998. *New York Times*, March 28, p. A16.
"Kevorkian Delivers 2." 1998. *Pittsburgh Post-Gazette*, April 18, p. A7.
"Kevorkian: Doctors' Aid Not Needed." 1994. *Houston Chronicle*, November 29, p. A6.
"Kevorkian Dresses as Jefferson at New Trial." 1996. *Boston Globe*, April 2, p. 8.
"Kevorkian Encountering Fewer Hurdles in Suicides." 1997. *New York Times*, October 17, p. A26.
"Kevorkian Explains Idea for Hitler Art Show." 1994. *New York Times*, May 22, p. 24.
"Kevorkian Faces Suicide Prosecution without a Law Being Cited." 1996. *New York Times*, April 17, p. A20.
"Kevorkian Forms Right-to-Die Group." 1995. *Pittsburgh Post-Gazette*, October 31, p. A6.
"Kevorkian Friend Aided Suicide, Lawyer Says." 1997. *Milwaukee Journal Sentinel*, December 13, p. 3.
"Kevorkian Gets Back Euthanasia Gear." 1998. *Milwaukee Journal Sentinel*, April 2, p. 5.
"Kevorkian Going on Trial for 4th Time in Suicides." 1996. *New York Times*, March 31, p. 29.
"Kevorkian Has a Lively Time Slamming the AMA." 1996. *Modern Healthcare*, August 5, p. 132.
"Kevorkian Has Kidneys to Give." 1998. *Pittsburgh Post-Gazette*, June 8, p. A4.

"Kevorkian Held Briefly After 2d Suicide in Day." 1996. *New York Times*, August 23, p. A15.
"Kevorkian Helps in Suicide." 1996. *Plain Dealer* (Cleveland), June 20, p. 8A.
"Kevorkian Helps Two More Take Their Own Lives." 1992. *Houston Chronicle*, December 16, p. A18.
"Kevorkian Inquest." 1993. *Pittsburgh Post-Gazette*, March 23.
"Kevorkian Intends to Be His Own Co-Counsel If He Is Tried Again." 1998. *St. Louis Post-Dispatch*, June 7, p. B4.
"Kevorkian Is Charged Again with Aiding a Suicide." 1993. *New York Times*, November 29, p. A18.
"Kevorkian Is Charged in Doctor's Suicide." 1994. *Chicago Sun-Times*, January 5, p. 11.
"Kevorkian Is Facing 2d Trial." 1993. *New York Times*, October 12, p. A21.
"Kevorkian Is Faulted in Suicide of Woman Labeled Incompetent." 1997. *New York Times*, September 8, p. A16.
"Kevorkian Is Freed After Pledging to Refrain from Aiding Suicides." 1993. *New York Times*, December 18, p. 8.
"Kevorkian Is Suing Police, Prosecutors." 1996. *Times-Picayune* (New Orleans), September 12, p. A12.
"Kevorkian Is Taken to Emergency Room With Pains in Chest." 1993. *New York Times*, December 13, p. B8.
"Kevorkian Jury Watches Tape of Patient Who Chose Suicide." 1996. *New York Times*, February 25, p. 28.
"Kevorkian Lawyer Says Client 'Went Too Far.'" 1998. *Washington Post*, June 30, p. A7.
"Kevorkian Leaves Hospital After Recuperating." 1993. *Gazette* (Montreal), December 22, p. D12.
"Kevorkian Leaves Jail After 3 Days." 1993. *New York Times*, November 9, p. A15.
"Kevorkian Leaves Prison for Hernia Surgery." 2005. *St. Louis Post-Dispatch*, February 4, p. A5.
"Kevorkian Legal Plan Faulted." 1998. *New York Times*, November 27, p. A31.
"Kevorkian Libel Suit." 1999. *Milwaukee Journal Sentinel*, August 11, p. 12.
"Kevorkian Likely to Get a Break." 1996. *Rocky Mountain News* (Denver), November 7, p. 66A.
"Kevorkian Loses." 2003. *Gazette* (Montreal), October 3, p. A18.
"Kevorkian Not Guilty." 1998. *Courier-Mail* (Brisbane, Australia), December 18, p. 13.
"Kevorkian Once Again Aids Suicide." 1995. *New York Times*, May 13, p. 6.
"Kevorkian Ordered Not to Aid Californians." 1993. *Washington Post*, March 12.
"Kevorkian Ousted from 'Obitorium' to Assist Suicides." 1995. *Times-Picayune* (New Orleans), June 28, p. A11.
"Kevorkian Plans Post-Prison Role." 2007. *Los Angeles Times*, May 27, p. A25.
"Kevorkian Pleads for Legalization of Assisted Suicide." 1994. *Washington Post*, January 31, p. A7.
"Kevorkian Promises Starvation If Convicted." 1998. *Milwaukee Journal Sentinel*, January 1, p. 6.
"Kevorkian Proposes Deal During His Arraignment." 1993. *Houston Chronicle*, October 27, p. A9.
"Kevorkian Prosecutor Won't Try To Appeal." 1990. *Oregonian*, December 15, p. E1.
"Kevorkian Provided the Gas for Woman's Suicide." 1992. *New York Times*, May 17, p. A21.
"Kevorkian Pushes Death Row Organ Giving." 1993. *New York Times*, October 17, p. A14.
"Kevorkian, Pushing for Jail, Aids in Suicide in His Home." 1993. *New York Times*, October 23, p. 8.
"Kevorkian Questioned in Death." 1997. *Gazette* (Montreal), December 29, p. B7.
"Kevorkian Returns to Jail, Refusing to Pay His Bond." 1993. *New York Times*, December 1, p. B10.
"Kevorkian Returns to Jail, Threatens to Starve to Death." 1993. *Atlanta Journal-Constitution*, December 1, p. A7.
"Kevorkian Rips Critics of Organ Donor Offer." 1998. *Atlanta Journal and Constitution*, June 10, p. 10A.

"Kevorkian Said to Aid Suicide as High Court Rules." 1997. *Atlanta Journal-Constitution*, June 28, p. 6C.
"Kevorkian Says He Aims to Ease Suffering, Not to Hasten Death." 1996. *New York Times*, March 6, p. A19.
"Kevorkian Seeks Ballot Vote on Suicide." 1993. *Chicago Sun-Times*, December 27, p. 8.
"Kevorkian Strikes Again." 1993. *Maclean's*, December 6, p. 25.
"Kevorkian Sued." 1999. *Gazette* (Montreal), July 11, p. A10.
"Kevorkian Takes Stand in Own Defense." 1994. *New York Times*, April 28, p. A16.
"Kevorkian Testifies Intent Was to End Victim's Suffering." 1994. *Houston Chronicle*, April 28, p. A7.
"Kevorkian There at Death of Skokie Woman." 1995. *Chicago Tribune*, August 21.
"Kevorkian to Appeal Ruling Against New Trial." 1999. *New York Times*, July 17, p. 14.
"Kevorkian to Await Ruling on Suicide Law." 1993. *Plain Dealer* (Cleveland), March 2.
"Kevorkian to Carry Gun." 1996. *Pittsburgh Post-Gazette*, September 27, p. A8.
"Kevorkian to Defy Ban." 1993. *Pittsburgh Post-Gazette*, March 12, p. A8.
"Kevorkian to Harvest Organs from Suicides for Transplanting." 1997. *Toronto Star*, October 23, p. A11.
"Kevorkian Trial Opens with a Surprise." 1994. *Gazette* (Montreal), April 22, p. A7.
"Kevorkian Trial Update." 1999. *Lancet* 353(9161): 1340.
"Kevorkian Vows to Keep Fighting Laws Barring Assisted Suicide." 1994. *New York Times*, December 18, p. 43.
"Kevorkian Will Be Sentenced Today on Murder Conviction." 1999. *St. Louis Post-Dispatch*, April 13, p. A3.
"Kevorkian Witness Again." 1993. *Globe and Mail* (Toronto), August 5.
"Kevorkian Won't Aid More Suicides." 1993. *Pittsburgh Post-Gazette*, December 27, p. A7.
"Kevorkian-Aided Suicide Investigated as Homicide." 1993. *New York Times*, February 26, p. A10.
"Kevorkian-Related Deaths Use Various Drugs." 1996. *Tampa Tribune*, August 18, p. 12.
"Kevorkian's Attorney Hints at Doctor's Involvement in Deaths." 1997. *Columbus Dispatch*, February 7, p. 6A.
"Kevorkian's Backers Outnumber His Foes at Michigan Protest." 1993. *New York Times*, February 27, p. 29.
"Kevorkian's Ballot Drive on Suicide Aid Stumbles." 1994. *New York Times*, July 6, p. A14.
"Kevorkian's Conviction for Murder to Stand." 2001. *Ottawa Citizen*, November 22, p. A15.
"Kevorkian's Latest." 1998. *Pittsburgh Post-Gazette*, March 7, p. A6.
"Kevorkian's Preliminary Hearing Ends." 1992. *Houston Chronicle*, February 18, p. A3.
"Kevorkian's Prosecutor Could Almost Defend Him." 1993. *New York Times*, August 26, p. A18.
"Kevorkian's Release Sought by Attorney." 2005. *Seattle Times*, November 20, p. A4.
"Kevorkian's Silence about Deaths Postpones Decision on Charges." 1991. *Houston Chronicle*, October 25, p. 14.
"Kevorkian's Sister, 68, Dies." 1994. *New York Times*, September 12, p. D10.
"Kevorkian's Suit." 1997. *Pittsburgh Post-Gazette*, May 28, p. A4.
"Kevorkian's Trial Ends in Disarray Yet Again." 1997. *Daily Telegraph* (Sydney, Australia), June 14, p. 25.
"Kevorkian's Trial Ordered." 1992. *Houston Chronicle*, February 29, p. A1.
Krauthammer, Charles. 1994. "Court Ruling on Physician-Assisted Suicide Has Chilling Implications." *Pittsburgh Post-Gazette*, May 16, p. B2.
Krieger, Tara. 2010. "A New Life for 'Dr. Death.'" *Legal As She Is Spoke*, November 2, http://www.lasisblog.com/2010/11/02/a-new-life-for-%E2%80%9Cdr-death%E2%80%9D/comment-page-1/.
Lasalandra, Michael, and David Weber. 1996. "Doc: Woman Had 6 Months To Live." *Boston Herald*, October 25, p. 6.
Laurence, Charles. 1997. "Assisted Death in Church Deepens Rift With 'Dr. Death.'" *Ottawa Citizen*, November 17, p. A10.

Lavi, Shai. 2005. *The Modern Art of Dying: A History of Euthanasia in the United States.* Princeton, NJ: Princeton University.

Lawder, David. 1994. "Jack Kevorkian Wields a Wicked Paintbrush." *Chicago Sun-Times,* October 8, p. 23.

———. 1996. "Kevorkian Urges His Patients to Skip Suicide, He Tells Court." *Chicago Sun-Times,* March 3, p. 27.

"Lawyer Asks Parole Board to Release Kevorkian." 2004. *Globe and Mail* (Toronto), November 9, p. A14.

"Lawyer: Kevorkian Got Involved Because Man's Doctor Wouldn't." 1996. *Chicago Sun-Times,* September 4, p. 26.

"Lawyer: Kevorkian 'Wants to Hurt Himself.'" 1998. *St. Petersburg Times,* November 27, p. 7A.

"Lawyer: Kevorkian's Life at Risk." 2006. *St. Petersburg Times,* May 21, p. 8A.

"Lawyer Puts Kevorkian Cases at 'Nearly 100.'" 1997. *New York Times,* August 14, p. A21.

Leavitt, Paul. 1995. "'Dr. Death' Appeal." *USA Today,* March 7, p. 3A.

Leavitt, Paul, and Donna N. Marsh. 1990a. "'Suicide' Doctor Released on Bail." *USA Today,* December 5, p. 3A.

———. 1990b. "Suicide Machine Charges Expected." *USA Today,* December 4, p. 3A.

Lee, Sandra. 1991a. "Cocktail from Dr. Death." *Herald Sun* (Melbourne, Australia), November 3.

———. 1991b. "'Doctor Death' Loses License." *Advertiser* (Adelaide, Australia), November 22.

———. 1991c. "Doctor May Face Murder Charge." *Advertiser* (Adelaide, Australia), December 21.

———. 1992. "Dr. Death 'Partied' While Woman Died." *Herald Sun* (Melbourne, Australia), May 19.

———. 1993. "'Dr. Death' Faces Jail." *Herald Sun* (Melbourne, Australia), May 18.

Leo, John. 1999. "Dancing with 'Dr. Death.'" *U.S. News & World Report,* March 22, p. 16.

Lessenberry, Jack. 1993. "Suicide Pioneer Takes on Death." *Guardian* (London), December 17, p. 13.

———. 1996a. "Dr. Kevorkian Says His Trial Is a Lynching." *New York Times,* May 7, p. A15.

———. 1996b. "In Latest Suicide Trial, Kevorkian Asserts 'Duty as a Doctor.'" *New York Times,* May 4, p. 10.

———. 1996c. "Jury Acquits Kevorkian in Common-Law Case." *New York Times,* May 15, p. A14.

———. 1996d. "Kevorkian Assistant 'Proud' to Be Charged in Assisted-Suicide." *Ottawa Citizen,* November 20, p. A13.

———. 1996e. "Kevorkian Goes From Making Waves to Making Barely a Ripple." *New York Times,* August 17, p. 6.

———. 1996f. "Kevorkian Helps 40th Suicide, Day After Police Tried to Intervene." *New York Times,* September 8, p. 38.

———. 1996g. "Kevorkian Is Arrested and Charged in a Suicide." *New York Times,* November 8, p. A19.

———. 1996h. "New Official in Quandary on Trying Kevorkian." *New York Times,* November 10, p. 21.

———. 1996i. "Police Break In on Patient's Meeting with Kevorkian for an Assisted Suicide." *New York Times,* September 7, p. 8.

———. 1996j. "Prosecutor Goes Against Tide in Going After Kevorkian." *New York Times,* November 25, p. A12.

———. 1996k. "Video May Lead to a Case Against Kevorkian." *New York Times,* September 21, p. 6.

———. 1999. "Kevorkian Calls His Jury 'Astonishingly Cruel.'" *Pittsburgh Post-Gazette,* March 29, p. A1.

Levesque, William R. 2003. "Schiavo's Wishes Recalled in Records." *St. Petersburg Times,* November 8.

Lewin, Tamar. 1994a. "Kevorkian Jury, Deliberating, Seems to Focus on Site of a Suicide." *New York Times*, April 30, p. 8.

———. 1994b. "Side Issue May Decide Kevorkian Verdict." *New York Times*, April 29, p. A14.

Lopez, Manny. 1997. "Kevorkian Is Costly to Detroit's Hotels." *Seattle Times*, November 3, p. A15.

Lusetich, Robert. 1998. "60 Minutes to the Dock for Dr. Death." *Australian*, December 11, p. 8.

Malone, Scott. 2011. "'Dr. Death' Kevorkian Remembered for Ascetic Side." Reuters, June 10. http://www.reuters.com/article/2011/06/10/us-kevorkian-memorial-idUSTRE7594A420110610.

Mansnerus, Laura. 1990. "The Suicide and the Doctor." *New York Times*, June 10, p. 7.

"Man Tells Kevorkian on Video: 'I Want to Die'" 1993. *St. Petersburg Times*, August 28, p. 5A.

Marchione, Marilynn. 1997. "Daughters at Her Side, She Chose to Die." *Milwaukee Journal Sentinel*, May 26, p. 1.

Marshall, Steve. 1993a. "'Dr. Death' Loses California License." *USA Today*, April 28, p. 3A.

———. 1993b. "Kevorkian Freed on $10,000 Bond." *USA Today*, September 15, p. 3A.

———. 1993c. "Michigan Challenges Suicide Law Reversal." *USA Today*, June 3, p. 3A.

Martin, Jeff. 1996. "Latest Kevorkian Case Is Classified a Homicide." *Houston Chronicle*, August 22, p. 11.

Mauro, Tony. 1990. "Justices to Join National Debate." *USA Today*, June 8, p. 6A.

McAdam, Doug. 1982. *Political Process and the Structure of Black Insurgency, 1930–1970*. Chicago: University of Chicago.

McCarthy, John D., and Mayer N. Zald. 1977. "Resource Mobilization and Social Movements: A Partial Theory. *American Journal of Sociology* 82:1212–41.

McGinn, Daniel, Matt Bai, Julie Weingarden, and Jeff Green. 1999. "A Defeat for Doctor Death." *Newsweek*, April 5, p. 45.

McPhee, Mike. 1997. "Suicide Note Blames MS." *Denver Post*, October 1, p. A3.

"McVeigh Conspirator, Kevorkian Among Rejected Top Court Cases." 2002. *Ottawa Citizen*, October 8, p. C17.

"Medical License at Issue for Kevorkian in Deaths." 1998. *New York Times*, July 19, p. 22.

Meehan, Brian T. 1990. "Doctor Made a Videotape Before Suicide." *Oregonian*, December 8, p. E1.

"Michigan Assisted Suicide Measure Rejected." 1998. *Plain Dealer* (Cleveland), November 4, p. 13A.

"Michigan Board Suspends License of Doctor Who Aided in Suicides." 1991. *New York Times*, November 21, p. D22.

"Michigan Court Upholds Ban on Assisted Suicide." 1994. *Chicago Sun-Times*, December 14, p. 28.

Michigan Department of State. 2014. "2008 Official Michigan General Candidate Listing." http://miboecfr.nictusa.com/election/candlist/08GEN/08GEN_CL.HTM.

Michigan Women's Historical Center & Hall of Fame. 2014. "Janet K. Good." http://hall.michiganwomen.org/.

Mishra, Raja. 1997. "A Fatal Slip by Kevorkian?" *Houston Chronicle*, December 7, p. A14.

"Mistrial Declared in Kevorkian Case after Lawyer's Statement." 1997. *New York Times*, June 13, p. A13.

"Mont. Court: State Law Doesn't Prevent Assisted Suicide." 2009. *Spokesman-Review* (Spokane), December 31.

"More Charges for 'Dr. Death.'" 1993. *Courier-Mail* (Brisbane, Australia), December 1.

Morello, Carol. 1998a. "Kevorkian Aims for Showdown." *USA Today*, November 24, p. 3A.

———. 1998b. "Kevorkian Sees Trial as Chance to Take Final Stand." *USA Today*, December 11, p. 6A.

Morganthau, Tom, Todd Barrett, and Frank Washington. 1993. "Dr. Kevorkian's Death Wish." *Newsweek*, March 8, p. 46.

Moss, Desda. 1990. "Inventor Proud of Suicide Device." *USA Today*, June 7, p. 2A.

———. 1992a. "'Dr. Death' Helps 2 More Die." *USA Today*, December 16, p. 3A.

———. 1992b. "Kevorkian May Face Indictment." *USA Today*, June 8, p. 2A.

Mueller, Mark. 1996. "Kevorkian Arrested on Disorderly Charge." *Boston Herald*, August 23, p. 6.

Mulvihill, Maggie. 1996. "Experts Doubt Kevorkian Will Face Criminal Charges." *Boston Herald*, August 20, p. 4.

"Murder Charges against Kevorkian." 1994. *Christian Science Monitor*, May 12, p. 2.

"Murder or Mercy?" 1998. *Maclean's*, December 7, p. 25.

Murphy, Brian. 1999. "'Consider Yourself Stopped.'" *Daily Telegraph* (Sydney, Australia), April 15, p. 22.

———. 2000. "Kevorkian Continues Crusade Behind Bars." *Houston Chronicle*, April 2, p. A2.

"Mutilation Alleged in Kevorkian Case." 1998. *Pittsburgh Post-Gazette*, June 9, p. A8.

Nano, Stephanie. 2000. "Study: Some Kevorkian Patients Not Terminally Ill." *Chicago Sun-Times*, December 8, p. 43.

"New Admission Puts Kevorkian Suicide List at 46." 1996. *New York Times*, November 5, p. A16.

"New Assisted Suicide Ban." 1997. *Pittsburgh Post-Gazette*, December 5, p. A26.

"New Charges on Deaths." 1995. *Herald Sun* (Melbourne, Australia), September 1.

"New Kevorkian Death." 1997. *Pittsburgh Post-Gazette*, September 4, p. A12.

"News Q&A." 2005. *Oregonian*, October 25, p. A2.

Nichols, Mark. 1996. "Dying by Choice." *Maclean's*, May 20, p. 47.

Nicol, Neal, and Harry Wylie. 2006. *Between the Dying and the Dead: Dr. Jack Kevorkian's Life and the Battle to Legalize Euthanasia*. Madison, WI: Terrace.

"No Freedom for Dr. Death." 2004. *Daily Telegraph* (Sydney, Australia), November 3, p. 29.

"'No Qualms,' Says Women in Video before Suicide." 1991. *Toronto Star*, October 29, p. A3.

"No Use of Suicide Device." 1990. *New York Times*, June 9, p. 6.

"Offering a Helping Hand to Those Who Long to Die." 1998. *Maclean's*, March 9, p. 52.

"Officials Debate How to Handle Kevorkian Case." 1993. *New York Times*, September 11, p. 7.

"Officials: Ill Woman Died with Kevorkian." 1997. *St. Petersburg Times*, December 31, p. 4B.

"Old Foe Takes Parting Shot at Kevorkian." 1996. *Atlanta Journal and Constitution*, November 1, p. 18A.

Olszewski, Lori. 1992. "Suicide Doctor Will 'Do It Again.'" *San Francisco Chronicle*, April 4, p. A6.

Oregon Health Authority. 2014. "Death with Dignity Act." http://public.health.oregon.gov/ProviderPartnerResources/EvaluationResearch/DeathwithDignityAct/Pages/index.aspx.

O'Shaughnessy, Patrice. 1998. "Death & Fame." *Daily News* (New York), March 22, p. 18.

Parker, Laura. 1999. "Assisted Suicide Backers Say the Cause Will Go On." *USA Today*, March 29, p. 9A.

"Patient of Kevorkian Is Found Dead in a Motel." 1997. *New York Times*, October 10, p. A19.

Peterson, Iver. 1995. "In One Doctor's Way of Life, a Way of Death." *New York Times*, May 21, p. 14.

"Police Search Kevorkian's Apartment." 1993. *Atlanta Journal-Constitution*, November 29, p. A4.

"Primetime Lawyer." 1999. *Lawyer*, August 9, p. 18.

Prodis, Julia. 1993a. "Kevorkian at the Scene of 18th Suicide." *Chicago Sun-Times*, September 11, p. 10.

———. 1993b. "Kevorkian's Fast, Like His Crusade, Stirs Dispute." *USA Today*, December 17, p. 8A.

———. 1993c. "Mich. Judge to Rule on Suicide-Aid Ban." *Chicago Sun-Times*, December 13, p. 18.

"A Prosecutor Drops Kevorkian Charges." 1997. *New York Times*, January 12, p. 20.

"Prosecutor Says He Won't Charge Kevorkian Now but Seeks Inquest." 1993. *New York Times*, March 6, p. 9.

"Prosecutor Seeking Tape of Lethal Injection." 1998. *Boston Globe*, November 24, p. A14.

"Prosecutor Seeks Murder Charges against Doctor." 1991. *New York Times*, December 20, p. A18.

"Prosecutors Are Ordered to Show Kevorkian's Intent Was to Kill." 1996. *New York Times*, April 7, p. 14.

"Prosecutors Search Kevorkian's Home." 1993. *Plain Dealer* (Cleveland) February 26.

Puente, Maria. 1998. "Fifth Trial Likely in Michigan for Kevorkian." *USA Today*, November 27, p. 3A.

"Quotations of the Day." 1990. *New York Times*, June 6, p. A2.

Reel, Monte. 1998. "St. Charles Woman's Death Is Linked to Kevorkian." *St. Louis Post-Dispatch*, April 15, p. A1.

Reid, C. 1990. "MD's Bedside Manner Shows His Fatal Charm." *Sunday Herald*, June 10.

"Released Kevorkian Jurors Favor Acquittal." 1996. *USA Today*, March 8, p. 3A.

"Reports from the Euthanasia Front." 1998. *Newsweek*, December 7, p. 32.

"Right-to-Die Advocate Brittany Maynard Ends Life." 2014. BBC, November 3. http://www.bbc.com/news/world-us-canada-29876277.

"Right To Die Doctor Fined." 1998. *Courier-Mail* (Brisbane, Australia), November 6, p. 19.

"Right-to-Die Group Stages a Rally for Kevorkian." 1993. *New York Times*, September 19, p. 36.

Risen, James. 1990. "'Dr. Death' Was Always Obsessed With Dying." *Toronto Star*, June 24, p. F4.

Robinson, Marilyn, and Kieran Nicholson. 1997. "Arvada Woman Finally Turned to Dr. Kevorkian." *Denver Post*, May 9, p. B1.

Robinson, N. 1993. "Suicide Doctor in Wait." *Courier-Mail* (Brisbane, Australia), December 16.

Rodick, Giza. 2007. "Dr. Death: Jack Kevorkian and the Right-to-Die Debate." In *Crimes and Trials of the Century: From Pine Ridge to Abu Ghraib*, vol. 2, edited by Steven Chermak and Frankie Y. Bailey, 101–22. Westport, CT: Greenwood.

Rollin, Betty. 1998. *Last Wish*. New York: PublicAffairs.

Rovner, Julie. 1998. "Kevorkian Arrested on Charge of First-Degree Murder." *Lancet* 352(9143): 1838.

———. 1999. "Kevorkian Convicted of Murder." *Lancet* 353(9160): 1250.

Rucci, Michelangelo. 1991. Untitled. *Hobart Mercury* (Tasmania, Australia), January 12.

———. 1992. "'Dr. Death' Charges Dismissed." *Herald Sun* (Melbourne, Australia), July 23.

———. 1993. "'Dr. Death' Helps Number 13 Die." *Herald Sun* (Melbourne, Australia), February 17.

Saltonstall, Dave. 1997. "Pals: Actress Longed to Die." *Daily News* (New York), November 23, p. 13.

"Schiavo's Parents Turn to Court of Public Opinion." 2005. *Tampa Bay Times*, February 15.

Schmidt, William E. 1990. "Prosecutors Drop Criminal Case against Doctor Involved in Suicide." *New York Times*, December 15, p. A10.

Schmucker, Jane. 1994. "Kevorkian Freed from House Arrest." *USA Today*, January 28, p. 3A.

Seelye, Katharine. 1992. "Kevorkian's 'Suicides' Share One Thing: They're All Women." *Toronto Star*, December 31, p. A13.

"'Sell Off' Organs." 1992. *Courier-Mail* (Brisbane, Australia), October 29.

Seven, Richard. 1990. "Did Doctor Murder Ailing Woman or Help Her Die? Case Sparks Euthanasia Debate." *Seattle Times*, December 4, p. B4.

Shapiro, Joseph P. 1998. "Kevorkian Tape Riles Activists." *U.S. News & World Report*, December 7, p. 56.

———. 1999a. "Casting a Cold Eye on 'Death with Dignity.'" *U.S. News & World Report*, March 1, p. 56.

———. 1999b. "Dr. Death Has Yet Another Day in Court." *U.S. News & World Report*, March 29, p. 37.

————. 1999c. "Dr. Death's Last Dance." *U.S. News & World Report*, April 26, p. 44.

Shin, Paul H. B. 1997. "Dr. Death's Client Had Liver Cancer." *Daily News* (New York), November 15, p. 8.

Shoichet, Catherine. 2014. "Brittany Maynard, Advocate for 'Death With Dignity,' Dies." CNN. http://www.cnn.com/2014/11/02/health/oregon-brittany-maynard/index.html.

Singleton, Don. 1998. "Dr. Death Arrest Is No Sure Thing." *Daily News* (New York), November 22, p. 5.

Sloat, Bill. 2002. "Kevorkian Withdraws Court Bid for Freedom." *Plain Dealer* (Cleveland), December 10, p. A19.

Slom, Celia. 1992. "Kevorkian Has Built Career on Unconventional Ideas." *Chicago Sun-Times*, March 1, p. 30.

Smith, Bill. 1993. "Law Stalling Kevorkian, 'Hero' or 'Serial Killer?'" *St. Louis Post-Dispatch*, March 7, p. 1A.

"State Suicide Ban Won't Stop Kevorkian." 1998. *Times-Picayune* (New Orleans), September 1, p. A8.

Stead, Geoff. 1998a. "Court Must Decide if Kevorkian Can Be Judge, Jury and Executioner." *Advertiser* (Adelaide, Australia), November 28, 1998.

————. 1998b. "Dr. Death on Murder Charge." *Courier-Mail* (Brisbane, Australia), November 27, p. 11.

Stephens, Scott. 1994. "Kevorkian's Lawyer Praises Client." *Plain Dealer* (Cleveland), June 29, p. 2B.

Stone, Andrea. 1993. "'Dr. Death' Helps Two More Die." *USA Today*, February 5, p. 3A.

"Stop Aid, State Tells Kevorkian." 1997. *New York Times*, April 5, p. 12.

Stout, David. 1997. "Janet Good, 73." *New York Times*, August 27.

Strauss, Gary. 2010. "Pacino Helps Viewers Get to Know Jack Kevorkian." *USA Today*, April 23, p. 7D.

Stryker, Jeff. 1996. "A Bedside Manner for Death and Dying." *New York Times*, May 19, p. 3.

"Student, 21, Ends Life with Kevorkian Help." 1998. *Atlanta Journal-Constitution*, February 27, p. 14A.

Suddes, Thomas. 1993. "Bill Seeks to Pull Plug on Kevorkian." *Plain Dealer* (Cleveland), January 14, p. 5B.

"Suicide Advocate Denied Bail." 2000. *Dominion* (Wellington, New Zealand), August 26, p. 4.

"Suicide Aid Ban Ruled Invalid by Mich. Court." 1994. *Chicago Sun-Times*, May 10, p. 3.

"Suicide Ban Back." 1993. *Pittsburgh Post-Gazette*, June 23, p. A8.

"Suicide Device Inventor Charged with Murder." 1992. *New York Times*, February 6, p. A21.

"Suicide Device on Trial." 1990. *Washington Post*, August 18.

"Suicide Doctor Gets a Trial Date, and a Warning." 1993. *New York Times*, September 24, p. 10.

"Suicide Doctor Goes Free." 1990. *Hobart Mercury* (Tasmania, Australia), December 17.

"The Suicide Doctor Is Convicted of Murder." 1999. *Maclean's*, April 5, p. 36.

"Suicide Doctor Warned on Use of Device." 1989. *St. Louis Post-Dispatch*, October 29, p. 13C.

"Suicide Help Ban Lifted." 1993. *Courier-Mail* (Brisbane, Australia), May 22.

"Suicide Law Still in the Dock as Kevorkian's Trial Nears." 1994. *New York Times*, April 4, p. B11.

"Suicide Rights." 1994. *Pittsburgh Post-Gazette*, May 1, p. A9.

"Suicide-Assist Ban in Legal Limbo after Kevorkian Acquittal." 1994. *Christian Science Monitor*, May 4, p. 10.

"Suicides in Michigan." 1992. *Maclean's*, December 28, p. 61.

Svoboda, Sandra A. 1996. "Kevorkian Assists at 32nd Suicide." *Chicago Sun-Times*, July 6, p. 20.

Tait, Nikki. 1999. "Kevorkian Convicted of Second-Degree Murder." *Financial Times* (London), March 27, p. 1.

Talbot, Mary. 1993. "An Interview with Dr. Death." *Newsweek*, March 22, p. 77.

Tangonan, Shannon. 1997. "Support Fades for Kevorkian as Trial Begins." *USA Today*, June 12, p. 6A.

"The Tape: 'I Want to Get Out.'" 1990. *Washington Post*, December 20, p. D2.

Taylor, Lynda. 2001. "Public Becoming More Accepting of Patients' Right to Die." *Pittsburgh Post-Gazette*, May 27, p. W3.

Taylor, Matthew. 1996. "Kevorkian Lawyer Breaks the News of Another Death." *Boston Globe*, September 30, p. B3.

Taylor, Verta. 1989. "Social Movement Continuity: The Women's Movement in Abeyance." *American Sociological Review* 54:761–75.

Teitell, Beth. 2011. "Kevorkian's Art Is Focus of Legal Tussle." *Boston Globe*, October 21, p. B1.

Terry, Don. 1993a. "Kevorkian Assists in Death of His 17th Suicide Patient." *New York Times*, August 5, p. A14.

———. 1993b. "While Out on Bail, Kevorkian Attends a Doctor's Suicide." *New York Times*, November 23, p. A1.

"Tethered to Home." 1993. *Herald Sun* (Melbourne, Australia), December 30.

Theimer, Sharon. 1993. "Prosecutors Are Pondering Kevorkian Murder Charge." *Chicago Sun-Times*, February 26, p. 3.

"Top Michigan Court Reinstates Assisted-Suicide Ban, for Now." 1994. *New York Times*, June 8, p. A21.

"Tragic Loss." 1998. *Jet*, March 16, p. 17.

"Trial Turns to Statements about Death on Videotape." 1996. *New York Times*, April 28, p. 21.

Ulrich, Roberta. 1992. "Kevorkian: Suicides Can Aid Living." *Oregonian*, October 28, p. C4.

"Using Surprise Strategy, Kevorkian's Lawyers Seek Acquittal." 1994. *New York Times*, April 22, p. A19.

"U.S. Suicides Doctor Quits 'Corrupt' Trial." 1996. *Hobart Mercury* (Tasmania, Australia), April 20.

Varner, Bill. 1996. "Kevorkian vs. the Prosecutor: A Last Attempt at Conviction by Thompson." *USA Today*, November 1, p. 3A.

Vogel, Nancy. 2007. "In Assisted Death, Model Is Oregon Law." *Los Angeles Times*, March 9, p. B3.

Vonnegut, Kurt. 1999. *God Bless You, Dr. Kevorkian*. New York: Seven Stories.

Wallace, Ryan. 2014. "One Woman's Quest to Die with Dignity—And What It Means for Us All." https://www.yahoo.com/health/one-womans-quest-to-die-with-dignity-and-what-it-means-99374572007.html.

Walsh, Edward. 1993a. "Eyes on Kevorkian as Law Takes Effect." *Washington Post*, February 27, p. B8.

———. 1993b. "Kevorkian's Lawyers Expect He'll Defy Law." *Chicago Sun-Times*, February 28, p. 24.

———. 1996a. "Jury Weighs Contrasting Views of Kevorkian." *Washington Post*, May 12, p. A4.

———. 1996b. "No Legal Action Is Anticipated as Kevorkian Suicides Multiply." *Washington Post*, August 24, p. A2.

———. 1996c. "Split Verdict on Assisted Suicide Trial." *Washington Post*, November 23, p. A3.

Warrick, Pamela. 1993. "Doctor Finds Few Allies in His Crusade." *Chicago Sun-Times*, January 24, p. 63.

Washington State Department of Health. 2014. "Death with Dignity Act." http://www.doh.wa.gov/YouandYourFamily/IllnessandDisease/DeathwithDignityAct.

Waugh, Bill. 1994. "Lawyer Uses Technical Defense for Kevorkian." *Chicago Sun-Times*, April 22, p. 9.

"'We Are All Terminal': Kevorkian Program Helps More People Die on Their Own Terms." 1998. *Ottawa Citizen*, March 2, p. A14.

"Weak but Defiant, Kevorkian Continues Jailhouse Hunger Strike." 1993. *New York Times*, December 8, p. B6.

White, Ed. 1996. "Kevorkian Arrested on Another Charge of Assisting Suicide." *Chicago Sun-Times*, November 8, p. 21.

———. 1997. "Rural Mich. Town Ready for Next Kevorkian Trial." *Chicago Sun-Times*, June 10, p. 64.

"Who's News." 1996. *ABA Journal* 82 (August):16.

"Wife Denies Man Asked Kevorkian to Stop." 1993. *Chicago Sun-Times*, February 27, p. 11.

Wilkerson, Isabel. 1990a. "Inventor of Suicide Machine Arrested on Murder Charge." *New York Times*, December 4, p. A1.

———. 1990b. "Kevorkian Says He'll 'Do It Again.'" *New York Times*, June 7, p. D5.

———. 1991a. "Opponents Weight Action against Doctor Who Aided Suicides." *New York Times*, October 25, p. A10.

———. 1991b. "Prosecutors Seek to Ban Doctor's Suicide Device." *New York Times*, January 5, p. A6.

———. 1993. "Suicide Doctor Tests Law, Stays With Man Who Dies." *New York Times*, May 17, p. A12.

Willing, Richard. 1999a. "Assisted-Suicide Supporters Lament Sentence as Harsh." *USA Today*, April 14, p. 21A.

———. 1999b. "Kevorkian Sentenced to 10–25 Years." *USA Today*, April 14, p. 1A.

Wilson, Jacque. 2014. "'Suicide Tourism' to Switzerland Has Doubled Since 2009." http://www.cnn.com/2014/08/20/health/suicide-tourism-switzerland/.

"Woman 'Aching to Die' Puts Suicide Machine to Test." 1990. *Hobart Mercury* (Tasmania, Australia), June 7.

Yeaman, Simon. 1990. "Dr. Death Heads Euthanasia Debate." *Advertiser* (Adelaide, Australia), July 4.

Yuhn, Amy. 1996. "Dr. Kevorkian Emboldened by 3 Acquittals." *Chicago Sun-Times*, June 22, p. 11.

Zernike, Kate. 1996. "New Case May Cost Kevorkian." *Boston Globe*, August 19, p. A1.

INDEX

CPSIA information can be obtained at www.ICGtesting.com
Printed in the USA
BVOW08*1918250615

405314BV00001B/1/P